DREAMERS & MISFITS

THE DEFINITIVE BOOK ABOUT RUSH FANS

ALEXANDER HELLENE

DREAMERS AND MISFITS:
THE DEFINITIVE BOOK ABOUT RUSH FANS
Copyright ©2020 by Alexander Hellene
All rights reserved.

This book or any portion thereof may not be reproduced, transmitted, or used in any form or manner whatsoever without permission in writing from Alexander Hellene, except for the use of brief quotations in a book review.

Cover art copyright ©2020 by Jesse White
(http://www.whiteknightsillustration.com)
Cover formatting and design copyright ©2020
by Manuel Guzman
(http://www.lolosart.com)
Formatting by Kevin G. Summers
(http://www.kevingsummers.com)

*To Geddy Lee, Alex Lifeson, and Neil Peart,
for the wonderful music they have created
and the indelible memories that endure.*

*To all Rush fans, past, present, and future,
who make the Rush fan community a family.*

*To all those who backed this book,
answered my fan survey, and support my work.*

And to my wife Demi.

OTHER BOOKS BY ALEXANDER HELLENE

Novels
A Traitor to Dreams
The Swordbringer
The Last Ancestor (Book One)
The Second Sojourn (Book Two)

Anthologies
Corona-Chan: Spreading the Love

As Editor
In Search of Sacha by Manuel Guzman

CONTENTS

Foreword: Rush Family 7

Preface: In A World Where He Felt So Small,
He Never Stopped Thinking Big 10

Introduction: Respond, Vibrate, Feedback,
And Resonate 23

Chapter I: Superior Cynics 34

Chapter II: Conform Or Be Cast Out 52

Fan Profile: David Andrade 87

Chapter III: Boys And Girls Together 89

Chapter IV: God And Government 118

Fan Profile: Tom Driscoll 159

Chapter V: The Freedom Of Music 164

Chapter VI: How Do We Make Contact
With One Another? 200

Fan Profile: Rob D. 240

Chapter VII: A Measure Of Love And Respect 243

Chapter VIII: Choices Got To Have Voices 276

Fan Profile: Michael Ostrich 309

Chapter IX: Because We're Here 311

Acknowledgments 320

Appendix A: Survey Results 322

Appendix B: Interview With Donna Halper,
February 11, 2020 323

Appendix C: Interview With Ed Stenger,
May 19, 2020 335

Appendix D: Interview With Metropolitan
Tikhon Mollard, August 15 – September 15, 2020 359

Appendix E: Interview With Marc Brennan,
September 28 – October 9, 2020 373

FOREWORD: RUSH FAMILY

"Art as expression,
Not as market campaigns
Will still capture our imaginations." [1]

IN THIS TOGETHER

There is no question that Neil Peart's lyrics are the reason I became a Rush fan at age twelve. Being a budding teenager enthralled with science-fiction, fantasy, and history, it was no surprise that his lyrics and Rush's music resonated with me so fervently. Over the years since that initial introduction I've also developed an intense respect and admiration for Peart's philosophical musings, work ethic, unparalleled skill as a drummer, and commitment to charity. He was my first and most influential musical hero.

---

1   Rush, "Natural Science."

In the hours and days following Peart's tragic death in early 2020, fellow Rush fans from across the world—many of whom I hadn't heard from in years—reached out to me for mutual comfort and solace, reminiscing about past Rush shows, and often sharing their deeply personal stories about how Peart's lyrical poetry coupled with Rush's powerful music helped them through a difficult time. Friends and family, whether Rush fans or not, passed along their condolences, making a point of telling me how sorry they were.

I became keenly aware of how intensely his death was affecting me; it went far beyond what I would expect to experience upon the death of a musical hero, leaving me somewhat rattled and confused. After the dust had settled, I digested the multitudes of online tributes to Neil, interacted with dozens of other fans, shed a few tears, and realized that I wasn't alone in my experience. The Rush fan community had reacted to Peart's passing like an enormous extended family of siblings and cousins who had just lost a respected father, revered uncle, or older brother, demonstrating how deeply Rush's music had touched all our lives. This struck me as a profound, and somewhat unusual, reaction for fans of a rock band.

Rush has often been called the "world's biggest cult band," but after this experience I realized that Rush fans are more like a family than a cult (see the popular online hashtag #RushFamily for an example of what I mean). Rush are the ideal patriarchs of this extended family of fans, sticking together through thick and thin for over four decades, without the drama or dysfunction associated with most rock bands. Classy, polite, and charitable, these three self-described brothers always went above and beyond for their fans, continually churning out masterful albums and elaborate stage shows, always with a sense of humor and great humility, and without ever compromising their integrity. Rush fans recognize these unique qualities in the band and inevitably end up developing a relationship with "Dirk, Lerxst, and Pratt" that goes beyond hero worship and into the realm of genuine affection, respect, and even love—like family. Like the typical family, we Rush fans all have our own unique personalities and differing opinions on all ranges of subjects, but Rush is the common thread that binds us together, and we all have that extra "YYZ" chromosome in our DNA. But what is it about the band that made us this way? What are our Rush fan *birth stories*, and how did we all find ourselves on the Rush family doorstep, swaddled in our Rush t-shirts and gripping copies of *2112* and *Moving Pictures*? Alexander Hellene attempts to answer these very questions in *Dreamers and Misfits* by going right to the source—Rush fans themselves. He enlisted the help of fans from across the globe via an online survey and personal interviews. Questions that the book tackles include, "what is the one song that best defines the typical Rush fan?", "is Rush a guy band?", and "are all Rush fans nerds?" The answers are mostly expected, but Hellene parses through them in meticulous detail, uncovering hidden layers of nuance that are both surprising and refreshing.

- Ed Stenger

Ed Stenger is a web developer from Cleveland, OH who runs the popular RushIsABand.com blog. He's been a Rush fan since discovering a beat-up cassette tape of 2112 in his older brother's closet back in 1982. His other interests include spending time with his family, running, Chinese martial arts, sci-fi/fantasy books/movies, and Cleveland sports.

PREFACE: IN A WORLD WHERE HE FELT SO SMALL, HE NEVER STOPPED THINKING BIG

"Any sense of adulation is just . . . so wrong." [1]

HOW TO EXPLAIN

My wife and I were driving through northern Greece one early morning over a decade ago. We were returning home after a night of partying. To stay awake, we had flipped on the radio and were cruising through stations. Let me tell you, there are few things as interesting as channel-surfing in a foreign country.

"Whoa, hold it!" I said when I heard a familiar clatter of wood hitting metal floating over rumbling bass-drums and machine-gun snare.

---

1 Neil Peart, *Beyond the Lighted Stage* (Documentary, 2010).

"What's that?" asked my wife, still my girlfriend at the time; she was driving, and I suggested the radio to help keep her awake on the long drive on that empty Greek highway.

"It's Rush. It's Neil's drum solo. From *Rush In Rio*." Yes, I'm such a dork that I recognized this particular version of Neil's concert-staple showstopper from this particular 2003 live album.

"Okay," my wife said, and rolled with it. She's not much of a rock n' roll fan, though she knew about my love of Rush before we were married.

The solo ended, exhilarating as always. I was awake now! The DJ came on, speaking something that sounded like Russian but was probably Bulgarian given our proximity to the mountains that formed the border between Greece and her northern neighbor. And then he played the version of "Natural Science" from the same album, the fantastic nine-minute-and-twenty-second closer to 1980's landmark *Permanent Waves*.

Permanent Waves marked somewhat of a reinvention of the band, mostly eschewing the multi-part, high-concept prog epics of past albums like *Caress of Steel*, *2112*, *A Farewell to Kings*, and *Hemispheres* in favor of shorter, punchier, though no less technically complex songs with more accessible lyrical subject matter.

Rush seemed to have pushed conceptual prog metal to its limits with the preposterously titled "Cygnus X-1, Book II: Hemispheres" from the *Hemispheres* album, sequel to the slightly less preposterously titled closer "Cygnus X-1, Book I: The Voyage" on the previous album, *A Farewell to Kings*. The duology details the adventures of an unnamed starfarer who sails his ship, the *Rocinante*,[2] into the titular black hole, emerging on the other side to become Cygnus, the God of Balance and ending the war between the heart and mind being waged by followers of Dionysus and Apollo, respectively, on some strange, distant world. The Greek in me appreciated the shout-outs to

---

2   How's *that* for a literary reference?

classical mythology, but much like Geddy Lee,[3] I could barely make sense of the story. I still can't.[4] All I know is that it rocks.

Permanent Waves had none of that. Songs were about the radio, free will, thunderstorms, and—gasp!—relationships! Like, between men and women! Relatively uncharted territory for Rush. The album also had mostly shorter songs than previous outings. There are more keyboards and synthesizers, more major-key non-blues-based melodies and harmonies, and guitarist Alex Lifeson's newer, shimmery, heavily chorused tone that seemed to usher in the decade. And in a striking shift, Neil Peart's lyrics were more personal and direct and less allegorical and obtuse than on Rush's five prior releases.

Of course, prog was still present. *Permanent Waves* had not one, but *two* lengthy, highly technical workouts clocking in well over the seven-minute mark: The underrated "Jacob's Ladder" in addition to the aforementioned "Natural Science."[5] It also had one of Rush's biggest hits, "The Spirit of Radio," which is also on *Rush In Rio*. But it was "Natural Science" that the Bulgarian radio station played that late night/early morning on the car radio of an old, well-maintained Mercedes-Benz (from a "better, vanished time," perhaps?) in Greece.

We listened and rocked out–well, *I* rocked out, though I kept the air-drumming to a minimum. Towards the end of this undeniable tour de force, my wife asked me, "What are the lyrics?"

Now, Geddy Lee had just sang the stanza: "The most endangered species: the honest man/Will still survive annihilation/Forming a world, state of integrity/Sensitive, open and strong."

I relayed this to my wife.

"Oh," she said. "What's that mean?"

What a question! Mind you, it was probably close to 4:00 a.m., I was slightly hung over, and we were coming off our sec-

---

[3] Michael Hann, "Geddy Lee on Rush's greatest songs: 'Even I can barely make sense of our concept albums,'" *The Guardian*, December 24, 2018, available at https://www.theguardian.com/music/2018/dec/24/geddy-lee-on-rush-greatest-songs, last accessed July 11, 2020.
[4] And *please* don't ask me to explain *Caress of Steel*'s "The Fountain of Lamneth."
[5] Three, if you count the mind-boggling instrumental freak-out in the middle of "Freewill."

ond or third night of epic partying in a row. But what *did* this mean? How could my fuzzy mind sum up this song in a succinct manner that someone completely unfamiliar with Rush's music and overall *raison d'etre* could digest?

It's tough to distill certain Rush songs into simple statements like "This is a love song" or "It's about family" or so on. If the radio station had played another track from *Permanent Waves*, like "Entre Nous" or something, it would've been a bit easier to do so. Neil Peart's lyrics were always purposeful and laden with meaning, but more often than not they could be taken many ways. "Natural Science" is a song about tide-pools and stuff like that, right? But the tide pools are just a metaphor for how people exist in little "tide pools" of our own, little personal universes separate from those of others, causing us to often miss the big picture. Simple enough, as far as Rush songs go. But the song is *also* about the music industry. And art. And making sure humankind never allows scientific progress to get out of hand and control *us* instead of vice versa. And the importance of staying true to your principles . . . you know, standard Neil Peart stuff that, in between the guitar solos and rumbling bass and symphonically precise and powerful drumming, gets the old noodle working.

I don't remember what I told my wife. I think I said something like "It's kind of hard to explain," because otherwise I'd have to embark on some long, dorky discussion that would have put my wife to sleep, defeating the purpose of us turning on the radio in the first place.

"Okay," she said, and we kept driving.

When the song was done, we resumed our station-surfing, but that blast of live Rush coming through over the wave on those roads in the hinterlands of Greece felt like a touch of home. That was the magic of Rush. "The Spirit of Radio" indeed.

LIKE WE ALL KNEW HIM

Neil Peart's passing meant a lot to people, because he and his band meant a lot to people. *Lots* of people.

Why? I don't know, and that's why I'm writing this book. But I'll give you my overarching theory. Keep in mind it's based on my own personal experience as a Rush fan, back when it was still uncool to be one. But I think I'm on to something:

Rush were one-hundred percent sincere. This is clearly reflected in their music and their lyrics. For example, let's talk about the rap section in the middle of "Roll the Bones," the title track from their 1991 smash-hit album.[6] Yes, Rush raps: Geddy Lee's synthesized vocals—portrayed by a sunglasses-wearing skeleton in the music video—spit Peart's rhymes about taking chances, not listening to "maniacs in polyester slacks" and getting out there to rock and roll the bones. After all, as we're reminded, "the night has a thousand saxophones." It's easy to mock, and many did, though *Spin*'s 1992 article interview with Peart calls the rap not "half as goofy as Michael Jackson's or Michael Stipe's."[7]

Knowing the band, one can imagine Peart hearing some rap on the radio and thinking, with a younger man's endearing earnestness, "Hey, this is cool! Maybe we can do some rapping in one of *our* songs!" And in fact, this is pretty much exactly the case:

> Yeah, that started off as a lyrical experiment for me; I was hearing some of the better rap writers, among whom I would include like LL Cool J or Public Enemy, musicality apart, just as writers, it was really interesting. And it struck me that it must be a lot of fun to do that; all those internal rhymes and all that wordplay and everything.[8]

How can you not love these guys?

This earnestness, devoid of smirking cynicism, nihilism, and ennui, shone through not just in their music and lyrics,[9] but

---

[6] Some fans might not remember, but *Roll the Bones* was Rush's first platinum album since 1985's *Power Windows*; see Andrew Olson, "Rush album and video sales (U.S.)," *Neil Peart News*, July 14, 2013, available at http://www.andrewolson.com/Neil_Peart/neil_peart_rush_album_sales.htm#:~:text=Quick%20facts&text=The%20best%20selling%20album%20is,Snakes%20%26%20Arrows%20(200%2C000)., last accessed July 14, 2020. It was *big*.

[7] Bob Mack, "Confessions of a Rush Fan: Our 1992 Interview with Neil Peart, March 1992, available at https://www.spin.com/featured/rush-neil-peart-1992-interview-confessions-of-a-rush-fan/, last accessed February 13, 2020.

[8] Neil Peart, "Rush - Roll The Bones Radio Special" (1991).

[9] "Neil and his bandmates were extraordinarily earnest. There was never a touch of

how Geddy, Neil, and Alex lived their lives. Rush were regular people taking their music seriously in an utterly ridiculous industry, and they always respected their fans. Yet by playing it straight—despite the band's goofier moments and sense of humor, evident mostly in their album liner notes and their on-stage antics and video clips—Rush made listeners feel like the band was on to something important and were inviting listeners along for the ride.

Plus, there's no artifice or pretensions with Rush, as pretentious as some find their lyrics.[10] As longtime friend of the band Donna Halper, current college professor and former radio DJ who broke Rush into the American market while musical director at WMMS in Cleveland, Ohio, is fond of saying about the band: "What you see is what you get."[11] And what you got seemed like three *regular guys* who just happened to be ridiculously good and hard-working musicians.

Vinay Menon of the *Toronto Star* recalls in a January 14, 2020 memorial about Neil Peart a story Peart told him about his audition with Rush to replace original drummer John Rutsey: "I remember us all lying down on the floor among the gear in the rehearsal room talking about *'Monty Python,'* talking about *'Lord of the Rings,'* but especially it was the humour right away that we shared that made me really want to be in that band . . ."[12]

---

irony or a wink at the fans in their over 40 years together . . . They were neither hip nor ironic enough to sneer at that view of the world as naïve, nor did they believe that success and happiness were impossible, which might thereby justify the nihilism and destructive hedonism that beset so many of their peers. They were just three guys from the Toronto suburbs who wanted to make the best music they knew how. And they meant everything they said and did." Steven Horowitz, "Everybody Got to Elevate from the Norm: The Enduring Appeal of Neil Peart and Rush," Libertarianism.org, January 15, 2020, available at https://www.libertarianism.org/columns/everybody-got-elevate-norm-enduring-appeal-neil-peart-rush, last accessed May 27, 2020.

10 Those who do are wrong, by the way.

11 "We've met politicians. We've met celebrities. Some of them, the way they seem on stage and then you meet them and you're like, 'Oh my God, what a disappointment.' With Rush, what you see is what you get. They were decent, compassionate human beings on stage, and decent compassionate human beings when you meet them in real life." Donna Halper, *The Bob Cesca Show Interview: Donna Halper on Neil Peart*, January 22, 2020, available at http://www.bobcesca.com/the-bob-cesca-show-interview-donna-halper-on-neil-peart-1-22-20/

12 "Talking to Neil Peart, and watching how he lived his life, inspires me still," Vinay Me-

I'll say it again: How can you *not* love these guys?

A SECRET CLUB

Fairly or not, Rush got slagged as a nerd band. Not only that, Rush was one of the few bands I can recall where critics and other music fans attacked their *listeners*. It's one thing for the uber-cool self-appointed tastemakers to dislike a band's *music*, but to dislike their *fans*? That's an entirely new level of condescension.

Remember: Rush found success when being a nerd (whatever that means) or being into nerdy pursuits (however those are classified) was a social stigma. But Rush were like those nerds at school who were *really good* at something, so good that even the jocks and the cheerleaders had to tip their caps, metaphorical or otherwise, and say, "Yeah, those guys are nerds, but they're kind of *cool* nerds" and leave them alone. Mostly. As Cool Nerds, an oxymoron if there ever was one, Rush were a safe haven for the rest of us Uncool Nerds who might have been socially awkward or featured some kind of physical or other characteristic that made us not quite as popular as our counterparts.

Yet Rush never talked down to their fans, never engaged in self-pity or angsty finger-pointing at the wider world. Neil's lyrics were a massive part of this. He wrote poetry, if you ask me, poetry set to music.

"Duh, Alex! That's what lyrics are!"

I know. But have you *heard* most rock lyrics? They're pretty dumb. Some are fun, and I love them dearly, but they're still dumb.[13] Neil Peart was different. Neil wrote, in part, about things like dystopian futures, fantasy battles, ancient Greek gods as a

---

non, *Toronto Star*, January 14, 2020, available at https://www.thestar.com/entertainment/opinion/2020/01/14/talking-to-neil-peart-and-watching-how-he-lived-his-life-inspires-me-still.html, last accessed February 10, 2020.

13   I say this as a fan of artists like Frank Zappa and Van Halen, two bands not exactly known for, shall we say, the *tastefulness and literary quality* of their lyrics.

metaphor for the battle between the heart and mind, growing old, losing hair, insecurity, alienation, uncertainty, teen suicide, fear, the weather, piloting spaceships through black holes, sentient trees, cities, civilizational decline, travel, the corrupting influence of money, recovering from tragedy, and the freaking *French Revolution*.[14] But above all else, Rush sang about *staying true to your principles*. That resonates with a *lot* of people, nerds and cool kids alike.

Rush's final album, 2012's *Clockwork Angels*, is a steampunk epic as a metaphor for the battle between utter chaos represented by the character of the Anarchist, and restrictive control "for your own good" represented by the character of the Watchmaker, all told through the airship-flying deeds of Owen Hardy as he finds adventure, wisdom, inner-strength, and the love of his life. And it's probably the best thing they ever recorded.

Bear with me: *Clockwork Angels* was a concept album, Rush's *first* overtly concept album if you can believe it. Unlike programmatic *songs* like "2112," "Xanadu," or the two parts of "Cygnus X-1," *Clockwork Angels* is connected not by broad themes like *Signals*, *Grace Under Pressure*, *Power Windows*, *Hold Your Fire*, *Presto*, *Roll the Bones*, or *Counterparts* but by an actual, honest-to-God, Pete-Townshend-would-approve *narrative*. Neil even co-wrote a companion novel with science-fiction legend Kevin J. Anderson.[15] But Peart was such a skilled lyricist that each song worked on its own, detached from the overarching story. Every track has its own mini-narrative with a beginning, middle, and end that works within and without the album's overall story arc. It's utterly brilliant, and if you're a Rush neophyte intrigued by the band due to the overwhelming outpouring of fan-grief over Peart's death, it's a fantastic place to start.[16]

14 And he made it *rock*.
15 The book is goofy as hell, but fun. And you can play "Spot the Rush reference!" in the prose.
16 I still recommend newbies give "Freewill" and/or "Limelight" a listen first to get their feet wet, but one could do worse than begin at the end with *Clockwork Angels*.

When Rush retired in 2015, it was due to Alex's arthritis and Neil's chronic tendonitis, foot injuries, and shoulder pain from his athletic drumming, as well as all three members' desire to spend more time with their families. Us fans appreciated the band's 41 years of fantastic music and wished them well. But we all secretly—and yes, I feel comfortable speaking for all Rush fans since we're very, very similar in so many ways[17]—thought that they'd surely get together again someday for a one-off show or another album, or even a single. Neil's untimely death put an end to those admittedly selfish hopes.

I generally find it sad when people base their entire lives on a genre of music or a particular musician. But hypocritically I make an exception for Rush. This is because Rush were a unique and utterly weird animal in the world of rock: Three regular guys who made thoughtful music, who respected their fans, and who achieved monumental success without selling their souls in the process. If you're going to have rock star idols, you could do *far* worse.

This matters because it's very difficult to separate the art from the artist no matter how we try. But it's impossible for an artist's personal life to *not* bleed into their art. We see this with Rush. The three members were faithful to their wives and devoted fathers. Geddy and Alex are still married to their high-school sweethearts. They are all family men. Other than youthful dalliances with marijuana, Rush was not a drug band.[18]

The Rush story is, by rock standards, really quite tame. There are no band-ending rows, no drug-fueled recording sessions or bitter legal disputes. Their story is bereft of any legendary encounters with weird groupies *a la* Led Zeppelin or Frank Zappa. Kiss and UFO used to make fun when they toured together for singing about dining on honeydew and drinking the milk of paradise, and not being interested in all the readily avail-

---

17 This is one of this book's central theses, after all.
18 Though there was that one time Alex Lifeson did ecstasy in the mid-90s . . . *See* Paul Elliot, "Alex Lifeson on God, police brutality and 'disco biscuits,'" *Classic Rock*, October 13, 2016, available at https://www.loudersound.com/features/interview-alex-lifeson-on-god-police-brutality-and-disco-biscuits, last accessed May 22, 2020.

able female attention.[19] Geddy Lee got interested in baseball because he was bored on tour and didn't party, and back in the 70s and 80s daytime baseball was still a thing so he'd watch games in his hotel room. Alex Lifeson would play his guitar. And Neil would read. A lot. As he put it, "What more perfect, portable education than having a lot of free time on your hands and bookstores everywhere?"[20] In the 2003 documentary *The Boys in Brazil*, Geddy Lee characterizes Neil as ". . . just a normal guy, you know? He's just got a big brain." Lee also warns viewers of the 2010 documentary *Beyond the Lighted Stage*: "Don't be surprised when you discover how boring we really are."

Sadly, Neil Peart's life is most well-known for its personal tragedy. In 1997, Neil's only child, his daughter Selena, died in a car accident at age 19. His wife succumbed to cancer 10 months later. He essentially quit the band to ride his motorcycle around North America.[21] When he returned in 2002, the band leaped back into action, releasing *Vapor Trails*, a pounding, vital album that showed Neil's renewed vigor and, somehow, optimism, in both his drumming and lyrics, although there is plenty of sorrow in songs like "Ghost Rider, "Vapor Trail," and "Earthshine," and perhaps Neil's most scathing bits of social and political criticism in "Ceiling Unlimited" and "Peaceable Kingdom."

The whole album is great, easily an 8-out-of-10 if you want to rate things numerically. The centerpiece, at least lyrically, is a song called "Secret Touch":

> You can never break the chain
> There is never love without pain
> A gentle hand, a secret touch on the heart
> You can never break the chain
> (You can never break the chain)
> Life is a power that remains
> (Life is a power that remains)

---

19 As Donna Halper put it when I spoke to her on February 11, 2020, when confronted with groupies, Geddy Lee would get flustered and leave the room, saying "I've got to call my girlfriend." And he would! (Appendix B).
20 Neil Peart, *Beyond the Lighted Stage* (Documentary, 2010).
21 At his daughter's funeral, Neil told Geddy and Alex "consider me retired." Neil Peart, *Ghost Rider: Travels on the Healing Road* (ECW Press, 2002).

A healing hand, a secret touch on the heart
A gentle hand, a secret touch on the heart

This is an oblique reference to Peart's newfound love. He would remarry, wedding photographer Carrie Nuttall, and he would have another child, his daughter Olivia. He remained a reader and a clean-liver with a strong work ethic who never complained about playing the hits like "Tom Sawyer" every show. He continually improved his craft. He kept reading and writing. He didn't do drugs. And he died at the age of 67 anyway while many of his chemically compromised colleagues shamble on in undeath.

Sometimes the world of rock n' roll doesn't make sense. Sometimes the *world* doesn't make sense.

GHOST RIDER

Neil Peart was famously private. Reading and watching interviews with him, especially when he was younger, revealed a rather prickly man who routinely got his words twisted by the low-consciousness music journalists he spoke to who really hated the band for not being trendy or for being fans of Ayn Rand.[22] He even eschewed meet and greets with fans due to shyness and a general dislike of adulation.

Later in his life, especially after he rejoined the band in 2002, Neil comes off as much more relaxed, although there's a part of him that still seems closed off, still the nearly-thirty-year-old thrust into the limelight due to the success of 1981's *Moving Pictures* who wrote the oft-quoted line "I can't pretend a stranger is a long awaited friend." Neil always seemed like he had to slow down his thoughts to communicate with normal

---

22 Barry Miles, "Is everybody feelin' all RIGHT (Geddit . . . ?), *New Musical Express*, March 4, 1978, available at https://www.theguardian.com/music/2015/may/13/rush-nme-interview-1978-rocks-backpages, last accessed May 6, 2020 ("They are actually very nice guys. They don't sit there in jackboots pulling the wings off flies. They are polite, charming even, naïve—roaming the concert circuits preaching what to me seems like proto-fascism like a leper without a bell.").

people, though he did so with a gracious demeanor and a smile on his normally stoic face.

In *Beyond the Lighted Stage*, there is a scene where the three members are sitting at a table in a fancy restaurant, eating a nice dinner and drinking fine wine. They're cracking jokes and having a good time, ostensibly discussing the next Rush album which Alex Lifeson describes as being a concept album about the life of Frankenstein. He and Geddy also stumble upon the title "Rise to Your Knees."[23] A part of me wishes they actually *had* made this album. But what struck me when watching this sequence is that, in addition to Neil laughing nearly the entire time and how damn *funny* Alex is, Neil still seemed like a bit of an outsider even though he'd known Geddy and Alex since 1974.

A part of this is inevitable: Geddy Lee and Alex Lifeson had been friends since they were thirteen.[24] They have that telepathy possessed only by those who have been friends nearly their entire lives. And even though Peart had been a part of the band for decades, it seems like he still couldn't penetrate that invisible wall. He laughed along with them, but when he interjected with jokes and comments of his own, they were somehow . . . off. Not bad, not wrong, not unfunny, just . . . it's hard to explain. Maybe the best way to put it is "too cerebral," as though even when telling jokes Neil thought *very deeply* and *very seriously* about them.

Geddy and Alex laugh along, of course, and build on his contributions—the classic improv comedy idea of "Yes, and . . ."[25] But there's no denying that Neil was a bit of an outsider, a misfit, even within the band of outsiders and misfits that was Rush. You have to watch the scene to get what I mean.

---

23   After a slightly inebriated Alex tells Geddy jokingly "As soon as I can get over there, I'm gonna rise to my knees and kick your *ass*!"
24   Paul Elliot, "The History of Rush by Geddy Lee & Alex Lifeson: The Early Years, *Louder Sound*, February 3, 2016, available at https://www.loudersound.com/features/rush-s-early-years-exclusive-interview-with-geddy-lee-alex-lifeson, last accessed February 14, 2020.
25   My favorite exchange: Neil: "You know what they say about if you put a hundred monkeys in a room with typewriters that they'll eventually, you know, produce the works of Shakespeare." Alex: "*Who's gonna clean those typewriters?*"

And yet that was one of the most endearing part of Neil: he never lost that young man's tendency to think *very deeply* and *very seriously* about everything. This is why his lyrics and drumming were so good. He never phoned anything in. Not even his jokes.

I don't care if Neil was an avowed atheist who even wrote a song called "Faithless." I like to think he's at peace and that his family will find some measure of peace as well. R.I.P. Professor, and God Bless.

INTRODUCTION: RESPOND, VIBRATE, FEEDBACK, AND RESONATE

"I am so appreciative of our fans. I bless their hearts every single day. But they're hard to analyze as a group because they're so different." [1]

A REMARKABLE BOND

This isn't a book about me, but I'm going to have to talk about myself a *little* bit, so please bear with me.

This isn't even a book about Rush, the beloved Canadian rock band that was *more* than a band to many of us, although Rush will be *in* it. There are enough Rush biographies and documentaries out there without me adding to the din. In fact, the 2016 film *Time Stand Still* is about Rush's final tour in 2015

---

1   Geddy Lee, *Beyond the Lighted Stage* (Documentary, 2010).

and the relationship the band had with its fans, who made their uncompromising four-decade career possible. Geddy Lee has expressed this sentiment many times, for example, in the liner notes to 1998's live album *Different Stages*[2] and in his speech during the band's induction into the Rock & Roll Hall of Fame in 2013:

> And on behalf of my two partners, I have to thank the most passionate, most dedicated, incredible fan base around the globe. That's you guys. For not only supporting and encouraging our musical progress over the years, but for the insistence of their voices which has most certainly led us to this evening. We share this honor with you. Thank you.[3]

So why write a book covering such well-trodden ground?

Because, as far as I am aware, there has never been a book detailing what it is about *certain types of people* that makes us so loyal to Rush. "Most bands have fans," writes *Toronto Star* journalist and friend of the band Vinay Menon. "RUSH has kindred spirits."[4] We know the fan base is intense in the emotional connection it feels to Geddy, Alex, and Neil and their music, but *why*? What makes your average Rush fan tick? Are all the stereotypes about Rush fans true? If so, what does that tell us about why the band's music appeals to them? And if *not*, what does *that* tell us?

In other words, is there a Rush fan *type*?

So this book is different. This book is about *you*, the Rush fan, the kindred spirit.

Over the course of 41 years, bassist/vocalist/keyboardist Geddy Lee, guitarist Alex Lifeson, and drummer/lyricist Neil

---

2 "... But most significantly, we would like to thank our many fans around the world for their long-standing support which, to our continuing amazement, has enabled us to hang around for so damn long - despite the inherent weirdness of our music!"
3 Rock & Roll Hall of Fame Acceptance Speech, April 18, 2013, available at https://www.youtube.com/watch?v=TKuO1FpCWRI, last accessed March 4, 2020.
4 Vinay Menon, *Rush: An Oral History* (Toronto Star Newspapers Limited, 2013), at 4.

Peart created some of the most exciting, complicated, and thought-provoking rock music the world has ever seen. I know the label "prog" gets attached to Rush, which I understand given their penchant for odd time signatures, ambitious compositions, and ridiculous skill at their respective instruments. But Rush was a *rock* band, whose main purpose was to write catchy, driving songs that would elicit a visceral, emotional response in their listeners. That their songs *didn't* focus on the typical rock fare of sex, drugs, and other forms of illicit behavior only endeared Rush to their legion of rabid fans.

Why? Why was there such a special connection between Rush and their fans than, say, Led Zeppelin and their fans, or Van Halen, or The Rolling Stones, or The Eagles, or U2 have with theirs? What is it about the fans of this critically reviled[5] but commercially[6] and popularly beloved trio of Canadian misfits that inspires such fervor? Why did the death of Neil Peart on January 7, 2020 at the age of 67 from glioblastoma affect so many of us so deeply?

Personally, I have never been affected by a celebrity death until Neil's. I mention this for two reasons: (1) I am not alone, and (2) it forms the impetus for this book.

In conversations after Neil's passing with my brother, a Rush fan himself,[7] we found ourselves wondering why we couldn't stop thinking about Neil Peart. We never met him! He didn't know that we existed outside of that amorphous, abstract concept he knew of as his fan base! Yet every time we listened to Rush's music, thought about Peart's lyrics, or watched an old interview with him, it felt like he was still alive. In interviews after Peart's death, longtime fan of the band Donna Halper, the woman in large part responsible for their long and illustrious career, expressed the same sentiment, finding herself talking about Neil in the present tense.[8]

---

5   Until recently.
6   "RUSH ranks third for most consecutive gold or platinum studio albums by a rock band, behind only The Beatles and The Rolling Stones." Vinay Menon, *Rush: An Oral History*, at 4.
7   Thanks to me.
8   Listen to, for example, her January 22 interview on *The Bob Cesca Show* podcast.

This was weird, right? I'm a fan of both David Bowie and Prince, yet their deaths did not affect me like Neil's. No, this was different. And like I said, a quick Internet search of newspaper articles, blogs, and social media postings shows that my brother and I are not the only ones who feel this way.

Rush *fans* are as interesting a beast as Rush *the band*. The Rush fan stereotype is a familiar one to anyone with a passing familiarity with the band: geeky, socially awkward white males who are bad with girls, play *Dungeons and Dragons* and video games, and probably have severe halitosis. In other words, Rush were a *nerd band*.

This is, of course, the portrait painted by the hipster-driven music press before they were even called hipsters. Yet my own experience was very different. There were all sorts of people who liked Rush. Some of them were the "cool kids." And yes, I hope you're sitting down for this one, but *even females were fans*.

Have you recovered from the shock yet? Good.

Now, none of this is news if you're a Rush fan yourself. I relate these anecdotes for the benefit of those picking up the book out of curiosity or who are new to the band and their music. Suffice it to say, the typical Rush fan shares many traits with other Rush fans, and yet comes from all sorts of walks of life. How do I know this? Not just from my own personal experience, but from a survey I conducted on-line to gather as much data as I could from Rush fans to see if these stereotypes were true or false, and to also determine what, if any, commonalities I could draw. Over 650 fans responded, giving me a picture of (mostly American) Rush fans that is *at least* as accurate as any political polling you see in the news media.[9] I get into the specifics of the survey and its results in each chapter dedicated to one or more of the popular conceptions/stereotypes of Rush fans, so the questions were devised with these stereotypes in mind. None of these were meant to pry, nor with the intent of sharing

---

[9] I am forever indebted to Ed Stenger of the great blog Rush Is A Band (www.rushisaband.com) for blasting the word about my survey out on Twitter and on his website. I never would have gotten the sheer volume of responses without his help.

any information fans did not authorize me to disclose. I'm a lawyer—I know how this works.

The survey[10] I asked Rush fans to fill out asked the following questions:

- Name
- Age
- Gender
- Race
- Ethnicity
- Country
- Education Level
- Area(s)/Field(s) of Study
- Occupation(s)
- Are you a musician?
- If yes to above, what do you play?
- Other hobbies/areas of interest
- Religion (if any)
- Politics (e.g., More Left? Right? Libertarian? Etc.)
- When did you first start listening to Rush?
- What was the first Rush song you heard?
- How did you become a Rush fan?
- Favorite Rush song (if you HAD to pick one)
- First Rush album you bought
- Favorite Rush album and why
- Favorite Rush era
- Have you seen Rush in concert?

---

10   Though I am no longer accepting answers, you can still see the survey on my website at https://amatopia.wordpress.com/2020/02/05/rush-survey-is-live/

- If yes, how many times and which tours?
- Favorite Rush concert memory or memories?
- What other kinds of music do you like?
- Do you enjoy what are considered "nerd" or "geek" hobbies?
- If "yes," which ones? (e.g., comic books, sci-fantasy, tabletop RPGs, etc.)
- How did you react to Neil Peart's death?
- What does Rush's music mean to you?

I'll provide a little teaser here by saying Rush fans are a more diverse lot than conventional wisdom would say. And there are several commonalities among fans, though not necessarily the ones you may be thinking of.

Let me give you an example of the power of Rush's music. One of my favorite things to do is watch reaction videos on YouTube. "Reaction videos" are a genre where the name describes them perfectly: videos showing people's reactions to experiencing certain things for the first time, be it a movie, a TV show, a video game, food or drink, or more germane to our purposes, music.

I'm a musician myself, as musicians are always fond of letting you know, so I enjoy watching musicians or people with deep knowledge and appreciation of music react to stuff they've never heard before and talking about why they do or don't like it. And there's a subset of reaction video I like to call, for lack of a better term, "Black Guys React."

Before you close the book, offended that I'm getting all racial on you, I beg your continued indulgence for a few more paragraphs as there *is* a point to this story.

Now, there are *all sorts of people of various ethnicities* who make reaction videos. But I'm discussing African-Americans since Rush has, fairly or not, been sneered at by some as a "white" band, as though having a primarily Caucasian fan base is intrinsically negative thing or reflects poorly upon *the band itself*, but that's a debate for another day. This may be more due to the fact that *progressive rock as a genre* appeals mostly to white males,[11] which we'll get into in Chapter III. A second reason is that there are, surprisingly, *tons* of Rush reaction videos made by black YouTubers.

Some of these were made before Neil's passing, some after, and a bunch were reactions to Neil's live drum solos. Before we begin—and if you're a Rush fan, you already know this so feel free to skip—but Neil Peart was leagues above his peers when it came to constructing and playing drum solos. "It is no exaggeration to say that Neil was one of . . . rock music's most respected drummers," wrote Donna Halper on January 21, 2020 in her hometown newspaper *The Patriot Ledger*. "Even drummers in other bands admired his work, and there were rock critics who didn't like Rush's music but still acknowledged Neil's talent."[12] In other words, in music as well as in sports, *talent will out* and *like recognizes like*.[13]

The drum solo has been mocked, and for good reason, as the part of a rock show when it's time to brave the crowds and detritus they leave behind to venture to the venue's fragrant lavatory, or maybe grab a beer or some other form of chemical enhancement before coming back to see the band play their next *real* song. It doesn't help that most rock drummers, while good at *keeping the beat*, aren't so good at playing all by themselves.[14]

Not Neil. Nope. It's not just that he had a gigantic drumset so big it had to rotate so he could play the whole thing. It's not just

---

11   *See, e.g.,* James Parker, "The Whitest Music Ever: Prog rock was audacious, innovative—and awful," *The Atlantic*, September 2017, available at https://www.theatlantic.com/magazine/archive/2017/09/the-whitest-music-ever/534174/, last accessed March 4, 2020.
12   Available at https://www.patriotledger.com/entertainmentlife/20200121/quincy-woman-who-discovered-rush-remembers-drummer-neil-peart, last accessed February 15, 2020.
13   I can't help but think of the deep and sincere respect rival basketball legends Magic Johnson and Larry Bird had for each other and the friendship they formed off the court despite their epic duels on it.
14   Ginger Baker, one of Neil's biggest influences, is a notable rock exception I can think of off the top of my head.

DREAMERS & MISFITS

that Neil, unlike many drummers (ahem, Nick Mason)[15] *actually used every last bit* of his gargantuan drumkit. And it wasn't just Neil's superlative skill that set him apart from his peers.

It was how Neil *constructed* his drum solos.

Lots of drummers are good *drummers*. Not a lot of drummers are good *composers*. Neil was. His solos were built, like his drum parts in general, in an orchestral fashion, playing rhythmic melodies. The solos move from fast snare work to tom-heavy fills, to African-inspired rhythms on his electronic drums, to a call-and-response between marimba and drum to a full on jazz workout accompanied by a pre-taped horn section Neil would trigger with samples tied to his electronic drums.

The solos last around eight minutes but whizz by since they're so damn *interesting*.[16] And watching them is utterly mesmerizing. I remember showing one such solo to my seven-year-old son shortly after Neil's death. My son's response: "He had a really special talent."

Yes he did.

When these YouTube reactors who'd never listened to Rush before watch Neil play, their faces become masks of bewilderment as they nod along, interjecting with their analysis and admiration of his playing. I particularly like a YouTuber named Jamel_AKA_Jamal's video about Neil's drum solo from Rush's concert in Frankfurt during their 30th Anniversary World Tour in 2004.[17] One of my favorite channels is called Lost in Vegas. The two gentlemen, George and Ryan, come from a rap and hip-hop background and through their channel delve deep into the world of rock and metal.[18] They offer very trenchant expla-

---

15   I say this with love—Pink Floyd is another band I could write an entire book about.
16   As much as I love Rush concerts from the *Clockwork Angels* and *R40* tours, with their shorter drum solos in the middle of certain songs, I miss the full solos of earlier tours.
17   Available at https://www.youtube.com/watch?v=jyPbaIxH0mc, last accessed March 4, 2020. As Jamel_AKA_Jamal puts it, "[Neil]'s your favorite drummer's favorite drummer."
18   *See, e.g.,*, Petr Knava, "These Two Guys Discovering Rock and Metal Music is the Most Heartwarming, Joyful Thing You'll See Today," *Pajiba*, March 6, 2018, available at https://www.pajiba.com/web_culture/lost-in-vegas-is-the-most-heartwarming-joyful-youtube-channel-around.php last accessed February 15, 2020.

nations about *why* a piece of music works . . . and they *really* seem to like Rush.[19]

The overwhelming sense George and Ryan convey in these videos is that Rush is *fire*. Music transcends barriers of culture and subculture, race and ethnicity, nation and continent. Even me writing this little anecdote is poking fun at the idea that some bands or some styles of music should be "white" and some "black," and that a black guy is incapable of enjoying and understanding Rush and a white guy is incapable of enjoying and understanding rap.[20] It's preposterous, and the kind of thing the band would likely agree with me about.

> *You and I, we are pressed into these solitudes*
> *Color and culture, language and race*
> *Just variations on a theme*
> *Islands in a much larger stream*
>
> *For you and me, race is not a competition*
> *For you and me, race is not a definition*
> *For you and me*
> *We agree*

"Alien Shore"

As you'll see through the course of this book, Rush fans run the gamut, although there are threads that seem to typify your average Rush fan, if any of us weirdos can be considered "average." Many are musicians. Many have backgrounds in science and engineering. Many were or still are into what are popularly called "nerdy" hobbies like role-playing games, computers, sci-fi, and fantasy. Many were politically center-left or libertarian. Many were atheist or agnostic. Many were male. Many were white.

---

19 One of the best parts is at the 6:30 mark of their "La Villa Strangiato" video when George expresses his belief that there's no way Rush is a trio. "Lies. Lies. Lies. There's eight people in this band. Y'all got a couple of motherfuckers underneath the stage . . ."
20 Of course, Rush and rap meet on "Roll the Bones."

But these are the superficial similarities. It's the deeper ones I'm more interested in.

We'll get into Rush's musicianship, lyrical content, and personality, and why it resonates so much with fans, later on, but suffice it to say Rush's songs fire the imagination and provide hope and comfort in ways few rock bands can.

I will close this introduction trying to answer the question "Why are we here?" with something other than "Because we're here." In fact, I will answer this question with three other questions:

1. What is it that binds Rush fans together? In other words, what is the "Rush fan" archetype?
2. Why does this band speak to so many of us so deeply? and;
3. Why did Neil Peart's death affect so many of us, who never knew the man but for his words and his drumming, in such a profound way?

The first five chapters get into question 1. Chapter I will look at popular and critical conceptions of Rush and their fans. Next, Chapters II, III, IV, and V will each focus on one or more stereotypical aspects—appellations or epithets, depending on your perspective—thrown towards Rush fans and exploring how accurate or not this is in light of my survey results. Chapters VI and VII will look at questions 2 and 3, respectively. Chapter VIII gets into the fanbase's favorite songs and albums, while Chapter IX will attempt to bring it all home, put a bow on it, and any other cliché you think is appropriate. The Appendices feature portions of survey results and interviews I conducted in writing this book.

The results of my research were illuminating, entertaining, poignant, and a little mind-blowing. I sincerely hope you will enjoy the fruits of my labor as we travel across the cosmos of Rush fandom, learning lessons, making memories, and having a few laughs along the way.

We sometimes catch a window
A glimpse of what's beyond
Was it just imagination
Stringing us along?
More things than are dreamed about
Unseen and unexplained
We suspend our disbelief
We are entertained

"Mystic Rhythms"

CHAPTER I: SUPERIOR CYNICS

"You rarely will find someone who used to be the high school quarterback to be a Rush fan, or the head cheerleader is rarely a Rush fan. But the band geek that you knew in high school, or the guy that was super-good at science is probably a Rush fan. So we're a very smart, artistic, and intelligent bunch, I would say, but with that comes maybe some social awkwardness." [1]

A VERY DIFFERENT DRUMMER

Every subculture attracts a certain type of person. Your fan of classical music tends *on average* to be different than your fan of death metal or hip-hop. Your fan of patchwork quilting tends *on average* to be different than your fan of motorcycles. Your

---

1   Jillian Maryonovich, *Rush: Time Stand Still* (Documentary, 2016).

fan of the New York Yankees tends *on average* to be different than your normal human being.² You get the idea. There is some overlap, but every group gathered around a different hobby or pursuit tends to have certain core commonalities, and these commonalities differ from those of other groups of fans, whatever it is they are fans of.

And sometimes, as was the case with Rush, a group of fans were despised by the music press.

I say this in the past sense because the hatred for Rush fans is pretty much non-existent nowadays. Sure, there is some light ribbing, but not the visceral dislike we saw in the 1970s and 1980s. Before we get into the similarities between Rush fans and see whether the popular stereotypes about them are valid, it's worth discussing why Rush fans themselves were the object of so much scorn, almost as much as the band itself, and how this may have shaped Rush fans' perceptions of themselves.

THE COOL KIDS' TABLE

"Rush weren't straight up prog," actor W. Earl Brown told me over Twitter. "Rush weren't straight ahead rock. Rush didn't fit. Nor did the fans. In the 70s and early 80s, there was no such thing as a cool nerd. Rush was nerdy yet powerful—they attracted a nerd herd of smart & interesting people. The cool kids scoffed."[3]

"Rush didn't fit the mold of a rock band," explains Ed Stenger, long-time Rush fan and proprietor of one of the biggest and best Rush websites, RushIsABand.com. "A lot of the reasons Rush fans are so passionate about the band is the same reasons these critics didn't like them."[4] Stenger elaborates:

---

2   I kid, I kid.
3   W. Earl Brown, May 13, 2020, available at https://www.twitter.com/WEarlBrown/status/1260602029145124865
4   Ed Stenger, interview with the author, May 19, 2020 (Appendix C).

> They were almost too serious for rock music from a lot of the critics' standpoints, too pretentious. What do they think they're doing, 20 minute songs. I think that was the key right there. They weren't used to seeing a band like this and they were like "Who are these guys?"[5]

I think Brown and Stenger are on to something. In particular, Brown's usage of the term "the cool kids" to describe the music press is perfect, particularly as it relates to their relationship to prog rock as a genre. We saw this in the 1970s, and we still see it to a degree now. One example of this phenomenon can be seen in the Chicago-based Pitchfork.com—the so-called "Most Trusted Voice in Music"—and their reviews of modern-day prog-metal behemoth Tool.

First, here's a bit from Pitchfork's review of Tool's 2001 album *Lateralus*, where reviewer Brent DiCrescenzo writes a story-within-a-review from the perspective of a young Tool fan:

> I feel like this record was made just for me by super-smart aliens or something, because it's just like a cross of 1971 and 1987. Imagine, like, Peter Gabriel with batwings or a flower on his head singing while Lars Ulrich and Rick Wakeman just hammer it down. It's the best Tool record because it's the longest. All summer I worked at Gadzooks, folding novelty t-shirts, and on each break, I would listen to *Lateralus* because the store just plays hip-hop and dance. My manager would always get on me for taking my breaks 20 minutes too long, but that's how long the album is and it just sucks you in.[6]

---

5   *Id.*
6   May 15, 2001, available at https://pitchfork.com/reviews/albums/8104-lateralus/, last accessed May 14, 2020.

The whole thing is rather snide, unsurprising given DiCrescenzo's 1.9-out-of-10 rating for the album. Note the sneering references to mall culture and the fictitious Tool fan feeling like nobody understands him.

Here's Jess Harvell reviewing Tool's 2006 album *10,000 Days*:

> Like most progressive rock and heavy metal—hell, maybe most popular music in general—suspension of disbelief is key with Tool. Taken at face value, with their song suites, meat puppet videos, and histrionic singer, they're pretty goofy. People make fun of Tool fans because they assume they take the band seriously—these spotty, greasy kids with bad shoes and worse hair who already wear an insult on their T-shirts. At 28, I'd feel funny mocking 15-year-olds still finding their place in the world. And as for taking them seriously—well, I take Tool about as seriously as I do black metal or Lil Jon or the films of Tsui Hark. Which is to say, not very.[7]

Harvell, at least, tempers the derision for Tool and prog fans with a little understanding of what it's like being young. But even still, Harvell has to throw in that he *totally* doesn't take Tool seriously, and that fans who *do* take them seriously are mock-worthy. Keep the usage of words like "spotty" and "greasy" in mind, because we will see them again later.

And finally, here's a bit from Jeremy D. Larson's review of Tool's 2019 album, *Fear Inoculum*:

> Tool are just King Crimson in Joker makeup. They thrive in an enormously popular world of polyrhythms and prurience; of Jungian philosophy and Bill Hicks memes; of pewter drag-

---

[7] May 1, 2006, available at https://pitchfork.com/reviews/albums/8105-10000-days/, last accessed May 14, 2020.

on statues with orbs in their mouths and guys telling you that DMT is actually a chemical in your brain. Forged in the mad-at-my-dad fires of '90s post-grunge and nu-metal, the progressive metal quartet has sustained a decades-long career on equal parts technical precision and psychedelic bullshit. Their multi-part songs are loosely about embracing pain, grief, desire, transgression, until all your chakras are open and you know exactly why the pieces fit. They've been a punchline for years.[8]

Now, Larson does go on to explain that *the band themselves* might not take themselves too seriously and are *in on the joke too*! Because bands like Tool *have* to be a joke. Nobody takes prog rock seriously, right?

SOME PEOPLE WILL JUST NEVER LIKE YOU

For whatever reason, Rush fans and prog fans in general were singled out by the music press just as much as the actual bands. Journalist David Weigel, most well-known for his political writing, penned a love-letter to the genre called *The Show that Never Ends: The Rise and Fall of Prog Rock*. Rush features prominently in the book, as is expected, but for our purposes it's Weigel's discussion of Rush fans and the backlash that *they* faced which is most interesting:

> Progressive rock was, at that exact moment [the late 1970s], being chewed up by a critical backlash. The fans showing up to hear Rush were the wrong kind of fans—the mockable ones,

---

[8] September 5, 2019, available at https://pitchfork.com/reviews/albums/tool-fear-inoculum/, last accessed May 14, 2020.

with mockable taste in music. "Rush failed to deliver the killer punch I had half-hoped was coming," Paul Morley wrote in *NME*. "Instead it was heads down for the first of their long Science Fantasy epics and, after that, epic after epic. As far as I could tell, there was little point to them." [9]

I do have a minor correction to Weigel's analysis: Morely wrote the first *half* of the article, whose full title is "The Rush Phenomenon: This Band Has Fans. Lots Of Them. They Sold Out The Free Trade Hall And Surprised Even The Promoter. PAUL MORLEY asks why, PAUL RAMBALI tries to answer."[10] Paul Morely wrote about the British fans gathered to see Rush, while Paul Rambali wrote a more in-depth concert review. The words Weigel quoted were actually written by Rambali. Again, a small quibble, but I want to be accurate because we're going to take a deep dive into this very same article.

In the *New Musical Express* piece, Morley expresses his sheer disbelief that Rush had any sort of fan base whatsoever:

> I AM ON THE TRAIN, sat uncomfortably among a load of moderately hairy, strangely excited, spotty young kids. They are wearing pre-faded denims, Levi jackets and tatty pumps, and I'm thinking that I must have accidentally jumped into a carriage containing some sort of school trip—until the train stops and all the kids herd onto the platform.
>
> I see T-shirts and garishly coloured embroidery on the backs of the Levi jackets, exclaiming Ted Nugent! Kiss! Blue Oyster Cult! And,

---

9 David Weigel, *The Show That Never Ends: The Rise and Fall of Prog Rock* (W.W. Norton & Company, 2017), at 161.
10 *New Musical Express*, June 11, 1977, available at http://www.2112.net/powerwindows/transcripts/19770611newmusicalexpress.htm, last accessed May 12, 2020.

> most Noticeably, Rush! Christ, they're going the same place I'm going—to see Rush.
>
> Rush have fans! I thought the only other people in the Free Trade Hall would be a few reluctant or curious fellow hacks. But of course Rush have fans. It's just that it's a bit of a surprise, is all. Quite unnoticed by anyone, it seems, maybe even Rush's followers themselves, the band has zoomed from obscurity through cult status to hover around superstardom. A phenomenon.
>
> The Free Trade Hall had sold out, apparently surprising even the promoters.

There is no mention of the fans' races or genders here, although we can assume they are male (see the adjectives "hairy" and "spotty"[11]) as well as white (this being Manchester, England in the 1970s), but the disdain Morley feels for the concertgoers is, though not vicious, certainly palpable.[12] You can sense this in his interactions with Rush fans as he tries in vain to understand what this phenomenon is all about:

> So what's it all about? I donned my investigative mac and trilby, swam merrily through the Free Trade Hall bar, and did my best to uncover . . . why.
>
> Most of the fans I talked to seemed unimpressed at my disbelief, seemed unimpressed moreover that Rush could fill the hall so effortlessly. "Could have played two night, I reckon," said one guy. My knees buckled slightly.

---

[11] To the English, "spotty" refers to acne and other skin blemishes on young people, usually young men, and connotes someone who is not worth taking seriously due to both their age and their hygiene.

[12] It will, however, turn vicious later on; see Chapter IV: God and Government.

There was a good number, too, who claimed that they'd discovered Rush way back in 1974 (which is a long time ago in terms of this audience—it was overwhelmingly school aged) by, apparently, listening to the radio or just "knowing by the cover of the album that they were a good rock band." A few remembered The Old Grey Whistle Test playing a Rush track, and took it from there.

Everywhere it was blatantly apparent that there is a rare fanaticism for Rush, and an insatiable appetite for any imported flash heavy metal. I must be mixing with the wrong people, because really this was all a revelation to me. I dug deeper, asking a number of milder looking fans why they actually liked Rush.

So, why? "Because they're good . . . It's really good music and it hits the brain . . . They seem to get better with each album . . . They're Canada's best rock group. . . People want to go to live shows and hear really heavy stuff that's gonna freak them out . . . I don't think you give them enough coverage . . . Are you Max Bell? . . . Their words are nice, they really get a lot of things across . . . Power and intelligence . . . They're different from Ted and Sabbath and all that lot . . . Because I want to. . ."

Reeling from all this, and from the remarks of one guy who put me firmly in my place when I asked: "Aren't they similar to Led Zep?"—he sternly replied, "Ah, but Led Zep are a quartet and this lot are a trio"—I found my seat.

For those of us who got into Rush fans in the late 80s, 90s, or later, it's interesting to see that the fierce loyalty among the fans was already firmly established at the time this piece was published: a year after the release of *2112* and three months before *A Farewell to Kings*.

As far as his thoughts on the band itself, Morley walked away impressed by their musicianship, but he still didn't "get" the acquired taste[13] that was Rush:

> It was a tense and crude atmosphere, obvious what was imminent—a rush to the stage as soon as Rush appeared onstage. Unfortunately I missed the no doubt almighty welcome for Rush because minutes before the big moment I was thrown out of the hall for assaulting its manager. But when I sneaked back in everyone was standing in the stalls, arms outstretched, plenty of V-signs, the odd Rush banner, and even a fairly large Canadian flag right at the front.
>
> It was no way a perfunctory response. The kids around where I was stood knew every note and lyric of each song. There were even odd attempts at lighting matches, a la American audiences.
>
> Rush played absolutely amazingly—no sloppiness, total control, all the flash licks, sharp riffs, Jerk-off guitar solos brilliantly executed, carefully placed breaks, classy pinnacle vocals that the crowd was thirsting for. Their light show was maybe the best I've ever seen.

---

13   *See, e.g.,* WMMR Philadelphia DJ Pierre Robert in the May 15, 2004 issue of *Billboard*: "Rush is a unique sound and some would say an acquired taste." (p. 55). There is also a popular meme that reads, over a shot of the band playing "Xanadu" in the mid-1970s, "Rush is an acquired taste. Don't like them? Acquire some taste."

It was loud, but very very clean. The band looked like puppets—they could play The Royal Variety Show and probably offend no one.

So what is it about Rush?

This concluding question was what Rambali tried to answer in his conclusion of the *NME* article. And he doesn't get it either:

> MAYBE IT'S SOMETHING to do with the cathartic effect of a big noise. Unlike other turn-of-the-decade phenomena, such as glitter and the introspective singer songwriter, heavy metal refuses to die the death.
>
> It isn't just a question of dinosaurs still being extant either—new heroes emerge with increasing regularity. Last year it was Ted Nugent and this year Judas Priest and, no two ways about it, Rush.
>
> They thunder into the opening number with all the power and subtlety of an earthquake, and the crowd roar in approval as Alex Lifeson and Geddy Lee roam around the stage in an endless series of guitar superhero postures and power-chord dynamics.
>
> This staunch observer was almost converted as the first three numbers (especially "Bastille Day") sledgehammered into the audience. But Rush failed to deliver the killer punch I had half-hoped was coming—instead it was heads down for the first of their long Science Fantasy epics and, after that, epic after epic.

As far as I could tell, there was little point to them. They were no more than a lot of riffs, mostly derived from Sabbath, Purple and Zeppelin, and loosely thrown together around various concepts. Titles like "By-Tor And The Snow Dog" and "The Fountain Of Lamneth"[14] give a fair indication of what to expect—the fairytale castles of Yes meet Sabbath's headbanger.

But never mind the content, just feel the dynamics. Each successive riff ploughed new depths of heavy metal dynamism, and the only unusual thing was Geddy Lee's strangled banshee vocals, which sounded like someone trying to sing like Robert Plant after an unfortunate accident. Alex Lifeson played elementary power chords and gimmick-laden solos, and Neil Peart's drums were exemplary heavy metal thunder.

However, Rush's ability in their chosen field is unquestionable. No matter how overworked the basic idea may be, they attack it with enough ferocious zest and almost obsessive dedication that the results really did sound alive and, to the crowd at least, fresh.

The degree of technological sophistication involved in Rush's stage show simply reflects the single-mindedness with which they approach their music.

---

14 No one, including the band, is quite sure if they actually ever played "The Fountain of Lamneth" live, and no live recordings of the song exist. This article gives credence to the theory that they did, but it is also equally possible that Mr. Rambali is mistaken.

> The epics were full of dramatic lighting (their own, specially flown in) and Lifeson was surrounded by echo units, phase shifters, digital delay and harmonizers—very expensive stuff that enabled him to seemingly double-track his guitar on stage.
>
> The PA (their own again) used digital delay to spread the sound out over the stereo columns, and the sound mixer knew exactly when to boost the volume—they didn't miss a trick, visually or aurally.
>
> Rush's dedication to their cause is about to pay off, the opinions of those who see it as some kind of sophisticated torture notwithstanding.

    I am not saying that rock critics have to like or understand a band, and Rambali is actually pretty fair in his assessment of Rush's music and on-stage presentation. This relative even-handedness is admirable given that Rambali, like Morley, was hip-deep in the decidedly anti-prog world of punk rock. But reading this, one can't help get the impression that, like Morley, Rambali also thinks the band's fans are easily amused rubes stunned by pretty lights, pummeling riffs, and puerile lyrics.

    "What are the two things that the cognoscenti of the Rock and Roll Hall of Fame or *Rolling Stone* magazine, which are one and the same, hate the most?" asks Martin Popoff, author of *Rush: The Illustrated History*. "They hate progressive rock, they hate heavy metal. Well, Rush invented progressive metal. They're both."[15] This genre snobbery definitely explains the rock press's disdain for Rush, which could *at best* be called "lukewarm." Obviously, this disdain spilled over to the kinds of people who would actually *like* this weird Canadian band with the super-high-pitched singing guy. People have to be a

---

15   *Rush: Time Stand Still* (Documentary, 2016).

bit touched in the head, or at least uncool, to tolerate this guy's voice, right?

And while we're at it, let's take an aside to talk about Geddy Lee's voice.

YES, HE SPEAKS LIKE AN ORDINARY GUY

Most Rush fans are aware of indie rock darlings Pavement's 1997 single "Stereo," which features frontman Stephen Malkmus pondering the following:

> *What about the voice of Geddy Lee*
> *How did it get so high?*
> *I wonder if he speaks like an ordinary guy?*
> *(I know him and he does)*

Well, I'm glad this got sorted out!

Malkmus's lyrics are a gentle rumination, a funny little wink at a very famous rock singer's distinctive voice. But contemporary reviewers of Rush just *could not get over Lee's singing*. I find this amazing considering the sheer amount of beloved high-pitched singers like the aforementioned Robert Plant, and flat-out *bad* singers like Bob Dylan and Bruce Springsteen and many punk rock singers who, quite literally, aren't even hitting the right notes, or any notes at all.

Luckily, a fantastic user of RateYourMusic.com named schmidtt compiled a multi-page thread titled "Rolling Stone's 500 Worst Reviews of All Time."[16] In his section on *2112*, he gathers all of the various critics' insults about Lee's vocals.

First, here's Alan Niester's review of *2112* for the 1979 *Rolling Stone Record Guide*:

---

16 Available at https://rateyourmusic.com/list/schmidtt/rolling-stones-500-worst-reviews-of-all-time-work-in-progress/1/, last accessed May 12, 2020.

> **Rating:** 2 Stars
> This Canadian power trio, which boasts a vocalist who sounds like a cross between Donald Duck and Robert Plant, reached its pinnacle of success the day it was discovered by Circus magazine and turned into fanzine wall-decoration material. Rush is to the late Seventies what Grand Funk was to the early Seventies—the power boogie band for the 16 magazine graduating class. Rush Archives, a reissue of the first LPs, is docked one star for pointlessness.[17]

And of course, there's more—note the appearance of some familiar faces in schmidtt's rundown of the Geddy Lee Two Minutes of Hate:

> Devoting a whole side of your album to a seven-part suite about the dystopian future of year 2112 (inspired by the writings of Ayn Rand, no less) was hardly a move likely to endear you to many rock critics in the 1970s, and indeed, it is hard to think of a band more despised than Rush were in that decade. Alan Niester's mocking entry in the first edition of the record guide was hardly atypical: much of the "criticism" of this band tended to consist of little more than a string of insults about Geddy Lee's voice. "God knows I've never been anything resembling wild about Led Zeppelin—and once, in fact, was famous for having said so—but even at their absolute crassest Page & Co. always throw in at least a little humor," John mendels(s)ohn wrote in the March '75 issue of *Phonograph Record*, in a review of Rush's second LP, *Fly By Night*. "To put it as succinctly

---

[17] schmidtt, https://rateyourmusic.com/list/schmidtt/rolling-stones-500-worst-reviews-of-all-time-work-in-progress/6/, last accessed May 12, 2020.

as possible, Rush sound—quite deliberately, one supposes—like Led Zeppelin with lobotomies, singer Geddy Lee like Robert Plant at 33 1/3 rpm." Meanwhile, Paul Rambali compared Lee's "strangled banshee vocals" to "someone trying to sing like Robert Plant after an unfortunate accident" in the 6/11/77 issue of *NME*. "If gnomes sang in rock bands it'd sound like this," Rick O'Shea concluded in a 5/5/79 concert review that ran in *Pop Star Weekly*. "Lots of special lighting tricks, explosions, robot voices, whirs, squawks and chirps couldn't disguise the fact that this was shallow, repetitive pompous nonsense."[18]

So yes, it's safe to say that critics really did not like Geddy Lee's voice. At least they were creative in their insults.

BACK TO THE FAN HATE

"By the time Rush emerged, progressive rock had entered its never-ending defensive phase," writes Kelefa Sanneh in *The New Yorker*. "[U]ncoolness is now part of the genre's identity."[19] This uncoolness may have been a music press creation. Our friend schmidtt does us a favor by pointing us to yet another Paul Morley hatchet job of Rush and their fans, his June 24, 1978 review of Rush's *Archives*, a collection of the band's first three albums (*Rush*, *Fly By Night*, and *Caress of Steel*).

Now, as we'll see in Chapter IV: God and Government, another *NME* writer, Barry Miles, concluded after his interview with the band that they were probably fascists—a fact Weigel finds "scabrous": "The leading music paper and taste maker

---

18   *Id.*
19   Kelefa Sanneh, "The Persistence of Prog Rock," *New Yorker*, June 12, 2017, available at https://www.newyorker.com/magazine/2017/06/19/the-persistence-of-prog-rock, last accessed May 8, 2020.

branded Rush's music—music partially composed by a Holocaust survivor's son—as 'fascistic.'"[20] This, of course, spilled over into assessments of Rush fans. How could it not, given the left-wing leanings of most critics—no wonder why punk was "embraced almost immediately"[21] by the critics, and bands like Rush disregarded at best and reviled at worst, their fans viewed as "slow-witted."[22]

Back to Morley. His review of *Archives* paints a particularly scathing portrait—a caricature, really—of Rush's fans. The music on the first three albums is "monotonous" and "pompous," "complete rubbish," and is "unimportant, derivative, false and above all else IMMATURE."[23] And clearly, this immature music appealed only to immature people:

> It's when the motivation for Rush becomes apparent, and the way it's translated into music (The Power And The Glory) and lyrics (Journeys For Pureness And Power) that the reason for Rush's actual popularity becomes clear. It's rooted in the immaturity of both the group and their fans. Immaturity of emotions, responses, ideals, character. A striving for something they'll both never have.
>
> Rush are musically a superficial splodgy mess of the stun [sic] of Led Zeppelin, the excessive structures of Yes and the melody of later Beatles. There's six sides of music here in this package, 24 songs and two suites. None, except for maybe the title track of "Fly By Night," has any genuine melodic and structural pres-

---

20   Weigel, at 163. And I am going to indulge in another minor correction of Weigel's otherwise excellent and fun book: *both* of Geddy Lee's parents survived the Holocaust *and* Nazi concentration camps: first Auschwitz, and then Dachau and Bergen-Belsen.
21   *Id.* Neil Peart's politics at the time didn't help either; more on this in Chapter IV, *infra*.
22   *Id.*
23   Paul Morley, "Power, Pomp, Purity, Pretension, Popularity . . . The RUSH Problem," *New Musical Express*, June 24, 1978, available at http://www.2112.net/powerwindows/transcripts/19780624nme.htm, last accessed May 12, 2020.

ence. The more usual workout comprises manic twisting riff progressions and an ultra-active rhythm section that drives the music along with the necessary macho propulsion. Acoustic and classical guitars give some slight textural variations; Geddy Lees' vocals are of the strained, painful, whining type.

The real point of the music, its major attraction, is its power. Thrashing about, nose-diving all over the place, thrusting and smashing. There are occasional reflective, acoustic songs that are interruptive, childish—really just token moments. Power is its popularity.[24]

We're getting deep down the rabbit hole here with references to power fantasies, populism, and male chauvinism . . . and yes, fascism. And all this from three nice Canadian suburbanites who just love playing rock and roll!

The striking thing, though, isn't the harsh word for the band. Bands are public figures and expect the slings and arrows of criticism to come their way. What stands out is the vituperative ire directed at *fans*, as though enjoying Rush's music puts one into a special class of undesirable. After all, "[t]he lyrics are calculated to appeal directly to the lonely, confused and immature," don't you know; they "naturally evade any diagnosis of any such problem." Peart's "words come from a direct male chauvinist viewpoint," and if they resonate with you, then you're clearly a male chauvinist. I mean, it goes without saying that "[t]he fantasies Rush concoct deal in mystical searches for pureness, strength and power, both physically and mentally." *Everybody* knows this, right?

If you like Rush, Morley continues, it's because you're *resentful*:

---

24 *Id.*

> Rush's fantasies are inspired by resentment—although the source of resentment in Rush's case is not easily definable—but a young fan can easily remodel that abstract and identify with it. This kind of resentment is not far from a spirit of revenge. Rush are certainly a strange substitute for power.

Don't you get it, Rush fans? Every time you rock out to "Bastille Day" or "2112" or even "Closer to the Heart," you're really seeking revenge on some great undefined "other" for your own powerlessness. And that's not all—you're probably also one bass fill away from your devotion to Rush transforming you into *literally Hitler*:

> Fascism lurking beneath the volume and noise? Sure. And the embarrassment to rock critics lies not in its implications but more in the naïvety of it all, an unawareness of what It Is Really All About. And I bet Rush fans revel in the works of Robert Heinlein.[25]

It's easy to mock Morley's paranoid hyperventilation and lurid fever-dreams as a product of his time, but then you remember that so many journalists, in the entertainment press and others, still think like this.

So we can conclude that Rush fans, as popularly conceived, are all white, male, and unpopular losers who can't think for themselves. These things are all problems, according to the coolest of the cool . . .

. . . *but are they true?*

---

25 Legendary sci-fi author Robert Heinlein transitioned from progressive politics to a more right-wing approach as he aged. Many on the left took umbrage with this transformation much the same way many on the right were not pleased when Neil Peart moved away from Randian Objectivism to a more center-left perspective.

CHAPTER II: CONFORM OR BE CAST OUT

"Neil, Geddy, Alex, They made it cool to be a nerd . . . long before it was cool to be a nerd. And I say that as a nerd." [1]

NERD IS THE WORD

Back in the early days of the Internet—I'm talking about the dark ages where if you were online, people couldn't *call your house* because there'd be a busy signal—there was a Rush message board I frequented. It was the forum on a larger site whose name I can't recall, but in addition to having extensive guitar and bass tablatures for every Rush album up to that point, the forum was full of knowledgeable, interesting people. I partic-

---

1   Bob Cesca, *The Bob Cesca Show Interview: Donna Halper on Neil Peart*, January 22, 2020, available at. http://www.bobcesca.com/the-bob-cesca-show-interview-donna-halper-on-neil-peart-1-22-20/.

ularly liked reading about other fan's concert experiences and going down the progressive rock rabbit holes to see what other bands a seventeen-year-old Rush fan might also find interesting. Anyway, there was a section where people would share less-than positive reviews about Rush, since many of them were funny, outrageous, and downright creative in their meanness. One guy posted a link to a website where "Limelight" was described as being catchier than AIDS (a joke now since removed), and where Rush's music—and their fans!—were routinely derided as being for "nerds," "losers," "dorks," and so on.

And Neil Peart was described as having "one vulva big ass drum kit."

The website was, of course, Mark's Record Reviews,[2] a now defunct music criticism/running diary of a music fan from New York City named Mark Prindle. The site is still up, though Mark stopped posting updates in 2011. But from 1996 until then, Mark's site was *hilarious* even if I didn't always agree with him.

So when I went to Mark's Rush page[3] and read this heading:

"Rush, featuring Geddy 'Crapvoice' Lee"

And the following introductory paragraph:

> Oh, Rush. Scourge of a nation. Murderer of a generation. Defamer of the eras. What is it with Rush, eh? You either love 'em or you hate 'em, right? Sure sure. It makes it easier to categorize them like that and not bother discussing their good points and bad. But dammit, I'm not an easy man. I'm a hard man. And I'm here to set the record (my own personal opinion) straight on Rush.
>
> Rush is a band for nerds. Sorry, hate to break it to you like that, but they are. Drummer Neil Peart writes lyrics like "High on the sacred

---

2   http://www.markprindle.com.
3   http://markprindle.com/rusha.htm, last accessed February 19, 2020.

mountain/Up the seven thousand stairs/In the golden light of Autumn/There was magic in the air." Singer/bassist Geddy Lee has the high geeky voice of a guy who, as my girlfriend puts it, "has been playing Dungeons & Dragons his whole life." And guitarist Alex Lifeson???? Well, he seems okay. Not sure what he's doing hanging out with those other two dorks.

Now let me get to the good points of Rush, those that may be—all three of them are top-notch at their instruments. Sometimes it's hard to tell, because their songwriting can be a bit simplistic, but if you sorta pay closer attention, you can hear that behind their silly overblown mystical nonsense, they've got a helluva nimble-fingered bassist, a crapuva lightning-speed beauty run ambiance guitarist who doesn't hog the spotlight, and one vulva bigass drum kit . . . You may have some lousy songs, but you have some great ones too! Plus, you're Canadian and one of you was on Bob and Doug McKenzie's "Take Off"! You're still a nerd band for loser dorks though.

    I could tell that it was largely done for comedic effect. And given my own relative level of immaturity, both then and now, I was hooked on Mark's site.
    A funny thing happened as these reviews went on, though: Mark gradually started to gain an appreciation for Rush's music. Though he was more of a fan of their earlier hard-rock albums and their resurgence in the 2000s, the reviews are still littered with asides that perfectly encapsulate the general view of Rush fans. There's this from Mark's *Fly By Night* review: "How could it not have occurred to Geddy and Alex that by making Neil

Peart their lyricist, they were giving up any possible chance of having sex with a girl?"[4]

Or how about this from his *A Farewell to King's* review: "And you've heard 'Closer To The Heart,' right? Short ballad? Really pretty? Maybe they played at your prom, if you want [sic] to a Nerd Science school?"[5]

And this one is a personal favorite, from the *Signals* review: "This is music by grown-ups for grown-ups. But relatively intelligent, mature grown-ups with a career! (Or, alternately, dorky loser science fiction teenagers with pony tails.)"[6]

Yet peppered throughout these reviews are references to catchy riffs, smart lyrics, and creative songwriting. That's what I always enjoyed about Mark's reviews: underneath all the manic humor and not-safe-for-work jokes, he knew his stuff and called it as he saw it. Sure, Geddy Lee's voice drove him nuts and other aspects of Rush's music weren't to his liking, but he wasn't afraid to point out the *good* in anything he listened to, even if the whole package wasn't his personal cup of tea. But eventually, Mark got over his aversion to being lumped with the nerds and the losers to consider himself somewhat of a fan.

I reached out to Mark to discuss his changing perception of Rush and their music, and while very busy with family life and work, Mark was gracious enough to speak with me via email and fill out my Rush survey. "I used to hate them," he says. "I didn't start listening to them as a fan until about 1998. The first [song] that made an impact was 'The Spirit of Radio.' It's possible I heard [other songs] first but didn't care enough to ask who it was."[7]

Permanent Waves, which received an eight-out-of-ten rating on Mark's site, seems to be the point where he starts to actually *enjoy* Rush's music rather than suffer through it:

---

4   http://markprindle.com/rusha.htm#fly, last accessed February 19, 2020.
5   http://markprindle.com/rusha.htm#farewell, last accessed February 19, 2020.
6   http://markprindle.com/rusha.htm#signals, last accessed February 19, 2020.
7   Mark Prindle, response to author's survey, February 5, 2020 (Appendix A).

> This is a dammed fine album incidentally. The production is light beers better than before (the band actually sounds like they're right in front of the mics, rather than in a bathroom way down the hall) and Geddy's voice has matured to something at least slightly resembling a normal range and frequency. The choppity chops and complex ideas had always been present in the collective Rush mind, but here for the first time, everything really meshes into a gel. Replacing bombast with radio-friendly catchy pop riffs, but leaving in the instrumental fortitude that separated them from the Foreigner/Bad Company animals, Rush erupted with one HELL of a hit single, "The Spirit of Radio" (THAT RIFF! MY GOD! GREATEST RIFF EVER!), along with a bunch of other calmed-down, well-composed rock songs (including "Free Will," which gets stuck in my head probably 2 times a day).[8]

"I bought a ton of their albums in cheapy bins for review purposes back in the mid-to-late '90s, and realized that a lot of it is better than I expected," Mark explained. "Even the keyboard pop years had some great songs."[9]

Hardcore fans will say that this is just the power of Rush. I agree to a point: To someone like Mark who knows and cares deeply about music, who understands *why* some music works and why some doesn't, it's only natural that he'd be able to pick out the good from the bad with Rush, as he does with most of the bands he reviewed on his site. And Mark is not what any would call a hardcore fan, but he certainly learned to enjoy what many call the "acquired taste"[10] of Rush:

---

8   http://markprindle.com/rusha.htm#permanent, last accessed February 19, 2020.
9   Prindle, response to author's survey, February 5, 2020 (Appendix A).
10 *See* Chapter I, footnote 13.

> Rush has never been one of my all-time favorite bands. I used to think it was nerd music for comic book fans who live in their parents' basements. And maybe it is—but it's also very good. They started off as Led Zeppelin rockers, then became hard rock prog artsters, then went all keyboardy, then came back to become extremely consistent creators of mature electric guitar-driven music. Plus, Neil Peart's lyrics were always interesting and intelligent, even when the morals were questionable (i.e. Ayn Rand). "Limelight" is especially good. It's extremely insightful, honest and poetic.[11]

And I think that's fair. The question you may have is, "Why spend so much time discussing one particular individual's personal opinion on Rush?" My answer is: Because Mark is definitely *not* what one would conjure in one's mind when asked to picture a "typical" Rush fan. Yes, he ticks some of the same boxes as many of the other survey respondents: mid-40s white male, musician, fan of other genres of rock. But Mark clearly seems, and sees himself, as different from those hypothetical, archetypical Rush fans—the nerds and the losers and so on.

That's why his slow turn towards Rush fandom, no matter how mild that may be, is so interesting.

So what *is* a "nerd," anyway? And why do so many of them seem to like Rush. *Are* most Rush fans stereotypical "nerds"? Just what the heck is going on here?

WHAT IS A NERD?

As with lots of words, the definition of "nerd" depends on who you ask. According to the venerable Merriam-Webster Dictionary, a "nerd" is "an unstylish, unattractive, or socially

---

[11] Prindle, response to author's survey, February 5, 2020 (Appendix A).

inept person, especially: one slavishly devoted to intellectual or academic pursuits."[12]

That's a pretty harsh definition! The equally venerable Cambridge Dictionary goes even further, throwing sex into the mix: "a person who lacks social skills, esp. Someone interested in technical things" goes one definition.[13] "[A] person, especially a man, who is not attractive and is awkward or socially embarrassing" goes another.[14] And finally, we have "a person who is extremely interested in one subject, especially computers, and knows a lot of facts about it."[15]

Ouch! Now let's look at some of the synonyms in the thesaurus appended to the Cambridge Dictionary entry for "Nerd": Here we see words like "accident-prone," "gauche,"[16] "ham-fisted," "lumpish,"[17] "functional illiteracy,"[18] "maladroit," and, uh, "lubber."

This does not paint a pretty picture of "nerd." In fact, when you, whether you rock out to Rush or not, hear the word "nerd," images of a scrawny, mouth-breathing asthmatic with slicked back hair, a runny nose and nasally voice, big front teeth, and acne wearing slacks just a *little* too high and a white button-down shirt—short-sleeved, of course—with a pocket-protector stuffed with pens. Oh, and you can't forget the thick black plastic glasses taped in the middle.[19]

12   https://www.merriam-webster.com/dictionary/nerd, last accessed February 21, 2020.
13   https://dictionary.cambridge.org/us/dictionary/english/nerd, last accessed February 21, 2020.
14   *Id.*
15   *Id.*
16   Not sure about this one.
17   Lumpish!
18   Not sure about this one, either.
19   True story: In grade school I had to wear thick plastic glasses as a kid because my vision was *so horrible* that regular thin wire-framed glasses couldn't hold my lenses. One time they broke in the middle, so in a pinch a teacher took some masking tape and "fixed" them for me so I could wear them home. Being a child of the 80s, every single other student knew *exactly* that these were stereotypical "nerd" glasses, and I didn't hear the end of it that day. In retrospect, I should've taken my chances fumbling around as blind as a bat and saved myself the angst.

For readers of a certain generation, I can just mention Robert Carradine and Anthony Edwards's characters in 1984's *Revenge of the Nerds* and you'll know exactly the look I'm talking about. Speaking of *Revenge of the Nerds*, have you watched that lately? It's aged *horribly*, and I'm not just talking about Hollywood's ideas of "nerds" as being people annoying enough who actually deserve the social abuse they take at the hands of the popular kids. There's that whole scene where Robert Carradine's character Lewis tricks the cute cheerleader Betty—girlfriend of the nerds' arch-nemesis, the jock Stan—into thinking *he's* Stan, and then has sex with her in the dark.[20] They also humiliate some popular girl (I don't remember if it was Betty or not) by distributing images of her topless all over campus. I mean, if they were trying to make the nerds sympathetic, I think they failed.

Anyway, where was I?

Right. Nerds. These popular ideas of what a nerd is are pretty hilarious, because they kind of fit what people think about Rush fans to a T: A shy, socially awkward guy who is into computers or some other solitary, not-that-popular-with-the-ladies hobby, and who probably dresses poorly. Here's another great cultural touchstone for the ur-nerd: the character of Steve Urkel as portrayed by Jaleel White in the popular 90s sitcom *Family Matters*.

One commonality about nerds is that they are walking, talking female-repellant. This commonly understood aspect of nerd-dom is also applied to Rush fans. The band themselves joked about this quite often, for example, during a video shown at the end of concerts on their 2010-2011 Time Machine Tour. In the video, the band is shown leaving the stage, but before they reach their backstage area for food, drink, and relaxation,

---

[20] Apparently, I'm not the only one to have made this observation. In an article about "misogyny in nerd-world" and the recent spate of sexual harassment allegations at tech companies, Jennifer Wright writes, "The most realistic part of 'Revenge of the Nerds' now seems to be the creepy scene where the nerd protagonist tricks a woman into sex." Jennifer Wright, "Opinion: Jocks Rule, Nerds Drool," The *New York Times*, August 11, 2018, available at https://www.nytimes.com/2018/08/11/opinion/sunday/nerds-lebron-james-elon-musk.html, last accessed March 4, 2020.

actors Paul Rudd[21] and Jason Segel, reprising their characters, best friends and huge Rush fans Peter Klaven and Sydney Fife, respectively, from the 2009 film *I Love You, Man*, get there first. They sneak into Rush's room, eat Neil's sandwich, and talk about how *awesome* Rush is while waiting for the band.

"I saw four in the mezzanine," says Geddy Lee as the band walks backstage.

"Yeah, I had three in the front row!" says Alex Lifeson.

"Seven females at a Rush concert!" Neil Peart comments as he opens the door. "Must be some kind of a world record!"[22]

The band seemed to find this a constant source of amusement. In 2018, Geddy Lee mentioned the predominately male nature of Rush's audience to *The Guardian*:

> Rush's commitment to noodling made them the dream band for an audience that was overwhelmingly male. "There's no getting around that," Lee says. "We would joke about it backstage. 'See any girls in the front row?' 'No. Some attractive boys. A lot of ugly boys.' When things started changing—and they did—we noticed: 'There's girls in the front row'. Or there'd be a sign in the back: 'Mythbusters: Girls who love Rush.'" Lee sighs, and laughs. "But we were too old to take advantage of it by that point."[23]

This brings us to another myth, the myth that women just do not like Rush. And although this chapter is about nerds and nerdiness, it makes perfect sense to delve a little bit into the ste-

---

21 In a nice bit of things coming full circle, Rudd provided narration for the 2016 documentary *Rush: Time Stand Still*.
22 Video available at https://youtu.be/iq3yjfoorsU, last accessed February 22, 2020.
23 Michael Hann, "Geddy Lee on Rush's greatest songs: 'Even I can barely make sense of our concept albums,'" *The Guardian*, December 24, 2018, available at https://www.theguardian.com/music/2018/dec/24/geddy-lee-on-rush-greatest-songs, last accessed July 11, 2020.

reotype that all Rush fans are dudes; we'll get deeper into this in Chapter III.

The way Rudd and Segel play their characters adds fire to this stereotype. The way they interact with each other before they even meet the band is, shall we say, uncomfortably awkward. Whether or not you've seen *I Love You, Man*, you'll cringe at this video, you'll laugh, and you might even relate a bit, even as a part of your brain says "Hey, wait a minute, I'm not like that . . . am I?"

I Love You, Man is a comedy about male friendship. After proposing to his girlfriend, Peter realizes he has no male friends to share the news with, or to even have as a best man. After some funny misadventures, Peter meets Sydney, and they bond in large part over their love of Rush. There are awkward jam sessions, discussions between Peter and his fiancée about Rush, and even an appearance by the band at a concert.

Rush appearing in a major studio picture, and *not* as an object of scorn and derision! Who would have thought it, right? But the power of time is an amazing thing. "The fans, the Rush fans of that era, grew up to be successful, influential people," says Ed Stenger. "They became movie directors or writers in magazines, or executives at companies. They were the ones in power . . . and they had a voice. They all liked Rush so it came out."[24] *I Love You, Man* director, John Hamburg, is a "huge Rush fan and he wanted Rush in that movie. He made it happen. That wouldn't have happened 20 years ago."[25]

Changing perceptions are a funny thing, and not only has nerd culture become a hot commodity over the past 20 years, so has Rush. "Somehow or another, we got legitimate," says Geddy Lee. "What I guess transpired is all these RUSH fans had time to grow up and get jobs and wanted to pay us back and wanted to fly their RUSH flag wherever they possibly could."[26]

South Park co-creator Matt Stone agrees with Lee's assessment:

---
[24] Ed Stenger, interview with the author, May 19, 2020 (Appendix C).
[25] *Id.*
[26] Vinay Menon, *Rush: An Oral History* (Toronto Star Newspapers Limited, 2013), at 48.

> There's a generation of guys like me and Paul Rudd and the comedy guys who are coming out of the closet and are unabashed about the band. RUSH was never quite cool in the way MTV wanted them to be. So now there's this generation of people like me who are successful and will just give it up publicly as a RUSH fan.[27]

"[O]nce Rush got that I wasn't poking fun at them, that I'm genuinely a fan and the main characters of the movie are fans and it's kind of a loving tribute to them, I think that's when they came on board," Hamburg explained.[28] Now, being a comedy, Rudd and Segel play up the modern-American-male-as-manchild trope, but they're so charming it *just* manages to avoid being offensive. But man, are these guys dorks.

Well, nerds to be accurate. Dorks, I'm reliably informed, are a different beast entirely. Based upon my research, a "dork" encapsulates all of the socially awkward and uncool aspects of a "nerd," but without the specialized knowledge and intelligence of the latter. "Dork" is also, from what I gather, a slang term for the male member.[29] So the less said about dorks, the better. Suffice it to say, "dork," like "geek," is interchangeable with "nerd" in modern parlance,[30] but since I'm a nerd about the English language, we're going to treat them as separate things for the purposes of this book.

27 *Id.*
28 Edward Douglas, "EXCL: John Hamburg Says I Love You, Man . . . Again!" ComingSoon.net, August 10, 2009, available at https://www.comingsoon.net/dvd/features/57873-excl-john-hamburg-says-i-love-you-man-again, last accessed May 27, 2020.
29 *See, e.g.*, "Nerd, dork or geek," *Grammarist*, available at https://grammarist.com/interesting-words/nerd-dork-or-geek/, last accessed February 22, 2020; *see also* "Geek vs. Nerd vs. Dork: What's the Difference," *Mental Floss*, September 4, 2008 ("This time, there's only one theory: The word dork originally meant "penis." (Specifically, human penis.) Popularized in the '60s, dork was probably derived from dirk, a penile name that was widely used until the short version of Richard became ubiquitous."), available at https://www.mentalfloss.com/article/19524/geek-vs-nerd-vs-dork-whats-difference, last accessed February 22, 2020. I'm really glad they specified *human* penis.
30 "Geek vs. Nerd vs. Dork," *Mental Floss*.

So from whence does the word "nerd" come? Would you believe me if I told you Dr. Seuss?

That's right: Everyone's favorite spinner of preposterous rhymes for young readers invented the word in his 1950 book *If I Ran The Zoo*. In this book, the narrator discusses how he wants to collect "A Nerkle, a Nerd, and a Seersucker too!" for his imaginary menagerie.[31] Apparently, kids liked the word so much, they began using it as an insult. Better that than "Nerkle," I guess. Another theory goes that at some point in the 1950s, students at Rensselaer Polytechnic Institute called other students who studied all the time "knurds," being "drunk" backwards, presumably differentiating them from the partiers.[32] Now, if kids who go to RPI, an engineering school, are calling you socially inept, then you *know* you're in a special class.

Whatever the true origin, the term took off in popularity so that by the time Rush burst onto the scene, and the appellation had been applied to the band, their music, and their fans. Even at the time of this writing when Rush has achieved mainstream acceptance and one no longer has to *secretly admit* to being a fan of the bands, articles complementary of Rush and their music are peppered with this particular n-word, particularly in tributes to Neil Peart after his death.

There is Drew Brown's February 15, 2020 piece in *Vice* called "For Small Town Nerds, Neil Peart Was A God"; it also calls Peart a "weirdo poet-philosopher" for good measure.[33] There is also *Rolling Stone*'s January 11, 2020 tribute which says of the song "Subdivisions": "Like the Neil Peart aesthetic as a whole, the song's drumming is at once profoundly nerdy and totally exhilarating";[34] how, exactly, drumming can be clas-

---

31   In case you're wondering what the good doctor's Nerd looks like, picture a typical Seussian creature with a pear-shaped body, floppy feet, and a bulbous head complete with long side-whiskers and a tuft of hair on the top. This Nerd has his (?) large hands, fingers laced, resting on its belly and is wearing a rather grumpy expression. You would too if there was a huge sign labeled "NERD" pointing right at you.
32   "Geek vs. Nerd vs. Dork," *Mental Floss*.
33   Available at https://www.vice.com/en_ca/article/dygp8x/rushs-neil-peart-was-a-god-to-small-town-nerds-like-me, last accessed February 22, 2020.
34   Hank Shteamer, "How Neil Peart's Perfectionism Set Him Free," *Rolling Stone*, January 11, 2020, available at https://www.rollingstone.com/music/music-features/neil-peart-

sified as "nerdy" is beyond me, but then again I'm not a bigtime professional rock journalist. Or how about Matt Miller's January 10, 2020 piece in *Esquire*, which states:

> [Rush's] virtuoso musical chops made it okay for them to be complete dorks. And no member of the band exemplified that more than Peart. He was two things at once: A total nerd and a musician of whom the legends were in awe. He made it okay to be both, he made it cool to be both. And he never stopped striving to be better.[35]

And lastly, here's a great 2015 piece from the *Houston Press* that seems to hit on all the stereotypical Rush-fan bullet points:

> Canadian rock trio Rush is an oddity in rock history. Somehow they managed to attract standard rock and metal fans along with lots of nerdier types who also found something to love about the band. Combining virtuoso playing and complex musical compositions that cover diverse material ranging from Dungeons and Dragons-style fantasy and science fiction to a variety of philosophical subject matter, the band has forged one of the strangest and most dedicated fan bases in rock and roll.
>
> I remember in the very early '80s, Rush still seemed to have a slight danger about them. Their fans seemed mostly to be the same types of hard-rock dirtbags who sold weed to junior-high kids and drove Camaros around town,

---

rush-drumming-tribute-936430/, last accessed February 22, 2020.
35 Matt Miller, "Rush's Neil Peart Found A Place For Sci-Fi and Other-Worldly Drumming in Rock Music," *Esquire*, January 10, 2020, available at https://www.esquire.com/entertainment/music/a30473801/neil-peart-dead-tribute-obit/, last accessed February 22, 2020.

but over the years that appeared to change a lot. The last time I was at a Rush concert, it looked like half the people in attendance probably owned a small software company somewhere, and a lot of them had brought their kids.

So why include Rush fans on a list like this? Because Rush is one of the most polarizing major bands in the world. People seem to either love Rush or hate them, with very little middle ground. Explaining the appeal to a non-fan is almost as futile as trying to convince someone that water isn't wet. People seem to universally agree that Rush are great musicians, but the folks who like them tend to love them, and everyone else tends to dislike them a lot. Rush is often characterized as the world's biggest cult band, and hardcore fans even have their own convention they can attend.

Pros: Fans might be able to help you fix your computer when it crashes. Cons: They might also launch into a lengthy discussion defending Geddy Lee's voice. Danger Level: Essentially nonexistent, unless you're threatened by people who play Dungeons and Dragons or work in the IT Department.[36]

There are more, but by now you get the idea. There are several takeaways from this repeated use of the word "nerd" when describing Rush's music and, particularly Neil Peart. Two stick out to me. One is that journalists all copy from the same playbook. But that's too cynical, right? There's no evidence to suggest that the fine members of the journalistic profession are all,

---

36 Chris Lane, "Five Bands Whose Fans Freak Outsiders Out," *Houston Press*, January 20, 2015, available at https://www.houstonpress.com/music/five-bands-whose-fans-freak-outsiders-out-6781915, last accessed June 11, 2020.

to a man, unimaginative hacks! The other is that maybe Rush really *is* "nerd music," and that Rush fans are, by extension, nerds.

And it's not just us regular folk or journalists who see this connection. None other than Les Claypool, bassist and vocalist for another oddball rock group Primus, and a self-professed massive Rush fan, has made a similar connection between Rush and various aspects of nerdiness.[37] In a piece for IFC's blog about The Three Stooges,[38] Claypool says the following: "Funny thing, RUSH and The Three Stooges = no chicks. Is it a coincidence that RUSH used to start their shows with the opening theme song from those old Stooges shorts? Ah, the profoundness of it all."[39]

As of this writing, Primus is gearing up for a summer tour called "A Tribute to Kings," where the band will cover Rush's landmark 1977 *A Farewell to Kings* album in its entirety (Primus had this planned before Peart's death; note also that, due to the COVID-19 pandemic, this tour has been postponed to 2021). On the "no women like Rush" stereotype, Claypool tells *Rolling Stone* "I've always joked that my wife is one of the few women I've ever met in my entire life that listened to Rush in her youth, and I always joke that that's why we've been married for so long."[40]

Lest you scoff at Claypool's bona fides as a Rush fan, Primus has been open about their Rush fandom since the beginning, playing snippets of their songs live—the first thing you hear on Primus' 1989 debut *Suck On This*, a live album, is the opening riff to "YYZ" before the band launches into "John the

37 Full disclosure: I am a *massive* Primus fan. I was a fan of Primus before I was a fan of Rush. So if I seem biased towards Mr. Claypool, you have been warned.
38 More full disclosure: I am also a *massive* fan of The Three Stooges. All the same disclaimers in the above footnote apply to any discussion of Curly, Larry, and Moe (and Shemp too, sure). You have been warned again.
39 Les Claypool, "Les Claypool guest blog: Primus frontman on the glory of the Three Stooges," December 30, 2011, available at https://www.ifc.com/2011/12/les-claypool-three-stooges, last accessed February 22, 2020.
40 Hank Shteamer, "Les Claypool on Primus' Rush Covers Tour: 'It's About Admiration for These Amazing Musicians,'" February 18, 2020, available at https://www.rollingstone.com/music/music-features/primus-rush-tribute-to-kings-tour-les-claypool-interview-953590/, last accessed February 22, 2020.

Fisherman." The drum intro is also the first thing you hear on the band's first studio album, 1990's *Frizzle Fry*, prior to opener "To Defy the Laws of Tradition." They've also been known to cover parts of "Cygnus X-1: Book 1" and "La Villa Strangiato" on tour. And Primus opened for Rush on the 1991-1992 *Roll the Bones* and 1994 *Counterparts* tours:

> [W]atching a band like Rush, especially when we were playing with them back then, it was not really cool to be a Rush fan. It was like a guilty pleasure. We actually got a lot of shit, especially from European press, for touring Europe with Rush. Because we were supposed to be this young, new . . . whatever the hell we were, but we were part of that alternative punk scene, and all of the sudden, here we were. I remember reading some British press, "What the hell's Primus doing playing with these old prog dinosaurs?"
>
> But perseverance wins the game and those guys . . . I remember watching them on the Colbert show and going, "Oh, my God, all of the sudden, now Rush is fuckin' hip!" [Laughs] They just got touched on the shoulder by the magic wand of hipness of Stephen Colbert. And it was a wonderful, wonderful thing. I've taken great pleasure in watching those guys become extraordinarily popular these last handful of years, and iconic. And even your entity paying more and more attention to them. Because back when I was a kid, you never read anything in Rolling Stone about Rush or very rarely even heard them on mainstream radio.[41]

---

41   *Id*. The admiration Claypool felt for Rush was mutual; *see* Hank Shteamer, "Rush's Geddy Lee: My 10 Favorite Bassist," *Rolling Stone*, July 2, 2020, available at https://www.rollingstone.com/music/music-features/rush-geddy-lee-favorite-bassists-inter-

So again we see Rush equated with being a nerd insofar as being a nerd means being terminally unhip and devoid of female companionship. But again I ask the question: *Is this true?* Is this what Rush fans are like?

Before digging into the meat of my findings, there are two more things about nerdiness we need to discuss. But first, I think the first entry of "Nerd" on the popular Internet repository of slang, Urban Dictionary, gives perhaps the best definition, and one you will see actually *does* ring true:

An individual who:

1. Enjoys learning
2. Does not adhere to social norms

A nerd is *not*:

1. A geek. The circles overlap, but they are not the same.
2. Someone who wears fake "nerdy" glasses
3. Someone who wears suspenders, fake glasses, and bowties on "nerd" day.
4. Someone who thinks of themself as a nerd, yet cannot hold an intelligent debate.
5. If you are reading this article to determine whether you are a nerd or not, you are not.

Nerds do not need to look up the definition of "nerd", it is a label with no consequence whatsoever, and nerds have better things to do than play along with societal stereotypes. That be-

view-1022134/, last accessed July 31, 2020

("He actually influenced me as a player to try to push the boundaries of my rhythmic abilities. I would say that tour I did with Primus was transformational for me. So as much I appreciated that, as a kid, he would come to Rush shows and want to do that, me, listening to him playing before us every night on that tour made me want to be a better player in a different way. So there was a wonderful exchange of respect going on there.").

ing said, if you merely want to see what people think of when they think of the word "nerd", because human thought processes, societal constructs, and philosophy are so interesting, consider yourself a nerd.

Synonyms include booksmart

Nerd is only a label. It doesn't matter whether you are one or are not one. Nobody cares either way, and you should not, either.[42]

WHAT NERDS DO

Defining "nerd hobbies" is one of those things where, to paraphrase Justice Potter Stewart from his famous concurrence to the United States Supreme Court's decision in *Jacobellis v. Ohio* with regards to hard-core pornography, you know them when you see them.[43]

First, I do have to point out that not all Rush fans are happy with the stereotype that they're nerds. "I hate the stereotype that Rush music is nerd music," says Mike W. "The first 4 albums they rocked as hard or harder than any hard rock band."[44] But as you'll see from the results of my survey, there's no denying that Rush's music is associated with all things nerd.

Now, I will not be as expansive as some may in defining nerd hobbies. People use the word "nerd" as an adjectival shorthand

---

[42] "Nerd," *Urban Dictionary*, available at https://www.urbandictionary.com/define.php?term=Nerd, last accessed February 21, 2020. I also like the definition immediately following this one: "noun: The most dangerous people in the entire world. Nerds have invented machine guns, assault rifles, armor piercing ammunition, high explosives, napalm, tanks, anti-personnel mines, torpedoes, cannons, surface-to-air missiles, fighter aircraft, bombers, submarines, destroyers, battleships, aircraft carriers, chemical and biological weapons, nuclear bombs, and ICBMs

Every weapon of mass destruction ever conceived [sic] *of or built was conceived* [sic] *of or built by nerds.*" Yikes!

[43] *Jacobellis v. Ohio*, 378 U.S. 184, at 197 (J. Stewart, concurring).

[44] Mike W., response to author's survey, February 6, 2020 (Appendix A).

for "being a fan of." There are surfing nerds, baseball nerds, make-up nerds, crossword puzzle nerds (okay, crosswords *are* pretty nerdy—just ask Don N.!),[45] motorcycle nerds, and so on. But when one thinks of a capital-N Nerd, surfing, make-up, and motorcycling do not come to mind.

Have you seen the Netflix horror-drama *Stranger Things*? Sure you have. *Stranger Things* takes place in the mid-1980s and the group of kids who comprise its main cast play *Dungeons & Dragons*. Because they're nerdy outcasts. The same dynamic can be seen with the short-lived TV series *Freaks and Geeks* (1999-2000) where the titular social outcasts also play *Dungeons & Dragons* and, yes, listen to Rush. In both examples, we see "Nerd" as not being synonymous with "a huge fan of something," but *Dungeons & Dragons* sure is used synonymously with "being a nerd."

Nerd hobbies, as commonly understood, include but are not limited to the following types of things:

- Tabletop roleplaying games like *Dungeons & Dragons, Shadowrun, GURPS, Traveler, Rifts*, etc.
- Science-fiction, fantasy, and horror books, movies, and TV shows such as *The Lord of the Rings, Dune, Dr. Who, Star Trek, Elric, The Hitchhiker's Guide to the Galaxy, Star Wars*, and *The Matrix*.
- Video games, both the console and computer variety.
- A strong interest in technology in general, whether this be tinkering with computers, audio equipment, or radios.
- Weird comedy that is very often, though not always, British in origin, such as *Monty Python* and *Red Dwarf*.

---

45   Don N., response to author's survey, February 5, 2020 (Appendix A).

- Comic books, whether typical superhero fare or the dark, edgy, and often bizarre world of independent and underground comics.
- Japanese anime, such as *Akira*, *Vampire Hunder D*, *Trigun*, *Berserk*, *Gundam*, and *Cowboy Bebop*.
- Boardgames, with an emphasis on fantasy or sci-fi themed wargames like *Warhammer 40,000* and anything else involving miniatures; painting said miniatures is another popular nerd pastime.
- Collectible card games like *Pokémon* and *Magic: The Gathering*.
- Certain types of music; nerds are really into heavy metal as well as quirky groups like *Devo* and *They Might Be Giants*.

In other words, most nerds aren't into football and beer. I suppose a "nerd" hobby could be *any* activity the quarterback and head cheerleader at your local high school are not apt to partake in, like birdwatching[46] or coin collecting.[47]

Now that we have our benchmark for what a nerd is, it's time to answer the eternal question of whether Rush fans are nerds. For that, we need to turn to the survey. My hypothesis going into this project was *of course Rush fans are nerds.* And the results of my research bear this out. I had a feeling that Rush fans were by and large into things like reading, history, science-fiction and fantasy, philosophy, video games, comic books, and RPGs. Turns out I was right.

46   Chad Hutchinson (response to author's survey, February 5, 2020), Michael (response to author's survey, February 5, 2020), and Richard Lucas (response to author's survey, February 11, 2020) all partake in this particular hobby (Appendix A). And so, as we'll see later, did Neil Peart.
47   John J., response to author's survey, February 5, 2020; Mike L., response to author's survey, February 6, 2020; Ken L., response to author's survey, February 7, 2020; and David C., response to author's survey, February 9, 2020, answer the burning question, "Are Rush fans into coin collecting?" with a resounding "Yes!" (Appendix A).

Out of 664 respondents, 653 answered the question "Do you enjoy what are considered 'nerd' or 'geek' hobbies?" Of those 653, 414, or 63.4%, answered "Yes" and 239, or 36.6%, answered "No."[48] So based upon my sample size, unscientific though it may be, I think it is safe to conclude that yes, most Rush fans are nerds. Rush, as it turns out, *is* a nerd band.

Digging into the responses to the opened-ended next question, "If 'yes,' which ones? (e.g., comic books, sci-fi/fantasy, tabletop RPGs, etc.)," 409 fans were kind enough to describe the types of nerd hobbies they enjoyed.

Before we get any deeper into these survey results, I'd like to discuss my decidedly lowbrow methodology. I'm no anthropologist or social scientist. I'm a sci-fi author and a nerd myself just trying to have fun and pen a tribute to my fellow Rush fans. So bear with me and please don't take this all as gospel. My methods include such scientifically validated techniques like reading the spreadsheet of survey results and making a note of every instance of every nerdy hobby respondents provided before tallying them up. Nifty, right? Just give me a crisp white lab coat, a clipboard, and maybe some crazy hair and I can be the proverbial "scientist pacing the floor."

Some of the nerd hobby categories people responded with are pretty big. "RPGs" and "collectables," for example. So for many of these I also noted specific properties or games or collectibles as subsets of the broader category, although if fans identified *Dungeons & Dragons* or specified "tabletop games" as a pastime but *not* "RPGs," I included it in the RPG bucket. Similarly, the response "gaming" is being put into the "video games" category, since I saw it coupled with "RPGs" but never with "video games."

Genres like "science-fiction/sci-fi," "fantasy," and "horror" were kept separate, as were "movies" and "TV." The category "board games" encompasses strategy games and wargames as well as stuff like checkers, but excludes tabletop RPGs like *Dungeons & Dragons*. Lastly, if respondents just said "all," I put

48   *See* Rush Fan Survey (Appendix A).

that into its own category which I almost called "Super-Nerd" but then thought better of it.

Got it? Good! So here are the results.

Sci-fi/fantasy and RPGs pop up most frequently. D. Boman's response is telling, as his experience with *Dungeons & Dragons* is tied to his interest in Rush:

> Back in the day the cousin that introduced me to Rush used to play Dungeons and Dragons for hours and days on end while listening to rock and heavy metal. Drove everyone else around us nuts because we were in our own world most of the time.[49]

Tod Waters makes a similar connection in his story of the first time he heard Rush's music:

> Heard 2112 and hemispheres at my friend elliot's house. I was hooked. It was sci fi. It was dungeons and dragons it was rock I[t] was smart. It was everything I wanted at the time.[50]

Some other fans were lucky enough for their nerdy pastimes to have really paid off . . . as in financially. W. Earl Brown lives a life many of us would envy:

> Again, my hobbies are my career. As a kid, STAR WARS and HALLOWEEN made me want to be in movies. I've been in MANDALORIAN and SCREAM, along with a bunch of others nerd-friendly genre things (PREACHER, REPRISAL, and others)[51]

Way to rub it in, Earl.

---

49 D. Boman, response to author's survey, February 8, 2020 (Appendix A).
50 Tod Waters, response to author's survey, February 8, 2020 (Appendix A).
51 W. Earl Brown, response to author's survey, February 5, 2020 (Appendix A).

Anyway, it's time for numbers. Nerds like numbers, right? This is what you've all been waiting for, so without further ado, here are some nerdy statistics for all of you stat nerds out there (there were a few):

Sci-fi: Coming as no surprise, 213, or 52% of nerdy Rush fans like to delve into deep space as fans of science-fiction, whether it be books, television shows, or movies in that genre.

Fantasy: 105, or 25.6% of fans, would rather travel through the land on epic quests, perhaps to defeat the Necromancer, as fans of the fantasy genre.

RPGs: When it comes to tabletop role-playing games (TTRPGs) *a la Dungeons & Dragons* and other pass-times where dice are slung and hit points are a precious commodity, 107, or 26.1% of Rush fans surveyed, loved to wield their d20 and fight some hobgoblins in the Temple of Elemental Evil. This comes as no surprise to me. I mean, just look at the album art for *Caress of Steel* and listen to "The Necromancer" and "The Fountain of Lamneth." Those are basically *D&D* campaigns set to music. Only 41, or 38.3%, of these 107 specifically name-dropped *Dungeons & Dragons* as their TTRPG of choice, meaning that *other TTRPGs exist!* Preposterous!

Comic Books: This was another big one, with 103, or 25.1%, of Rush fans surveyed being comic fans, or readers of graphic novels, if you want to be sophisticated about it. One respondent, Mark Irwin, actually works in the comics industry![52]

Reading: 96, or 23.4%, of Rush fans counted reading as a nerd hobby. I don't know if I buy that a devotion to the written word is nerdy. Some liked fiction, some non-fiction, but nearly a quarter of these self-styled "nerds" tend to have their nose in a book.

Video Games: 73 Rush fans surveyed, or 17.8%, described themselves as being into vidya.[53] This is no surprise: I've seen

---

[52] Mark Irwin, response to author's survey, February 5, 2020 (Appendix A). Mr. Irwin has done work as an artist, colorist, and inker for Marvel, DC, and Image Comics, currently runs Insight Comics, and has his own series with artist Dan Panosian called *Jack Secret*. So yeah, the guy's legit. And legit nerdy. In other words, *my kind of guy*.

[53] "Vidya game," *Urban Dictionary*, available at https://www.urbandictionary.com/define.php?term=vidya%20game (last accessed April 27, 2020).

the video for "Subdivisions." That kid is the ur-Rush fan, though he needs to work on his skills at *Tempest*.[54]

Movies and TV: Lots of Rush fans dug moving pictures, whether they be on the large screen or the small. 68, or 16.6% of fans enjoyed movies, while 13, or 3.1%, preferred TV.

Board Games: 31, or 7.5% of Rush fans surveyed, expressed their enthusiasm for board games of all types. These ran the gamut from well-known games like *Monopoly* to more advanced strategy games, war games, resource-management games, and the king of all board games, chess. And 1 of you does tournament cribbage![55]

Computers: 12 Rush fans surveyed, or 2.9%, are into computers, whether for recreational use or for tinkering and programming, enjoying technology high on the leading edge of life. And though not in answer to this particular question, 25 of the total 664 respondents, or 3.7%, work in the field of computer science.

Science: 26 Rush fans surveyed, or 6.3%, responded that they loved science. I'm sorry, I mean *SCIENCE!* This includes those who specified which type of science: Astronomy, physics, and so on. This was quite surprising to me—I expected far more than 17—but then I remembered that some either may not consider science to be "nerdy," or do science as their job,[56] whereas I asked for hobbies here. I feel you on the astronomy; I, too, wonder what it would be like to sail a spaceship into a black hole.

Collectables: 22 of you, or 5.3%, collect one thing or another. You didn't all specify but those of you who did specified things like baseball cards, CDs, action figures, actual NFL football helmets, *Star Wars* stuff, license plate, music memorabilia,

---

54 The band themselves might be video game fans, or at least of ancient 1970s arcade cabinets. *See* Vinay Menon, *Rush: An Oral History* (Toronto Star Newspapers Limited, 2013), at 25 ("Geddy Lee: I remember one period we were holed up at the Sunset Marquis Hotel in LA between tours. We couldn't really afford to bring everything back to Canada. We didn't have any gigs and we were there for like a month. We got really good at the Space Invaders game in the hallway because we had nothing else to do.").
55 Lisa LaFlame, response to author's survey, February 10, 2020 (Appendix A) Yes, I know cribbage uses cards, but I'm counting it as a board game. It has a board, doesn't it?
56 Does one really "do" science? There has to be a better verb . . .

and of course, Rush memorabilia. History: 12 Rush fans surveyed, or 2.9%, like to turn the pages of history. I'm not surprised. Rush fans are an intelligent lot, after all.

Tech: 10 Rush fans surveyed, or 2.4%, listed "tech" as a hobby. I don't know exactly what this means, except that technology is really cool.

Lego: That's right: Lego. Technically the plural isn't "Legos" but just "Lego." You can trust me--one of my best friends is from Denmark, and I've built (and stepped on) my fair share of the little plastic bricks. Anyway, 9 Rush fans surveyed, or about 2.2%, consider Lego building one of their hobbies.

Other Nerdy Pastimes: There are a lot, and some of them were only mentioned once, but here are some of the other wonderful hobbies Rush fans put in response to my borderline-intrusive questions: Models, Writing, Vintage Stereo/Vinyl, Horror, Trivia Competitions, Math, Anime, Audiophile, Stamp Collecting,[57] Photography, Hiking, Superheroes, Coin Collecting,[58] Crossword Puzzles, HAM Radios, Politics, Music Tech/Gear, Puzzles, Poetry, Cosplay, Speed Cubing,[59] Sudoku, Renaissance Fair/Medieval Reenactment, Hot Wheels, Weather, BMX Biking, Football Manager, Hiking, Philosophy, Piloting, Conventions, Marching Band, Reading Wikipedia, Beer Brewing, ISS Tracking, Pop Culture, Electronics, DIY Projects, Rugs, Fantasy Sports, Robotics, Geocaching, Animated Christmas Lights, Cornhole,[60] Genealogy, PEZ collecting, UFOs, Bigfoot, Disc Golf, Drawing, Wrestling, Sports Stats, Birdwatching, Conspiracy Theories, Recording Music, Occultism, Filmmaking, Flying Drones, Art, Lyric Writing, Model Trains, Video Editing, Building Movie Props, Woodworking, Latin, Air Hockey, Fan-Fiction, and Gardening. What a diverse lot!

Specific Properties: Many of you did highlight specific nerdy franchises, authors, movies, TV shows, and IPs, so with-

---

57 "Philately," if you enjoy strange words nobody around you will understand.
58 "Numismatics," if you like sounding incomprehensible to your friends.
59 "Speed cubing" is solving a Rubik's Cube puzzle *really fast*. I'm almost 40 and I *still* can't even solve one at regular speed.
60 Maybe it's because I'm immature, but the name of this game *still* makes me laugh every time I see it.

out further ado, let's run them down: *Dungeons & Dragons* (41), *Star Wars* (28), *Star Trek* (17), and *Lord of the Rings* (6), were the big ones, but Rush fans are also enjoy Marvel movies, Isaac Asimov, *Dr. Who*, *Magic: The Gathering*, *Harry Potter*, Pokemon Go, Guy Gavriel Kay, *Elfquest*, Batman, *Stranger Things*, *Halloween*, *World of Warcraft*, Stanislaw Lem, Ray Bradbury, William Gibson, *Jeopardy!*, William Shakespeare, Disney, Robert Heinlein, Harlan Ellison, Wonder Woman, DC Comics, and *Monty Python*.

So what does this all mean?

First, let me say that I was both unsurprised *and* a little bit surprised by these results. They were how I expected them to be in large part, but there were some quote-unquote "nerdy" hobbies I was expecting to see more of. In particular, I was mildly shocked there weren't more respondents who listed art, philosophy, history, poetry, astronomy, or science in general as their hobbies of choice.

But digging deeper into the survey results reveals that 356 of 664 respondents, or 53.6% of Rush fans, studied either science, medicine, engineering, law, philosophy, English, literature, and the humanities in general. And 159 out of 664 respondents, or 23.9%, work or had worked in what are broadly classified as STEM fields (Science, Technology, Engineering, and Medicine). So I think it's safe to say that *most* Rush fans have these interests stereotypically associated with fans of Rush.

None of this, of course, is to say that those who *don't* study or work in these particular fields are somehow "lesser." The only point the data explains is that Rush fans are nerdy.

What I got in this first facet of the stereotypical Rush fan was more of a *pop culture* view of nerdiness than an actual *hard science* view. To use an analogy from *The Simpsons*, some nerds are like Comic Book Guy, and some nerds are like Professor Frink. A lot of Rush fans fall more into the former category. This is not a bad thing, it is just an interesting and unexpected observation. My brother is a PhD chemist, and in his studies and work life he's met *tons* of scientists and engineers who are into Rush.

So in building our profile of a Rush fan, I think I have demonstrated that it is safe to conclude that *he or she is a nerd.*

You might be interested in *my* answers to this question, you sneaky devil. You're trying to get me to talk about myself. For shame. But all right, you've twisted my arm. Here's where I fall on the Alexander Hellene Scale of Rush Fan Nerdiness:

I am into science-fiction and fantasy, predominately reading and writing, but the occasional movie or TV show. Some of my favorite authors include J.R.R. Tolkien, C.S. Lewis, Robert Jordan, Tad Williams, Jack Vance, Robert E. Howard, Edgar Rice Burroughs, Rafael Sabatini, Frank Herbert, and Dan Simmons. I'm into old *Star Wars* and *Star Trek*, the *Lord of the Rings, Monty Python* and classic British humor generally. I used to be a *massive* comic book fan and artist with designs on working in the industry, but those fell by the wayside. I am a musician and music lover, with my genres of choice being all things rock and classical, with the occasional jazz album thanks to my years playing jazz music in high school and college. I played TTRPGs back in the day, but only got into *Dungeons & Dragons* within the past two or three years (vintage 1st Edition). I was a pretty big video gamer as a kid, but now play mostly retrogames, i.e., old Nintendo, Sega, PlayStation, and PC games, with my son. I'm *huge* into history, having majored in early American history in college. I also like astronomy and am fascinated by outer space, though I have no formal training in the field. Lastly, I consider myself a medium-sized fan of poetry and philosophy.

So yes, I am like 63.4% of you awesome people who responded to my survey: a Rush fan *and* a huge nerd.

WHY NERDS?

I have a theory why nerds like us gravitate towards nerds like Geddy, Alex, and Neil and the music they make. As I've shown, I'm not the only one who felt, both as a youngster and now, that Rush's music appealed to a certain type. And maybe *male* nerds specifically, though many dispute this assertion, including Donna Halper herself.[61]

However, it's also undeniable that most so-called nerd hobbies, for whatever reason, appeal to boys and men, whether they be video games or tabletop role-playing games or science-fiction. Many of these hobbies are created by people who devote a lot of time and attention to the little things, the details and aesthetics that tie the entire package together. They're heavily laden with things like backstory and lore, their own separate lingo, and the need to spend a *lot* of time unlocking their secrets, which rewards persistent fans and practitioners. Much the same way someone really into the *Dune* books by Frank Herbert, or someone who loves woodworking and the time it takes to both get good and to add the little flourishes that really make the finished product shine, Rush's music is *more* than just the music, though there are conceptual attributes that tie song to song and album to album that Rush fans love. What fan *hasn't* debated the backstory of Prince By-Tor, or tried to figure out the allegory of "2112," or just what the hell really happened when the pilot of the spaceship *Rocinante* sailed into that black hole at the end of "Cygnus X-1: Book I: The Voyage" and how he became Cygnus, the God of Balance in "Cygnus X-1: Book II: Hemispheres"?[62]

Ed Stenger agrees with me on this score. Ed was gracious enough to speak to me when I reached out to him, and had this to say:

> There are plenty of "cool people" that like Rush too. You just read their lyrics, the subject matter, especially their early records, very science fictiony, fantasy stuff, really heavy stuff that generally appeals to males I guess. Then just their musicianship, just how good they were and how proficient they were at their instruments and how much care they took in writ-

---

61   Interview with Bob Cesca, January 22, 2020.
62   Admit it: if you're reading this, you've done all of these things, and more.

ing their songs. Just them as individuals. Neil Peart, he's a nerdy guy, he always was. Always nose in a book, real quiet. Those guys didn't have a reputation for partying or doing drugs or trashing hotel rooms, that kind of thing.[63]

So does Brian Hiatt, senior *Rolling Stone* writer[64] and podcast host:

There's something about the music and the iconography of Rush that certainly attracts and invites that sort of geeky, for lack of a better word attention. The musicians in Rush are so detail oriented it invites that sort of detail oriented appreciation, so I think it's a possible . . . a circle of geekdom going on here.[65]

Maybe the solitary, introspective nature of these hobbies appeals to men in particular—something you can do alone with extreme focus that doesn't require interacting with other people. We are told time and again that women have better social skills than men and find social interactions more rewarding.[66] Therefore, is it any wonder that more men than women would be drawn towards things like model building, comic books, and video games? The fact that these things are considered "cool" now changes nothing.

Oh yeah: Nerdiness is in, and has been for a while.[67] I suppose things like the TV show *The Big Bang Theory* played a part

63 Ed Stenger, interview with the author, May 19, 2020 (Appendix C).
64 Hiatt is younger—about my age—so he represents a *very* different generation of *Rolling Stone* writer.
65 *Rush: Time Stand Still* (Documentary, 2016).
66 *See, e.g.,* "Females find social interactions to be more rewarding than males, study reveals," ScienceDaily, January 30, 2019, available at https://www.sciencedaily.com/releases/2019/01/190130175604.htm, last accessed May 6, 2020.
67 *See, e.g.,* Jake Draugelis, "The 4 cool hobbies that used to be nerdy," *ClickOnDetroit.com*, April 30, 2018, available at https://www.clickondetroit.com/entertainment/2018/04/30/the-4-cool-hobbies-that-used-to-be-nerdy/ (last accessed April 30, 2020).

in this, but the less said about that show the better.[68] I think it's more the fact that many of this current generation of tastemakers and creatives in the mainstream entertainment industry were Rush fans, and now that they are in control they're unafraid to let their nerd flag fly.[69] Further, more and more women have been getting into these hobbies over the last few decades, and contrary to popular belief, women have long been a part of sci-fi and fantasy *and have been embraced by male fans*. If you're trying to tell me there's a boy's club that ignores or scorns authors like Leigh Brackett—who was one of the writers of *The Empire Strikes Back*—Louise McMaster Bujold, Anne McCaffrey, Susan Cooper, or, I don't know, J.K. Rowling or Suzanne Collins, I'm calling you a liar.

The mainstreaming of nerd culture can be seen in *Beyond the Lighted Stage*. The documentary boasts an impressive cadre of celebrity Rush fans who most certainly are *not* nerds, or at least not *treated* by nerds. Not anymore. Luminaries such as Smashing Pumpkins frontman Billy Corgan, Nine Inch Nails leader Trent Reznor, and actor Jack Black openly express their love of and admiration for the band. Taylor Hawkins, drummer of the Foo Fighters who, along with bandmate Dave Grohl inducted Rush into the Rock and Roll Hall of Fame in 2013, expresses a sentiment relatable to most all Rush fans of a certain age: "It wasn't for everybody, you know? It wasn't necessarily cool. You were kind of like a Rush geek, you know? A music nerd, uh, a kind of nerd. It was kind of nerdy music, I suppose."

There are those words again, "geek" and "nerd." But all us Rush fans knew it. We all felt it. I think to a degree we still do. Fan Mel Santa Cruz sure does: "[Rush's] music spoke to me and made me feel like it is ok to be a 'geek' or a nerd about how cool music can be and that there are other misfits out there who are just as intense into music."[70]

---

68 Nothing against the show or fans of it, but it always struck me as what people who aren't really nerds think nerds are like for a non-nerd audience.
69 Yes, I know this contradicts the above footnote. Oh well, it's my book.
70 Mel Santa Cruz, response to author's survey, February 8, 2020 (Appendix A).

For me and many others, the song and music video for "Subdivisions," the second single from Rush's 1982 album *Signals*, hit the sweet spot of the alienated young man who felt like nobody understood him. Neil's lyrics described with painful accuracy the pressure to conform and fear of being cast out at school in suburban developments that seemed to deaden the spark of life within the young. Interspersed with the band playing, an awkward young man wearing jeans, a plain white T-shirt, and large 1980s eyewear walks alone through the halls of his high school. He see cooler kids, boys and girls, ignore him as they go off to do whatever it is the cool kids do, before he heads into the city, that "timeless old attraction," cruising for action before hunkering down alone at an arcade where he promptly loses at the game *Tempest*.

See? Nerdy Rush fans play video games. Even the band knew it at the time the video was made.

That song and video spoke to me in a way that no teen-angst anthems by Korn or Limp Bizkit or Linkin Park or other popular bands at the time did. Neil's lyrics were so spot-on they hurt. It was like he knew about *my* life and was speaking directly to *me*. As Ed Stenger put it, "[Peart] nails the teenage psyche in that song . . . that song really affected [teenagers] in a good way. It made you feel like you're not alone."[71]

Ed and I aren't the only ones who got this sense. Two Rush fans interviewed for *Beyond the Lighted Stage* share remarkably similar stories. Christopher Shneberger had this to say:

> It was in the "Subdivisions" [video], and it just seemed exactly my life you know? I was that kid who was watching the car drive away with all the cool kids going off to a party that I wasn't invited to. It was just nice to feel like there was a rock song out there that spoke to my experience trying to be cool and worrying about being cast out of a group of friends if you weren't cool. I wasn't very cool but luckily

---

71 Ed Stenger, interview with the author, May 19, 2020 (Appendix C).

> I had a group of friends that was equally not cool.[72]

I can relate, Christopher. I can relate. Fan Kelly Paris adds this:

> ... I remember watching the ["Subdivisions"] video and went, "Damn that represents me right there." This one person walking around not really being in a group. It seemed like it was this person that nobody really could relate to.[73]

A person that nobody could relate to. That's it. That's the crux of Rush's appeal right there.

Survey respondents likewise felt the appeal of "Subdivisions." Fan GHP states that "Subdivisions" was the [p]erfect anthem for where I live in Northern Virginia."[74] Susan C-C reminisces that "I was definitely a nerdy kid in high school, so 'Subdivisions' really spoke to me."[75] "Neil's lyrics so often illuminated ideas and feelings that I had felt, but never really articulated," recalls fan Darren Hightower. "When I heard the lyrics to 'Subdivisions,' that song was specifically about me at that exact moment in time (and many like me)."[76] And fan ADLC became a Rush devotee after watching the "Subdivisions" video,[77] as did Sam Undag.[78]

However, not everybody's experience with being a Rush fan and the stigma being one used to have was the same. Ed Stenger's experience is unique, given the time and place he grew up in:

---

72 *Rush: Beyond the Lighted Stage* (Documentary, 2010).
73 *Id.*
74 GHP, response to author's survey, February 6, 2020 (Appendix A).
75 Susan C-C, response to author's survey, February 5, 2020 (Appendix A).
76 Darren Hightower, response to author's survey, February 5, 2020 (Appendix A).
77 ADLC, response to author's survey, February 5, 2020 (Appendix A).
78 Sam Undag, response to author's survey, February 6, 2020 (Appendix A).

> Where I grew up, I grew up not in Cleveland but outside Cleveland, closer to Toronto on the lake. There were a lot of Rush fans in my school growing up. It was never uncool to like Rush . . . being a Rush fan I was never ridiculed or anything. Plenty of the cool people liked Rush too. I didn't experience that as much as people in other parts of the country maybe from my experience from talking to people.[79]

Rush, from what I can gather, was always more popular in Canada; not that they didn't sell millions of records and concert tickets in the United States and the UK, but Canadians really seemed to take to the three men of Willowdale without the funk of nerdiness being attached.[80] Apparently, the same was true in Cleveland, the town where Rush broke first in the U.S. thanks to Donna Halper giving "Working Man" a chance on WMMS, a song she called "a perfect record for Cleveland."[81] Being a factory town, the track resonated: "Every listener in the audience felt like that."[82]

Younger readers of this book, especially those born after the year 2000, might have difficulty imagining a time before the Internet, where any subculture, and I mean *any*, could find like-minded people who shared their hobbies, their philosophies, and their outlook on life. Today, you can play *Dungeons & Dragons* with people across the planet. Back then, you had to find a group of fellow nerds who shared your love of pen-and-paper RPGs, or your interest in history or, yes, birdwatching. And you had to keep it *secret* for fear of being mocked at school.

It's no coincidence that it's a line from "Subdivisions" that gives this book its name. But it's so fitting. The word "dreamers" has an easily understandable connotation. Kids with active

---

79 Ed Stenger, interview with the author, May 19, 2020 (Appendix C).
80 Any Canadian readers who have different experiences, please email me at alexanderhellencauthor@gmail.com so I can correct this, if needed, in a future edition of this book.
81 Donna Halper, *Rush: Beyond the Lighted Stage* (Documentary, 2010).
82 *Id.*

imaginations outside the norm can find it difficult to indulge in "normal" hobbies like sports. And the word "misfit" doesn't necessarily mean a juvenile delinquent ne'er do well who'd sooner set fire to the school than head to the arcade. The meaning I'm speaking of, and that, presumably, Neil Peart was too, was that the misfit *does not fit* in with the rest of his or her peer group. They are out of step, a square peg in a round hole. Peart's lyrics "really appeal to that misfit persona."[83]

Rush spoke to that in, "Subdivisions" and in so many other songs ("The Pass" comes to mind). But these songs gave us strength. As Donna Halper put it to me, the message of Rush's songs was about standing up for yourself, thinking for yourself, and doing what was right:

> If you've ever felt like an outsider, if you've ever felt not understood, if you've ever felt different, if you've ever felt not taken seriously, there's a Rush lyric for you. And, the Rush lyrics tend not to be self-pitying, they tend not to be like, let's all blame this group or that group. They tend to be about thinking for yourself, about making your own decisions, about not being over-reliant on the will of the group, and like I said, I think that resonates with a lot of people who have felt like nobody spoke to them.[84]

Popular liberal podcaster Bob Cesca expressed as much to Ms. Halper in their January 22, 2020 interview:

> Neil, Geddy, Alex, they, they made it cool to be a nerd long before, long before it was cool to be a nerd. And I say that as a nerd. The main character in the "Subdivisions" video, I felt like that kid, that kid walking by himself through

---

83 Ed Stenger, interview with the author, May 19, 2020 (Appendix C).
84 Donna Halper, interview with the author, February 11, 2020 (Appendix B).

the hallways of high school, I mean, I feel I like that was me, that spoke to me, that characterization spoke to me, the lyrics of that song spoke to me in a deeply personal way.[85]

I don't know if Rush made it *cool* to be a nerd, but they certainly made it feel *okay*. Okay to be different from others. Okay to be comfortable with who you are. And the band never talked down to their fans. They spoke to them like wise older brothers who had been through the same things the listeners had and had come out the other side stronger. The song, and the band in general, gave fans a sense that *everything would be just fine if you stay true to who you are*. And that meant so, so much to all of us "trapped between the bright lights and the mass production zone."

---

85   Interview with Bob Cesca, January 22, 2020.

FAN PROFILE: DAVID ANDRADE

Name: David Andrade
Location: Connecticut, USA
Age: 49
Gender: Male
Occupation: Educational Technology

David Andrade, like so many others, became a Rush fan thanks to the band's seminal 1981 album: "I heard Moving Pictures in middle school and got hooked." His fandom is a special one, in that he has gotten to share it with his family: "I got my wife to become a fan, have gone to concerts with large groups of friends, and my seven-year-old daughter has been a fan for years and sings along with me in the car. Her favorite song is 'Presto.'" It's not surprising, then, that the family aspect of Rush fandom is a huge part of the appeal for David. Rush fans obviously share their love for the band with their spouses and children and siblings, but fans feel a strong sense of family among each other, as though to be a Rush fan is to be a part of a secret club. "I enjoy the music and lyrics, and listen to it every day," David says, "but also the fan camaraderie. I have been a part of the Rush fan community since college when I was on the National Midnight Star newsgroup."

David's recollection of the Rush fan stereotype reflects how most people think of the band's devotees: "Rush fans are usually more 'intellectual' and male. It is a majority of men, but as time went on I saw more and more female fans as well and now it is a great, diverse group." Growing up, David remembers that Rush were not as popular as other bands of the day, "but respected as musicians. I had a few friends who were fans and that was enough. Rush got more popular with the internet and bulletin boards and then the web. The National Midnight Star was an amazing resource for Rush fans in the late 80s, early 90s." Some of David's interests tracked with Rush's lyrical content, but listening to Rush also got him into music as a participant and not just as a listener: "It got me more interested in playing guitar as a hobby. I was already into sci-fi, science and technology and was an engineer, school district CIO and now Educational Technology consultant (Sr. Education Strategist at CDWG)."

At the end of the day, for David, it's all about the music. "I love the fact that Rush kept changing their sound while keeping certain things constant and kept fans engaged. Rush's music has gotten me through many tough times and great times. Different songs fit different situations and feelings: 'The Spirit of Radio,' 'Half the World,' 'Dreamline,' 'Presto,' 'The Garden' . . ." Given this deep connection with Rush's music, so common among fans of the band, it's no wonder that David was an enthusiastic concert-goer when the band was still touring: "I have seen Rush live 27 times, from Hold Your Fire to the last tour. Every time is amazing and a memorable experience. I did get soaking wet at one outdoor concert but it was still fun. I have seen Rush with so many different friends and family, turning them on to the music. A friend of mine is friends with the band and has seen them way over 100 times and I've gone to shows with him. Great experience." At the end of the day, Rush's music has become the soundtrack of David's life. "No matter my mood or activity, there are Rush songs that fit. Rush has been, and continues to be, a huge influence on my life.

CHAPTER III: BOYS AND GIRLS TOGETHER

"In the early stages, it was very young, almost 100 percent male, and then as the years went by, it remained 100 percent male." [1]

NO GIRLS ALLOWED?

Rush is a "guy band." Everybody knows that. As we touched upon in Chapter II, Rush fan par excellence Les Claypool, and even the band itself, admit that women just aren't into Rush.

"Chicks did not really dig it, you know?" says Foo Fighters drummer Taylor Hawkins.[2] "I still don't throw on *Caress of Steel* that often with my wife around."[3] "In one way, Rush is a lot like Shaun Cassidy, Teddy Pendergrass and *Super Vixens*," wrote Steve Pond in a 1980 concert review for *Rolling Stone*, "its audience is made up almost entirely of one sex. In Rush's case, it's nearly all males—or more precisely, judging from this crowd, nearly all sixteen-year-old males with long hair, faint mustaches and adrenalin to burn."[4] Steven Horowitz of Libertarinism.org has a different take, wondering why Peart's cerebral lyrics didn't make Rush *more* appealing to women:

> The puzzle here is that Neil's lyrics are notable for the complete absence of the misogyny that affects so much rock and other popular music. If women are put off by the typical male rock star take on sex, love, and cars, they should have seen Rush as an escape from that.[5]

The stereotype of Rush being a band for males is an interesting one to ponder. After all, there are other out-there bands with the fairer sex comprising a sizable percentage of their fan bases. Blogger Trevor Nicholson, writing at JamBands.com, compares Rush fans with those of two such bands, Tool and Phish, and reaches some interesting conclusions:

> [A]ll three bands have peculiar lyrics, coupled with baffling song arrangements and complicated time signatures.
>
> Most importantly, all three bands are known for excellent musicianship and not known for anything superficial like their sex appeal, or stage presence.

---

4   Steve Pond, "Rush's Heavy-Metal Sludge," *Rolling Stone*, May 15, 1980, available at http://www.2112.net/powerwindows/transcripts/19800515rollingstone.htm, last accessed June 10, 2020.

5   Steven Horowitz, "Everybody Got to Elevate from the Norm: The Enduring Appeal of Neil Peart and Rush," Libertarianism.org, January 15, 2020, available at https://www.libertarianism.org/columns/everybody-got-elevate-norm-enduring-appeal-neil-peart-rush, last accessed. May 27, 2020.

If Rush can't get any female fans, how can Tool and Phish? I explored the bands lyrics, and stage persona to see if I could get any answers.[6]

Why indeed. Nicholson's conclusions sound familiar to anyone with a passing familiarity with Rush:

> Tool has morbidly dark lyrics; Phish's lyrics run the gamut from mythical stories, to goofy lyrics about an ugly pig.
>
> Rush's lyrics have J.R.R Tolkien references, anagrams in songs and stories of futuristic societies.
>
> I think that Rush overly dorked themselves in the lyric department attracting the D&D playing, male fan-base. Phish came close but squeaked by and got placed in the quirky and witty lyric category.

Ouch! I think Nicholson's observation about Rush's lyrical content is somewhat incomplete and reductionist, but he's not the only one with a distaste of the fruits of Neil Peart's pen. I mean, I can count only two Rush songs that have anything to do with Tolkien: "Rivendell" from 1975's *Fly By Night*, and "The Necromancer" from that same year's *Caress of Steel*. Heck, I can count *three* Led Zeppelin songs inspired by *The Lord of the Rings*: "Ramble On" from 1969's *Led Zeppelin II* references both Gollum and the land of Mordor, and on 1971's untitled album, "Misty Mountain Hop" is named after the Middle-Earth mountain range and "The Battle of Evermore" might as well be one of Tolkien's epic battle set to music. Zeppelin also has a high-pitched singer and bombastic riffs and was similarly

---

6   Trevor Nicholson, "Rush: Why No Female Fans?" JamBands.com *The Loop* (blog), August 10, 2010, available at https://jambands.com/the-loop/2010/08/10/rush-why-no-female-fans/, last accessed May 7, 2020.

disliked by rock critics at the time, yet their reputation quickly *grew* in stature as time went on while Rush remained nerd music. A function of Zeppelin's overt sexuality, perhaps?

Yet Peart's lyrics, not Robert Plant's are the ones so often singled out for ridicule. *Blender* once ranked Peart as the second worst rock lyricist *of all time*, with only Sting being worse:

> *An ace on the rototoms, a train wreck on the typewriter.*
> Drummers are good at many things: exploding, drowning in their own vomit, drumming. But the Rush skinsman proved they should never write lyrics—or read books. Peart opuses like "Cygnus X-1" are richly awful tapestries of fantasy and science fiction, steeped in an eighth-grade understanding of Western philosophy. 2112, Rush's 1976 concept album based on individualist thinker Ayn Rand's novella Anthem, remains an awe-inspiring low point in the sordid relationship between rock and ideas. Worst lyric: "I stand atop a spiral stair/ An oracle confronts me there/He leads me on light years away/Through astral nights, galactic days" ("Oracle: The Dream")[7]

This stings (no pun intended) pretty hard for those of us who find Peart's words so heartening and inspiring. I mean, are you telling me that the lyrics to songs like "The Pass," "Subdivisions," "Entre Nous," "Ceiling Unlimited," "Losing It," "Time Stand Still," "Resist," "Nobody's Hero," and "The Garden" are *trainwrecks*? There's no need to get upset, since taste in music and lyrics is subjective, but *Blender* is wrong.

---

[7] The original *Blender* piece is no longer available; this was taken from NeilPeartNews.com, October 11, 2007, available at http://neilpeartnews.andrewolson.com/2007/10/neil-peart-is-2-on-blender-list-of.html, last accessed May 7, 2020.

> Back to Nicholson:
>> Maybe it has to do with the onstage presence of the band. If females see bands live because of their looks and onstage sex appeal then obviously Rush is out. I say obviously because as great as Rush sounds live, there's not much else going on besides exceptionally well played music. When Geddy and Alex do decide to do more than the occasionally leg kick or toe tap, they usually do some syncopated head nod that's quite cringe-worthy.[8]

Nicholson isn't the only one to take umbrage with Rush's stage presence. In his infamous *New Musical Express* interview, Barry Miles noted that Rush "seemed to make no effort to put their individual personalities across to their audience to show anything of themselves"[9]; especially when contrasted with other acts like "the Stones or Zappa, who are also very professional, that the individual personalities come across, whereas Rush behaves as *one*."[10]

I'm not sure sex appeal is the *only* thing that allegedly keeps women at bay from Rush, but perhaps it is *a* factor.

Nicholson does something admirable then: He asks women for their opinions about Rush. Their answers are unsurprising:

> I interviewed three female friends who have a strong knowledge of music and all three of them said the same thing. They couldn't get past Geddy's sopranoish, banshee-wail. One female friend described his voice as "the sound of a starving baby bird waiting for mommy to come to feed him." Which I felt was a bit harsh,

---

8 Nicholson, "Rush: Why No Female Fans?"
9 Barry Miles, "Is everybody feelin' all RIGHT (Geddit . . . ?), *New Musical Express*, March 4, 1978, available at https://www.theguardian.com/music/2015/may/13/rush-nme-interview-1978-rocks-backpages, last accessed May 6, 2020
10 *Id.*

but amusing and certainly worth adding to this article.

Another friend made a good point when she said that her first Rush experience was watching the concert film, Rush: Exit Stage Left. Her first image was Geddy Lee, with his mane of hair and hook nose belting out some awkwardly high pitched lyrics about different Trees (The Trees) getting into a war and thinking to herself, "I can't get past this dudes voice, but the story in the song isn't helping sell the band either."

All three female friends could care less about the sex appeal of the band that they are going to see. One girl even called me a "chauvinistic knucklehead," for thinking that played a role in why a female adult would see a band live.[11]

I don't think it's fair to cast aspersions against Mr. Nicholson and accuse him and his hypothesis of some latent misogyny; after all, men and women *do* have different tastes—and that's okay! But I find it telling that Rush's lyrics and Geddy Lee's voice might be off-putting to women. Hell, they're off-putting to many *men*. Still, this lends credence to the stereotype of Rush's fans as being bearers of two different chromosomes. When I spoke to Ed Stenger, he speculated that "their lyrics, the subject matter, especially their early records, [were] very science fictiony, fantasy stuff, really heavy stuff that generally appeals to males I guess."[12]

Back to these sex differences: on February 27, 2017, a Quora user named John Wolforth posits a similar explanation as to why Rush fans all seem to be dudes:

---

11 Trevor Nicholson, "Rush: Why No Female Fans?"
12 Ed Stenger, interview with the author, May 19, 2020 (Appendix C). Once again, we see that the male/nerd overlap isn't just a figment of my imagination.

> In my opinion, Rush audiences tend to be primarily male because Rush music is not only progressive, it is what I refer to as Thought Rock. That is not to say that women do not think, I mean that the style and lyrics of Rush tend to focus on more lofty and convoluted subjects than what many women are interested in contemplating. Hell, many men don't like Rush either.
>
> From my experience - and whatever "scientific" evidence I have been able to gather through the years, women are more interested in "emotional" music; songs that talk about love and romance, or other emotional challenges of everyday life.
>
> It's like science fiction, most women are not deeply into it. Of course, I happen to think that Rush music is also full of emotion, just of a different, more eclectic kind.
>
> That is not to say that ALL women fall into that category, it just seems to be the case more often than not.[13]

This is some spicy subject matter, as gender differences tend to be, but it is important and necessary to consider in building a profile of the typical Rush fan. And of course, we want to find out if it's true.

---

13 John Wolforth, "Why does Rush have an audience that's primarily male?" Quora.com, February 27, 2017, available at https://www.quora.com/Why-does-Rush-have-an-audience-thats-primarily-male, last accessed May 8, 2020.

RUSH IS LIKE ANAL (?)

W. Earl Brown is an actor, a musician, a filmmaker, and a huge Rush fan. His vast list of credits includes the television shows *Deadwood*, *The Untouchables*, *Psych*, *Burn Notice*, *Ellen*, and *CSI*, and he has appeared in movies like *There's Something About Mary*, *Deep Impact*, *Scream*, and *Draft Day*.

In 2018, Brown wrote, produced, and starred in a short film called *Dad Band*, which details the travails of a middle-aged garage band of misfits who just want a one last chance at rock stardom . . . if they can get out of each other's way. Among its stars are Eric Stromer as Neal, the drummer (get it?) whose garage serves as the titular band's rehearsal space. The film also features Alice In Chains guitarist Jerry Cantrell as bassist Terry—once a guitarist in an *actual touring band,* Ted Kamp as affable keyboardist Abel, and Brown as Jimbo, lead guitarist and Neal's friend . . . and a Rush fanatic. In fact, Jimbo shows up to rehearsal in a Rush t-shirt. He also resents it *very* much when Terry picks up his axe and starts to play a few riffs.

It's a funny movie, and instantly relatable to any middle-aged family man past his prime who had a history of playing rock n' roll in their youth (like your humble author). Amidst a plot involving competing artistic visions, trying to catch the eye of Neal's hot neighbor and, uh, the theft of a pair of panties, there's one exchange that's both hilarious and particularly germane to the topic of Rush fans and their demographic breakdown:

> Jimbo: Then you come back in 8/12 time. Think "Cygnus-X1: Book 2." No, no—better yet . . . think "The Fountain of Lamneth"—first section.
>
> Terry: Dude, I love Rush too, but face it—chicks don't. Alright? It took me longer to get my first wife to go to a Rush concert than it did to try anal. And she said never again.

Abel: To the concert?

Terry: It's one of the reasons we got divorced.

Jimbo: This is not Rush though.

Neal: Dude, it sounds like Rush.

Terry: No chick is gonna fuck you to a Rush song. Definitely not up the ass.

Neal: I'm not saying we can't do originals . . . something simple.

Jimbo: "Tom Sawyer".

Neal: No! Simpler . . . and not Rush.

It's crass, but funny. And bonus points for the reference to "The Fountain of Lamneth," Rush's first 20-minute epic song.[14]

"A friend of mine passed it along to the band's TM [tour manager]," Brown told me when I reached out to him on Twitter. "I was told that Lerxst [Lifeson] and Dirk [Lee] loved it. I don't know if Pratt [Peart] got to see it or not."[15]

Brown was kind enough to share the genesis of this joke with me:

> Funny footnote: my wife and I go to a lot of live music. Rush is the only band I love that she does not (and Slayer). I had tickets to the final Rush show at the Forum—none of my friends could go with.[16] I talked C [Brown's wife Carrie Paschall] into going with me. After

---

14 No wonder Taylor Hawkins doesn't play this album for his wife!
15 W. Earl Brown, March 19, 2020, available at http://www.twitter.com/WEarlBrown/status/1240667925578534913
16 *Id.*, http://www.twitter.com/WEarlBrown/status/1240670796474798086

the show, walking back to the car, I was totally fanboying about the many deep tracks played and how I was finally coming around to their mid-late period keyboard-based material, and how . . .

"Look, I know you love them I appreciate[17] their skills as musicians . . . I'm glad you had a great time."

We walked in silence for a bit, I replied "it took me longer to get you to go to a Rush [concert] than it did to try anal. You seemed to have enjoyed each equally."

Stifling a laugh, she said "DON'T YOU EVER TELL THAT JOKE."[18]

So naturally, it ended up in the movie. And lest you think *I'm* being unfair to Ms. Paschall, I explicitly asked Brown if I could share this anecdote in the book and he gave me the okay.[19]

What this anecdote shows is that, even in their later, more popular period, Rush still appealed mostly to men. The trio, it seems, suffers from the same woes as the fictional band Spɪnäl Tap when asked about their fans by documentarian (mockumentarian?) Marty DiBergi, played by Rob Reiner:

Marty: Let's talk about your music today . . . uh . . . one thing that puzzles me . . . um . . . is the make-up of your audience seems to be . . . uh . . . predominately young boys.

---

17 *Id.*, http://www.twitter.com/WEarlBrown/status/1240671304711168001
18 *Id.*, http://www.twitter.com/WEarlBrown/status/1240671988802150400
19 *Id.*, May 7, 2020, available at http://www.twitter.com/WEarlBrown/status/1258491138048057344 ("I'd be honored. Yes.")

David: Well it's a sexual thing, really isn't it? Aside from the identifying the boys do with us there's also a reaction to the female . . . of the female to our music. How did you put it?

Nigel: Really they're quite fearful—that's my theory. They see us on stage with tight trousers we've got, you know, armadillos in our trousers, I mean it's really quite frightening . . .

David: Yeah.

Nigel: . . . the size . . . and, and they, they run screaming.[20]

THE UNBEARABLE WHITENESS OF RUSH

In addition to being a guy band, Rush is a very white band. Like all progressive rock, Rush fandom is not only male-dominated but *white* male-dominated. For whatever reason, this sort of music only attracts and appeals to this particular demographic. And this is a bad thing, or so the conventional wisdom goes.

"The Whitest Music Ever," proclaims James Parker's piece in the September 2017 issue of *The Atlantic*.[21] "White" is clearly used as a pejorative, the way the color of no other group of people would in any respectable mainstream publication. "Prog rock was audacious, innovative—and awful," reads the sub-

---

20 *This is Spinal Tap* (1984). The entire script is available here: http://www.awesomefilm.com/script/thisisspinaltap.txt, last accessed May 8, 2020.

21 James Parker, "The Whitest Music Ever: Prog rock was audacious, innovative—and awful," *The Atlantic*, September 2017, available at https://www.theatlantic.com/magazine/archive/2017/09/the-whitest-music-ever/534174/, last accessed May 8, 2020.

heading. There is, of course, a line about Rush featuring the "trapped, eunuch ferocity of Geddy Lee's voice, squealing inside the nonsense clockwork," which is, quite frankly, a pretty hilarious turn of phrase. But there is an odd racial fixation in Parker's survey of a genre of music he just does not like.

A lot of it gets into what "rock and roll" and "progressive rock" are. Rock, it is widely known, is a mixture of African-American blues melded with Scotch-Irish folk, rhythm and blues, and elements of country and jazz. It evolved from a melting pot of various musical styles, styles considered "low" by the upper crust, but rock is generally accepted to owe a great debt of gratitude to black music.

Prog rock, on the other hand, is defined as being more "out there" in the sense that the musicians involved are very talented and enjoy showing it, with long and complex song structures, dizzying displays of skill on their instruments, and thematic lyrical content involving the mythic and deeply philosophical. In other words, like Rush. Other bands in this genre include Yes, Genesis, King Crimson, Caravan, and Emerson, Lake & Palmer. More recently, with the advent of prog metal and even pop-prog, bands like Dream Theater, Queensrÿche, Tool, Porcupine Tree, Primus, Mastodon, and Coheed and Cambria have picked up the progressive rock mantle.

But really, according to Parker and others, prog rock is what happened when rock jettisoned any black influence and leaned more upon *classical* music for inspiration.[22] As Parker boldly proclaims: "Thus did prog divorce itself from the blues, take flight into the neoclassical, and become the whitest music ever."[23] But don't tell Tosin Abasi of Animals as Leaders that he's not supposed to be into prog! Or the members of Living Colour that Rush isn't for them!

---

22 *See, e.g.*, Edward Macan, *Rocking the Classics: English Progressive Rock and the Counterculture*, (Oxford University Press, 1997).
23 Parker, "The Whitest Music Ever."

This, of course, raises a few questions:

1) So what?

2) Is this *by default* a bad thing? and

3) *Is this even true?*

Thinking about prog rock bands off the top of my head, the only one who seem to remotely have "divorced" themselves of the blues and hitched their wagon to classical music is *maybe* Emerson, Lake & Palmer, and even then there is still blues influence in their music (they *did* cover Modest Mussorgsky's "Pictures at an Exhibition" in its entirety live in 1971, but that's not the sum-total of their work[24]). But were ELP "divorced" from black music? Was Jethro Tull, with Ian Anderson's flute flourishes and Martin Barre's delicate fingerpicked guitars contrasting with some absolutely filthy heavy blues riffs completely bereft of any black influence?

Is *Rush* beholden to classical music?

Methinks Mr. Parker and other critics of prog need to get a grip. There is a habit in modern times to see nearly everything through the lens of race. And I mean *everything*. The fact that I have to bring this up in a book beyond making a general observation that most Rush fans are stereotypically thought of as being of European descent is a testament to this. There has to be some *broader meaning* behind that fact, right? Some *power dynamics* or whatever that prove a style of music which appeals mostly to the *dominant colonial power* or something is *oppressive to minorities*.

I kind of want to puke just writing this kind of stuff, even in jest.

The whiteness of Rush fans is, according to writer Steven Horowitz, the result of Geddy, Alex, and Neil's suburban mid-

---

24   They also had an album called *Tarkus* which was, in part, about a giant armadillo-tank and its battle against mythical creatures like a manticore, so yeah, not very bluesy.

dle-class upbringings and their embodiment of those values, including striving for upward mobility via the pursuit of personal excellence:

> Rush's middle-class, middle-brow rock unsurprisingly appealed to the very same kinds of people they were. When I look around at many of my fellow fans who I know well, one of the things we tend to share is a similar suburban upbringing in the 70s and 80s. This, I think, also explains why their fan base remains overwhelmingly white (well-known rap stars and the members of Living Colour duly noted as exceptions).[25]

Indeed, writer Christopher J. McDonald wrote an entire book on this subject, noting that "suburbs socially reflected a continued desire for exclusivity among the American white middle class, who used the suburbs to create new pockets of socioeconomic and ethnic homogeneity."[26] Therefore, it can hardly be surprising that a band like Rush, whose members grew up in white, suburban areas, would make music and comport their lives reflecting the values inculcated by this background and therefore appeal primarily to an audience of a similar background. And for our purposes, Canadian culture is close enough to American culture for the point to remain valid.

I leave it up to the reader to decide whether this is a good thing or a bad thing. My conclusion is that it is unsurprising, uncontroversial, and no different than the fact that rap and hip-hop, for example, and before that jazz, appeal to the black, urban audience from which those styles of music sprang.

Let's get back to the music, shall we?

25   Steven Horowitz, "Everybody Got to Elevate from the Norm: The Enduring Appeal of Neil Peart and Rush," Libertarianism.org, January 15, 2020, available at https://www.libertarianism.org/columns/everybody-got-elevate-norm-enduring-appeal-neil-peart-rush, last accessed May 27, 2020.
26   *See* Christopher J. McDonald, *Rush, Rock Music, and the Middle Class: Dreaming in Middletown (Profiles in Popular Music)* (Indiana University Press, 2009).

In writing about the disconnect between prog *critics* and prog *fans*, the *New Yorker*'s Kelefa Sanneh points out the obvious fact that "[t]he genre's primary appeal . . . was . . . technical."[27] On the issue of prog and *race*, Sanneh offers a few of the hypotheses floating around:

> Why, then, did this music seduce so many Americans? In 1997, a musician and scholar named Edward Macan published "Rocking the Classics," in which he offered a provocative explanation. Noting that this artsy music seemed to attract "a greater proportion of blue-collar listeners" in the U.S. than it had in Britain, he proposed that the genre's Britishness "provided a kind of surrogate ethnic identity to its young white audience": white music for white people, at a time of growing white anxiety. Bill Martin, the quasi-Marxist, found Macan's argument "troubling." In his view, the kids in the bleachers were revolutionaries, drawn to the music because its sensibility, based on "radical spiritual traditions," offered an alternative to "Western politics, economics, religion, and culture."

There's no doubt the idea of race and culture is provocative, but I think we can all discuss it as adults. The fact is, since at least the 1970s, a piece of pop culture's whiteness is directly proportional to its uncoolness, at least in the eyes of the tastemakers and gatekeepers. These days, the same types of tastemakers and gatekeepers would use the word "problematic."

Once again, we see that Rush has Spinal Tap-syndrome:

---

[27] Kelefa Sanneh, "The Persistence of Prog Rock," *New Yorker*, June 12, 2017, available at https://www.newyorker.com/magazine/2017/06/19/the-persistence-of-prog-rock, last accessed May 8, 2020.

Marty: You play to predominantly, uh predominantly a white audience, you feel your music is racist in any way?

David: no!

Nigel: No, no, of course not . . .

David: We pro . . . we say, we say "love your brother"—we don't say it, really, but . . .

Nigel: We don't literally say it.

David: No, we don't say it . . .at all.

Nigel: No, we don't literally mean it, but we're not racists.

David: No, we don't believe it either, but . . . that message should
be clear anyway.

Nigel: We're anything but racists.

A GUY THING

Of the 664 Rush fans who responded to my survey, 658 disclosed their gender. Of these, 586 indicated that they were male, and 71 indicated that they were female. One respondent indicated that they were "nonbinary/Agender"; I debated including them as both, but given that the prefix "a" means "without" in Greek, I decided not to use them in calculating my numbers. Therefore, I am using 657 as my overall number of respondents to the gender question. I know I am running the risk of offending this Rush fan, but I hope that, if they are reading this book, they know that this was not my intention. Additionally, one Rush fan indicated that they were a male-to-female transgender, which I am including in the "female" tally.

Doing the math, then, my decidedly unscientific survey of Rush fans reveals that roughly 89% of you are, rounding up, male, and 11% of you, also rounding up, are female. This essentially means that nine-out-of-ten Rush fans are male. Based on the concerts I've been to and the people I've met who are into prog rock, I'd say that this reflects reality pretty accurately. It is also, like the high proportion of Rush fans being nerds, is not surprising.

Interestingly, Rush manager Ray Danniels saw the female proportion of Rush fans change as the band charged into the 21st century:

> We went from less than 10 per cent of our average house being female to suddenly it was 30 per cent. That came from women watching the documentary [Beyond the Lighted Stage] with their boyfriends or husbands and connecting it all. They were like, "Oh, I know that song and that song and that song." They actually knew five, six, seven RUSH songs but hadn't connected that they were RUSH.[28]

Also not surprising are the responses to the question about the race of the average Rush fan. Given that I am an American surveying Rush fans in the U.S., as well as a decent amount from Canada, Europe, and Australia, 581 of 664, or 87.5%, of respondents were white. The remaining 12.5% of Rush fans surveyed were Hispanic (11); mixed-race (9), Asian (4), African-American (2), Native American (2), Persian (1), and Indian (1), while 53 did not specify.

Again, as with about roughly 90% of Rush fans being male, roughly 90% of Rush fans being white also tracks with my own experience and observations. I'm sure this would be different if

---

28   Vinay Menon, *Rush: An Oral History* (Toronto Star Newspapers Limited, 2013), at 50.

I were, say, of Asian extraction and hung out with Korean and Japanese prog fans, but given my own background and social milieu, I'm declaring this stereotype, much like the nerd and male stereotypes, true.

So does this matter? And what does it say about Rush fans, and the band itself, that it appeals primarily to white men?

I'll answer the first question quite simply: This matters only because it's a fun and interesting thing to discuss. I know many people get touchy about race, especially in the United States, but I asked this question solely in the spirit of discovering what preconceived notions of the "typical" Rush fan are like so I can push aside these superficial aspects and get to the more interesting reasons why this band brings so many people together. As such, I'm not going to focus on the racial breakdown of Rush fans any more, since of all the Rush fan stereotypes out there (male, nerd, atheist, libertarian, musician, into science), race matters the *least*.

So that leaves us with the question of why Rush appeals primarily to men.

LADIES FIRST

First of all, no less an authority on the band than Donna Halper calls it a "myth" that all Rush fans are men:[29]

> [I]n the original incarnation of the band, yes. The vast majority of Rush fans were male, agreed . . . . But that was true about rock and roll in general . . . As time went on, and the members of the band got more into different kinds of lyrical manifestations, different kinds of songs, there are some beautiful songs that Rush have done. "Entre Nous." "The Garden."
> I mean, come on, it's not all, you know, heavy

---

29   Donna Halper, interview with the author, February 11, 2020 (Appendix B).

metal thunder. And I think gradually, people got apprenticed into Rush that hadn't been apprenticed into it before, maybe it was through a boyfriend, maybe it was through a husband, maybe it was through a father, but these days? Yeah, Rush fans are just about everything, gay, straight, black, white, green, purple, and male and female.[30]

I would also like to point out that the founder of Rushcon, the world's biggest convention for Rush fans, is a woman named Elizabeth "Eddy" Maxwell. Further, Rushcon's entire staff[31] is female: Auction coordinator Holly Smith, logistics manager Mary Jo Plews, special projects lead Kristy Williams, and creative director Jillian Maryonovich. Maxwell seems to enjoy pointing out that Rushcon was started by "a core group of strong, dedicated women," which punctures the stereotype of *all* Rush fans being male.[32]

Jillian Maryonovich is featured in the 2016 documentary *Time Stand Still*, and throughout the film you see lots of other hardcore female Rush fans, a counterintuitive phenomenon given the stereotypes about Rush's music and fan base. "The female fans, they're more outgoing and they seem to be more involved," Ed Stenger told me. "I think the fact that the Rush Con organizers are all women kind of speaks to that, in my experience."[33] Respondent Susan C-C's experience reflects Stenger's assertion: "Female Rush fans have always been there, even when outnumbered by guys maybe 6-1 or more. Because we're seen as the exception rather than the rule, I've found we Rush chicks are particularly passionate about the band."[34]

30 *Id.*
31 http://rushcon.org/staff/index.html, last accessed May 14, 2020.
32 Matthew Sherwood, "The gathering of the cult of Rush: Rushcon 12 brings the band's most dedicated acolytes out to YYZ," *National Post*, October 16, 2012, available at https://nationalpost.com/entertainment/the-gathering-of-the-cult-of-rush, last accessed May 14, 2020.
33 Ed Stenger, interview with the author, May 19, 2020 (Appendix C).
34 Susan C-C, response to author's survey, February 5, 2020 (Appendix A).

Clearly, something in Rush's music speaks to women as much as it does to men. "I grew up in Milwaukee," Maryonovich told Toronto's *National Post*. "[A]t my upper-class high school, everyone was into stupid bubble-gum music. Because everyone else hated Rush, it made it cooler for me to like them . . . Their lyrics were about atheism and science and rebellion and conformity—topics that really spoke to me at that time of my life."[35]

It was also Rush's lyrical content which grabbed Williams:

> Williams . . . remembers her life was "in a state of flux" when she had her Rush conversion moment. In 2003, at 23, she was stuck in rural Victoria [Australia] with her boyfriend after their car was hit by a wallaby; they happened upon a Rush DVD in a department store. She was taken by the lyrics to Roll the Bones: "Why are we here? Because we're here." Says Williams, "Those words just grabbed me, and it was hook, line, sinker, and a copy of Angling Times, to quote Red Dwarf."[36]

More recently, philosophy PhD Liz Stillwaggon Swan penned a piece for *Psychology Today* describing how Rush's music helps her get through the nationwide—hell, *world*wide—lockdowns mandated by various governments in reaction to the global coronavirus pandemic:

> The past couple of months have been incredibly trying times. They've been filled with darkness, fear, confusion, panic, illness, uncertainty, and emotional pain. As a philosopher, I've traveled into the deep recesses of my mind, replaying certain insights from influential philosophers I've studied, trying to eke out some inspiration. Long walks in the sunshine with these thoughts

---

35 Sherwood, "The Gathering of the cult of Rush."
36 *Id.*

have been therapeutic. But long walks in the sunshine while listening to Rush—my favorite philosophical muse—have been freakin' amazing.[37]

Among her favorite songs: "By-Tor and the Snow Dog," "The Necromancer," "The Fountain of Lamneth," and "Jacob's Ladder." "I believe Neil Peart was well acquainted with the idea of seeking the light in dark times," Swan continues, "of shaping a brighter reality if only in one's mind, of seeing the proverbial light at the end of the tunnel and running full-speed ahead toward it."[38]

But tell me again that Rush's music doesn't appeal to women.

There is something universal at work with Rush's music and Neil Peart's lyrics, something that might appeal *mostly* to men but is in no way lost on the fairer sex. Before moving on to discussing some possible reasons why Rush fans are mostly men, I would like to share a female Rush fan's response to Mr. Wolforth's post on Quora discussing this very same subject:

> Female perspective here! I thought I would pop in because it seems much needed. I am not trying to make this the "I'm not like other girls" argument that is honestly really harmful, but so are the broad sweeping brush strokes that NO women like prog music" and "women only like pop." That is almost as ridiculous as me flipping that argument and saying that all men like prog music and no men like pop. It would be ludicrous to argue that as the truth, and if it was the world would be super boring.

---

37 "If Rush Could Wave Their Magic Wand: They'd make everything all light in a time of darkness," *Psychology Today*, April 29, 2020, available at https://www.psychologytoday.com/us/blog/the-philosopher-is-in/202004/if-rush-could-wave-their-magic-wand, last accessed May 17, 2020.
38 *Id.*

Rush is my favorite band and it has proven to be a great bonding experience for my father and I. In the cases it comes up in conversation I sometimes get some weird looks, probably because I am both a teenager and a female.

From my personal experiences I would say that Rush isn't isolated in this primarily male audience. I would say it has something to do with outdated and frankly ridiculous notions that anything that isn't bubble gum pop is "too complex/hard/edgy etc." for the oh so delicate female mind. These notions are incredibly ingrained in our society and it irritates the crap out of me. Some of us don't listen to it because we have been told that it isn't for us, and we just listen. With Rush being a band with such a devoted following who has followed them from the start, a lot within the prototype of the outcast teenage boy, which Rush were and likely relate to, thus that is the fan base that we see as the norm.

If any of you think that because of my gender I am not intelligent enough to understand the lyrics or "enjoy the musicality" I will be pisssssssssed. I read both The Fountainhead and Atlas Shrugged to better understand Ayn Rand and objectivism, in turn to be able to better understand the philosophy and basis of many of Neil's earlier songs.[39]

---

39 A. Tucker, "Why does Rush have an audience that's primarily male?" Quora.com, April 18, 2019, available at https://www.quora.com/Why-does-Rush-have-an-audience-thats-primarily-male, last accessed May 14, 2020.

And yet, clearly Rush speaks to men a *lot*, their female fans notwithstanding. I wonder if this clannish devotion to the band is related to the innate male desire to belong to a gang.

THE WAY OF THE GANG

What is it about large groups of like-minded young men that sends the powers that be into a tizzy of a fear? Perhaps it's what philosopher Jack Donovan in his 2012 book *The Way of Men* calls "the way of the gang." "You have to define your group," Donovan writes. "You need to define who is in and who is out ."[40]

First, Donovan explains some male tendencies that our modern civilized society tries to suppress:

> Boys are scolded even for their violent fantasies—for the violent stories they want to hear, the violent books they want to read, the violent games they want to play. Male "demonism" is punished, pathologists, and stigmatized from cradle to campus. Even the good guys are treated like bad guys for ganging up, for being "xenophobic," patriotic, or too exclusive. Video games, fighting sports, and movies are decried for being "too violent." Football is deemed "too dangerous" by many overprotective parents. Everyone is supposed to agree that violence is never the answer—unless that violence comes from the cutting edge of the State's ax.[41]

In modern times, the role of men as using their dangerous propensity for violence to tame the wilderness and beat back barbarian hordes has been greatly curtailed. This has resulted in much confusion about what being a man is, and for a society

---

[40] Jack Donovan, *The Way of Men*, (Dissonant Hum, 2012), at 5.
[41] *Id.* at 105.

of geldings without chests, to paraphrase C.S. Lewis, to understand what to do with them. Especially in large gatherings.

Adversity, hardship, and the time-honored tradition of busting balls: These are the things that make men. "A woman simply is, but a man must become," writes scholar and professor Camille Paglia, who more than many men can articulate what being a man is all about. "Masculinity is risky and elusive. It is achieved by a revolt from woman, and it confirmed only by other men. Feminist fantasies about the ideal 'sensitive' male have failed. Manhood coerced into sensitivity is no manhood at all."[42]

This is interesting to ponder, since Neil Peart's lyrics are certainly not the typical macho bragging about his sexual notch count the way many hard rock bands' tend to be. Peart is definitely a sensitive soul, sensitive about nature and the overall human condition, and this sensitivity clearly informed his lyrics. Yet Peart was also fiercely independent, willing to stand up for his beliefs, and no doubt demonstrating other stereotypically masculine traits. And Rush was, obviously, his gang.

As far as "the way of the gang," Donovon describes it as a bifurcation between "being a good man" and "being good at being a man." Indeed, this is the premise of *The Way of Men* and much of his subsequent writing. And one of the virtues men value is *mastery*. Is there something about Geddy, Alex, and Neil's mastery of their instruments that resonates so deeply with men? Does this appreciation for Rush's musical wizard help create this "us versus them" bond that many men crave? Do smug, dismissive rock critics and other people who just don't get Rush make the tribe of Rush fans *more* appealing? Does Rush fandom provide an outlet for this innate male desire to form gangs and cause havoc?

It very well might.

As I've shown, neither Rush nor their fans actively *exclude* females. But it's a fact that their music attracts men in large quantities. And some, including critics like Barry Miles, seem to have a problem with this.

---

42 Camille Paglia, *Sex, Art and American Culture: New Essays* (Vintage Books, 1992) at 82.

Perhaps it's residual fear of fascist movements which animated Barry Miles's ridiculous assessment of Rush's music as basically appealing to brownshirts-in-waiting. We see this fear of large gatherings of men, mostly young ones, in the modern incel movement (if being an "involuntary celibate" can be considered a "movement") that has resulted in some tragic mass shootings and other misogynistic violence that puts mainstream society on edge. Whatever the case, when things are described as "male dominated," it almost always carries a negative connotation. Now, fandom of a rock group usually doesn't lead to acts of wonton destruction, *especially* Rush, but then again nobody considered rock critics to have the best sense of perspective.

We've established in Chapter II that Rush fans are nerds, and historically most nerds and nerd pursuits have been male-dominated. I think it's safe to say that it was mostly teenage boys who identified with the social outcast protagonist in the "Subdivisions" video. Yet we've also seen that Rush's lyrics appeal to women. Nerdiness and maleness tend to overlap. So if it's not the *lyrics* which make Rush appeal mostly to men, is it the music itself?

YOU CAN'T FORGET THAT THERE ARE NOTES INVOLVED

Another stereotype that I think is true is that males are generally more interested in heavy, bombastic, and often bludgeoning music than in softer sounds. Speaking from my own perspective as a musician playing with a lot of hard rock bands, and encountering lots of groups in the metal, hard-core, math rock, and death metal scenes, there aren't all that many women *playing* this type of music, at least in the clubs, though to be fair there was a decent number of female fans. But an endless series of anecdotes does not a serious analysis make, so let's talk some music theory.

Rush is an entirely different beast when it comes to classification—are they metal? Hard rock? Prog rock? Prog metal? They are heavy, no doubt, but they display a melodic sense that adds a lot to their appeal—how many bands can switch times signatures and moods so often and so effortlessly while still retaining a logical through line so expertly crafted that you don't even notice the musical insanity? But think about it: politically correct or not, men and women will both describe a song or a melody or a chord or what have you as being either more masculine- or more feminine-sounding.

Musicologists refer to these harmonic qualities in terms of *intervals*, the relationship between the different notes in a given chord or scale. Here's the quick and dirty version: Every basic chord consists of three tones, the *one*, the *three*, and the *five*. These numbers refer to the notes of a scale.[43] We all know "Do, Re, Mi, Fa, Sol, La, Ti, Do," right? Well, think of "Do" as the *one* of a chord, "Mi" as the *three*, and "Sol" as the *five*. You put them together and you get a major chord. It's hard to explain this in writing, writing about music being like dancing about architecture and all of that, so maybe the best thing for you to do is to find a piano and play a C, an E, and a G at the same time. That's C major.

Now let's move that third, the E in our example, down a half step so it's E-flat. E-flat is the *minor* third, which turns the chord from C major to C minor. It has a very different characteristic, sounding sad or mournful, or you might even say *heavy*. "Even though most nonmusicians can't name a chord on hearing it, or label it as major or minor," writes musicologist Daniel J. Levitin, "if they hear a major and minor chord back to back they can tell the difference."[44] If you tried this just now, I would be shocked if you do not agree. And your *brain* could tell the dif-

---

43   *Most* scales, and most *Western* scales at that. Indian music, for example, features micro-tones between half-steps, the smallest interval in Western music. And some Western scales, such as the various diminished scales, feature *more* than eight notes (the seven notes with the octave repeating itself), while others like the pentatonic and whole-tone scales feature fewer.
44   Daniel J. Levitin, *This Is Your Brain on Music: The Science of a Human Obsession* (Dutton, 2006), at 267.

ference as well as your ears: "[A] number of studies have shown that nonmusicians produce different physiological responses to major versus minor chords, and major versus minor keys." This is how harmonies can affect the mood of a piece of music. You can play with just the three and the five and get all sorts of interesting chords. Things get even more interesting when you add the *seven* ("Ti"), whether major or minor, and other extended tones.

Here's a germane example any Rush fan will understand: Think about the verse to "The Spirit of Radio." It's very major, upbeat and "happy" sounding, for lack of a better word. Contrast this with the entirety of the song "Distant Early Warning." Or "Red Sector A," or most of the *Grace Under Pressure* album, really. Those songs sound dark and almost oppressive. They have that minor key vibe that is very different from a song like "The Spirit of Radio."

"Limelight" provides a great example of this dichotomy within the same song. Think of the main riff and the verse, and then think of that wonderfully evocative and emotional chorus. The verse is *major*, and the chorus is *minor*. This push-pull between the two qualities, and how they heighten the message of the lyrics, are one of the things that makes the song so interesting.

Before we continue, if you are a musician and are already knowledgeable about music theory, please forgive any errors in this section, or repetition of things you already know. And if you're a musical neophyte, I greatly appreciate your patience. This has a point. Trust me.

What this has to do with Rush being "guy" music as opposed to "girl" music is that, like it or not, we think of the dark stuff as being male in the light stuff as being female. This may be innate, or it may be culturally ingrained, or it may be a little bit of both. If you want to play a quick game of association, do you consider Slayer a guy or a girl band? Do you consider Maroon 5 a guy or a girl band? Do you see what I'm getting at? It's very difficult to articulate these ephemeral, musical, intangible things into words, especially when playing with the powder keg that is gender differences. I'm doing the best I can, and I greatly appreciate your patience.

So what does this have to do with Rush? Rush uses all sorts of musical moods, but the popular image of Rush isn't a song like "Grand Designs" or the entirety of the *Hold Your Fire* album.[45] Most people think of Geddy Lee's banshee shrieking vocals and a thunderous, bone crunching, bombast that stands toe-to-toe with Black Sabbath and Led Zeppelin. One also thinks of a style of music that involves a lot of hairy, sweaty men. Probably with mustaches.

"But wait!" you might say. "Women loved Sabbath and Zeppelin!" That was true! Women also loved Pink Floyd, which, like Rush, get put into the "brainy" camp. So what gives?

As discussed earlier, Led Zeppelin had a lot of sex appeal, and in their way, so did Black Sabbath. Much like the Rolling Stones and other rock 'n' roll groups of their era, Led Zeppelin sang a whole lot of songs about sex. Ru.32sh did not.

A band singing about breaking their fast on honeydew and drinking the milk of paradise, the French revolution, and flying a spaceship into a black hole doesn't really ooze with sexuality. Contrast this to Pink Floyd who, in addition to having a more accessible sound, did have a certain sexiness to their music, thanks mostly to David Gilmour's slinky guitars and soulful vocals that made their lengthy songs and weighty subject matter palatable to a very wide audience of men *and* women.

Whether this accurately describes the phenomenon I will leave up to you, dear reader. But suffice it to say I think the tag of "guy band" got attached to Rush accurately, but in an unfair manner designed as a slight instead of a fact. Because it *is* a fact that most Rush fans are male. I still stand by my assertion that there is nothing inherently wrong with a band having a predominately male fan base, but many critics disagree.

Still, I think it's telling that one of Rush's first fans and their biggest booster was female: Donna Halper. As she told me, she did not drink or do drugs or engage in other high risk pursuits

---

45   For my money, *Hold Your Fire* contains some of the most beautiful music Rush ever recorded.

and was mocked and marginalized, not surprising given her career in the music industry.[46] In Rush, she found a community of like-minded people who accepted her as is: "What Rush did for me . . . it gave me a fan community and it gave me friends that I didn't have before."[47]

That is the power of Rush, my friends. Without getting maudlin, there's something special about this band. In Donna's words, and it's a theme that will come up again and again in this book, "Rush brings people together."[48] And it's not a nerd thing or a male thing or a female thing. Rush fans are often misfits. We're all looking for our fellow misfits, and we found our own island of misfit toys in Rush and their music.

I'm sorry. I promised I would not get maudlin and then I go and drop a reference like that.

---

46 Donna Halper, interview with the author, February 11, 2020 (Appendix B) ("I don't smoke . . . I don't do drugs . . . I was mocked, I was made fun of, I was ridiculed, I was really treated quite unkindly at some of the stations I worked at.")
47 Id.
48 Id.

CHAPTER IV: GOD AND GOVERNMENT

"Nothing used to get Neil crazier . . . than people who were upset with him when he walked away from Ayn Rand." [1]

OBJECTIVELY SPEAKING

"With acknowledgement to the genius of Ayn Rand."
    With those eight words in the liner notes to 1976 is landmark *2112* album, Rush sealed their fate as personae non-grata in the largely left-wing world of the music press.
    Don't believe me? Let's take a deeper dive into the March 4, 1978 *New Musical Express* article written by our old friend, Mr. Barry Miles:

> I got the job of interviewing Rush because I was the only one on NME who knew who Ayn Rand

was—simple as that. Ayn Rand? Oh, she's an obscure ultra-right-wing American cult writer of the late 30s and early 40s and, yes, Rush follow her ideas. The epic 2112 is a rewrite of her book Anthem and they also name their Canadian record label after the same book. But more about her later . . .[2]

Yes, and more about her later in *this* book as well.

To a Rush fan in the 21st century, this is all somewhat bewildering as Rush can barely be considered a political band, or a religious one, the meme declaring "Rush: Zeppelin for Canadian Atheists" notwithstanding. It's no stretch to assume from Neil's lyrics—and the fact that in 2012, the band's legal team filed a copyright and trademark dispute against conservative American talk show legend Rush Limbaugh to stop using "The Spirit of Radio" as bumper music[3]—that the band is more on the left-side of things. And yet, the songs that *do* delve into political issues tend to be quite nuanced. In fact, Rush is said to be neither right nor left, but *libertarian*. What "libertarian" means is another thing we will get into later, but suffice it to say the stereotype that Rush fans are *libertarian atheists* exists for a reason. As with all of these stereotypes, though, the purpose of this book is to discover whether this is true.

To do so will require dealing with the large shadow cast by Ms. Ayn Rand.

THE ANTHEM OF THE SHRUGGING ATLAS

If Ayn Rand—and libertarians in general—could have a credo, it would be Rand's assertion in *Capitalism: The Unknown Ideal*, that "[T]he smallest minority on earth is the individual. Those who deny individual rights cannot claim to be defenders of minorities."[4] It doesn't take a great detective to see this influence in Neil Peart's lyrics.

Born in St. Petersburg, Russia in 1905 as Alisa Zinovyevna Rosenbaum, Rand and her family fled Russia shortly after the 1917 Bolshevik Revolution, emigrating to the United States in 1925.[5] Unsurprisingly, Mr. Lenin and his comrades left Ms. Rand with a sour taste in her mouth when it came to anything and everything resembling socialism.

We don't need to delve any deeper in Rand's background except to mention that she became a famous—some may say infamous—writer and philosopher. What made Rand stand out was that she was one of the few public intellectuals of her era to take an ardently *right*-wing stance on economic, social, and moral issues. Rand developed a philosophy called Objectivism, which has "selfishness" as its core virtue. Now, Rand defined the term a little differently than what we commonly think of when we hear the word "selfish." Like most philosophies, it is nearly impossible to boil Objectivism down into a few sentences, but this is what AynRand.org, maintained by Rand's longtime colleague Leonard Peikoff, has to say about selfishness:

> Ayn Rand wrote volumes urging people to be selfish.
>
> What? Aren't people already too selfish? Just do whatever you feel like, be a thoughtless jerk,

---

[4] Signet, 1986.
[5] Wikipedia, "Ayn Rand," available at https://en.wikipedia.org/wiki/Ayn_Rand, last accessed May 22, 2020.

and exploit people to get ahead. Easy, right? Except that acting thoughtlessly and victimizing others, Rand claims, is not in your self-interest.

What Rand advocates is an approach to life that's unlike anything you've ever heard before. Selfishness, in her philosophy, means:

- Follow reason, not whims or faith.
- Work hard to achieve a life of purpose and productiveness.
- Earn genuine self-esteem.
- Pursue your own happiness as your highest moral aim.
- Prosper by treating others as individuals, trading value for value.

At the dawn of our lives, writes Rand, we "seek a noble vision of man's nature and of life's potential." Rand's philosophy is that vision. Explore it for yourself.

Objectivism, a philosophy for living on earth.[6]

Note well that Rand was an *atheist*, an *individualist*, and advocated for *reason* above all else. She was also a capitalist in the sense that she believed any form of taxation was an immoral theft.

Sound like any Canadian musician, a drummer perhaps, that you know?

Rand wrote a multitude of essays and treatises on her philosophy and hit the lecture circuit hard throughout her life, but is most well known for her quartet of novels: *We the Living*, *Anthem*, *The Fountainhead*, and *Atlas Shrugged*.

---

6 "Introduction to Objectivism, available at https://aynrand.org/ideas/overview/, last accessed May 22, 2020.

Needless to say, just a glance at the titles of these books is enough to make any Rush fan realize where the inspiration for certain songs came from.

Let's start with the lyrics to "Anthem," the hard-hitting assault that kicks off Rush's second album, 1975's *Fly By Night*. As an aside, and no disrespect to the late John Rutsey[7] who was a damn fine stickman, but has there ever been a one-album upgrade due to the replacement of *one guy*[8] like there was between Rush's self-titled debut and *Fly By Night*? It completely changed the complexion of the band from a meat-and-potatoes rock outfit—albeit one with far better chops than most—to the prog-metal legends we all know and love.

Anyway, those lyrics:

> Know your place in life is where you want to be
> Don't let them tell you that you owe it all to me
> Keep on looking forward, no use in looking 'round
> Hold your head above the crowd and they won't bring you down
>
> Anthem of the heart and anthem of the mind
> A funeral dirge for eyes gone blind
> We marvel after those who sought
> The wonders in the world, wonders in the world
> Wonders in the world they wrought
>
> Live for yourself
> There's no one else more worth living for
> Begging hands and bleeding hearts
> Will only cry out for more

---

[7] Rutsey tragically died of a heart attack due to complications from diabetes in 2008. He was 55 years old. R.I.P., Mr. Rutsey!

[8] A replacement for Rutsey was sought both for reasons of differing musical direction, as Alex Lifeson explains in *Rush: Beyond the Lighted Stage*, and for health reasons, as Rush's former manager Vic Wilson says in the same film.

Anthem of the heart and anthem of the mind
A funeral dirge for eyes gone blind
We marvel after those who sought
The wonders in the world, wonders in the world
Wonders in the world they wrought

Well, I know they've always told you
Selfishness was wrong
Yet it was for me, not you
I came to write this song

Anthem of the heart and anthem of the mind
A funeral dirge for eyes gone blind
We marvel after those who sought
The wonders in the world, wonders in the world
Wonders in the world they wrought

"Anthem," very much like the book of the same name, essentially spells out the tenets of Objectivism, the key lines being "Begging hands and bleeding hearts will only cry out for more" and "Well, I know they've always told you selfishness was wrong," but there are also strong allusions to imposing one's will on the world, another Objectivist belief.

Anthem, Rand's 1938 novella, depicts a dystopian world where the collective has entirely subsumed the individual to the point where nobody even has *names* and are instead identified by numbers. The story's protagonist makes some scientific discoveries on his own and is forced to flee, escaping the collective to found a new society based on the rediscovered power of the individual.[9]

Anthem features passages such as:
> I shall choose friends among men, but neither slaves nor masters. And I shall choose only such as please me, and them I shall love and

---

9   Synopsis courtesy of everybody's old friend Wikipedia, available at https://en.wikipedia.org/wiki/Anthem_(novella), last accessed May 23, 2020.

respect, but neither command nor obey. And we shall join our hands when we wish, or walk alone when we so desire.[10]

And, "There is nothing to take a man's freedom away from him, save other men. To be free, a man must be free of his brothers,"[11] "And now I see the face of god, and I raise this god over the earth, this god whom men have sought since men came into being, this god who will grant them joy and peace and pride. This god, this one word: 'I',"[12] as well as what might be Objectivism's fundamental credo, which closes the book:

> And here, over the portals of my fort, I shall cut in the stone the word which is my beacon and my banner. The word which will not die, should we all perish in battle. The word which can never die on this earth, for it is the heart of it and the meaning and the glory. The sacred word: EGO.[13]

It's impossible to miss the influence Rand had on Peart. It is also impossible to miss, given Barry Miles' referencing the above passage in his 1978 *New Musical Express* piece on Rush, that Peart's adherence to Objectivism did not endear Rush to the primarily left-wing music press: "[A] lot of that [popular] music, especially at that time was really liberal. Anything that even touched on anything that was conservative or libertarian or whatever set them off."[14]

And now, in trying to figure out if Rush is really a right-wing band appealing primarily to right-wingers, or a libertarian band appealing primarily to libertarians, we need to address the

10 Ayn Rand, *Anthem* (Cassell, 1938).
11 *Id.*
12 *Id.*
13 *Id.*
14 Ed Stenger, interview with the author, May 19, 2020 (Appendix C).

awesome, epic, ass-kicking elephant in the room, *2112*, both the album and the song.

AYN RAND . . . *IN SPACE*

Rush fans, male or female, left-wing or right-wing, nerd or not, already know the premise of the song "2112," title track of Rush's big commercial breakthrough. Hot off the heels of the ambitious, underperforming *Caress of Steel*, Rush's record label wanted something more basic, more commercial, more singles-oriented, and more like their first album, "leaning on us at our weakest."[15] Rush's response essentially boiled down to "Yeah, no."

It was actually more nuanced and thoughtful than that. "We talked about how we would rather go down fighting than try to make the kind of record they wanted us to make," Geddy Lee explained.[16] "We made *2112* figuring everyone would hate it, but we were gonna go out in a blaze of glory."[17]

Alex Lifeson's recollection was similar: "We decided we would rather go back to our jobs working on a farm or working as a plumber's mate for my dad, or whatever, than give in and just be something everybody else wants us to be."[18]

Peart, as might be expected, put this period of defiance and strident refusal to listen to the will of the collective—the collective being their management and record company—in rather Objectivist terms:

> We did summon that strength of character to say "No, we won't do that, we're doing it our way, and if this is the last hurrah, fine." You know, back to the farm or the dealership for me. It was a big no. "No, we're not doing any of

[15] Neil Peart, *Rush: Beyond the Lighted Stage* (Documentary, 2010).
[16] *Id.*
[17] *Id.*
[18] *Id.*

that! No, you can't tell us what to do! And no, we don't care!"[19]

Rush doubled down on the instincts that animated the more ambitious parts of *Caress of Steel*, and the gamble paid off. *2112* proved to be the big break the band needed, which is fascinating when you consider the title track's subject matter, *and* the fact that, as Lifeson put it at the time, "We don't want to change what people think about rock & roll, we just want to show them what we think about it."[20] This uncompromising attitude is in part what endears Rush to fans, but the music and its sheer scope help as well.

"2112" was a hard-charging conceptual song suite. On a distant world lay the sprawling Megadon City, ruled by the priests of the Temples of Syrinx. The priests control every aspect of human life, right down to the "the words you read, the songs you sing, the pictures that give pleasure to your eyes,"[21] a parallel to Soviet central command if there ever was one. Behind a waterfall, the unnamed protagonist discovers a guitar, a "toy that helped destroy the elder race of man."[22] Excited, he shows it to the priests, who destroy the guitar and send our hero on his way, because after all one has to "think about the average"[23] who have no need to make music of their own. Our hero has a vision of how much different and better the world could be, thanks to an Oracle he sees in a dream. Despondent, he kills himself as visions of this world dance before his eyes at the moment the elder race returns to reclaim their world and, presumably, usher in a golden age Ayn Rand would be proud of.

It's simultaneously heady and goofy, the perfect encapsulation of rock and roll. But it was *earnest*, and fans understood it. Peart's lyrical skill lay in imbuing each song with layers of meaning. On the surface, "2112" is an objectivist sci-fi story.

19   *Id.*
20   "About *2112*," Rush.com, available at https://www.rush.com/albums/2112/, last accessed May 24, 2020.
21   "2112, Part II: The Temples of Syrinx."
22   "2112, Part IV: Presentation."
23   *Id.*

Dig a little deeper, and it's an allegory of the need for individuals to buck the collective and blaze their own trails to avoid cultural and personal stagnation, a message science-fiction authors like Frank Herbert and Dan Simmons would be proud of. Even deeper than *that*, "2112" can be seen as being about the band itself: It is Rush's artistic manifesto and the allegory of one band defying their record label to make the art they want, willing to kill their career in order to show the world what rock and roll could be, is pretty obvious. And while *2112* didn't resonate with the critics, it struck a major chord with fans who bought the album in mass quantities and flocked to see Rush play it live.

As intense as the subject matter was, it alone was not the driving force behind "2112"'s popularity: The music *kicks ass*. The riffs twist, turn, and pummel, with dramatic dynamic shifts and tricky rhythms. "2112" is a mission statement for Rush which showcased Lifeson's fleet-fingered precision, Peart's complex orchestral drumming, and Lee's fantastic bass-work and wailing vocals. The striking cover, designed by long-time Rush collaborator Hugh Syme, depicts an ominous red star—representing communism, perhaps?—and inside the album, the "Starman" facing this star would become the band's most iconic logo:

> Initially, that logo didn't begin as an identity factor for the band, it just got adopted. We didn't consider it a mascot overall icon of representation for the band at the time.
>
> What I did do with that particular cover was read their lyrics, and understand that there is a good force and a bad force: the good force was music, creativity, and freedom of expression-and the bad force was anything that was contrary to that.
>
> The man is the hero of the story. That he is nude is just a classic tradition . . . the pureness of his

person and creativity without the trappings of other elements such as clothing. The red star is the evil red star of the Federation, which was one of Neil's symbols. We basically based that cover around the red star and that hero.

Now, that hero and that kind of attitude about freedom of expression and the band having that kind of feeling . . . at the time, it never really occurred to me, to be honest with you, that they would adopt it quite so seriously as a logo. Because it's appeared just about everywhere, thereafter.[24]

The song, that image, the album's dedication . . . whether intended or not, "2112" became the band's calling card, and Objectivism its credo. A more unlikely hit has never exploded amidst the record-buying public. Unsurprisingly, showcasing a side-long, seven-part prog-metal paean to Objectivism raised the hackles of the left-leaning rock press. It was what the doyennes of political correctness these days would call "problematic."

Later, Peart would downplay the debt the band owed to Ms. Rand and her philosophies: "All it means is the abstract man against the mass. The red star symbolizes any collectivist mentality," he told *Creem* in 1982.[25] And in 1991, Peart backed away from Rand's influence further:

Inspiration behind it ["2112"] . . . it's difficult to trace those lines because so many things tend to coalesce and in fact it ended up similar to a book called Anthem by the writer Ayn Rand, but I didn't realize it while I was working on

---

24 Hugh Syme in Jeffrey Morgan, "From Brainwaves to Tidal Waves: The Story Behind Rush's Album Covers," *Creem*, Spring 1983, available at http://www.2112.net/powerwindows/transcripts/19830320creem.htm, last accessed May 24, 2020.
25 http://www.angelfire.com/ok3/rush/albuminfo.html, last accessed May 24, 2020.

it. And then eventually as the story came together the parallels became obvious to me and I thought "Oh gee I don't want to be a plagiarist here" so I did give credit to her writings in the liner notes it is explainable in a sense because that album came out of a time of turmoil for us, where a lot of people were trying to tell us what to do and how to commercialize our music, and how we ought to be doing this and doing that. Basically for us "2112" was a statement of rebellion, "we're going to do it our way."[26]

But the damage was done. And it does seem slightly disingenuous to say that a dedication to the "genius" of Ayn Rand—Peart's words!—was merely a bid to avoid a plagiarism lawsuit. Strong language for a CYA.[27] I find the explanation Peart gives, and those of Lee and Lifeson as well, in the 2010 *2112 and Moving Pictures* Classic Albums documentary more convincing: it wasn't about politics and it wasn't about economics with "2112." It was about Rand's artistic manifesto, and owed a debt more to *The Fountainhead* than to *Atlas Shrugged*. And as said above, it doesn't take a huge leap to realize that the suite is also a shot at the music industry: who do you think the priests in "The Temple of Syrinx" represent in this metaphor?

Still, one has to give Rush credit for never scrubbing the dedication from subsequent editions of *2112*. Whether you like Rand or not, the band sticking to its guns is both admirable in the era of "cancel culture" and a powerful reminder that Rush respects its audience's intelligence and ability to separate *art* from an *artist's personal politics*.

Anyway, the rest of the *2112* album is damn good as well, which I'm sure helped sales. "A Passage to Bangkok" became a

---

26 "Neil Peart on Rockline For 'Roll The Bones,'" *Rockline*, December 2, 1991, available at http://www.2112.net/powerwindows/transcripts/19911202rockline.htm, last accessed May 24, 2020.
27 A technical legal term, meaning "cover your ass."

concert favorite, as did closer "Something For Nothing," which could be seen as another ode to Objectivism.

All of this is a set up to the 1978 *New Musical Express* interview with Barry Miles, published a few months before the release of *Hemispheres*. I'm sure Miles similarly found "The Trees," another libertarian anthem, distasteful, what with lyrics like these:

> There is unrest in the forest
> There is trouble with the trees
> For the maples want more sunlight
> And the oaks ignore their pleas
>
> The trouble with the maples
> And they're quite convinced they're right
> They say the oaks are just too lofty
> And they grab up all the light
> But the oaks can't help their feelings
> If they like the way they're made
> And they wonder why the maples
> Can't be happy in their shade?
>
> There is trouble in the forest
> And the creatures all have fled
> As the maples scream, "oppression"
> And the oaks just shake their heads
>
> So the maples formed a union
> And demanded equal rights
> "The oaks are just too greedy
> We will make them give us light"
> Now there's no more oak oppression
> For they passed a noble law
> And the trees are all kept equal
> By hatchet
> Axe
> And saw

Libertarians really glommed onto this song, including U.S. Senator Rand Paul (R-Kentucky), one of the United States Senate's only open libertarian, who quoted "The Trees" during speeches... until Peart sent him a cease-and-desist letter.[28] That wasn't all: for a variety of reasons, Peart claimed that it's "very obvious" that Paul "hates women and brown people."[29]

Well, *that* escalated quickly.

Chalk this up to Peart's evolution away from Randian Objectivist to "bleeding-heart libertarianism."[30] But the fact of the matter is, like it or not, Rush, and Peart's lyrics specifically, inspired a whole host of Rush fans to venture into the right side of the political spectrum.

THE WORLD'S FIRST—AND ONLY?— LIBERTARIAN ROCK BAND

Politics, like religion, are the two things we are told never to talk about. That said, I personally like author G.K. Chesterton's assertion that he *only* talks about politics and religion since "[t]here is nothing else to discuss."[31]

Here in the United States, politics are particularly funny. Unlike Canada, many European nations, and countries across the world with parliamentary systems granting proportional representation to all parties receiving a qualifying amount of votes,[32] American politics is a two-party, winner-take-all blood-

---

28   Brian Hiatt, "From Rush With Love: Is this the end of the road for the geek-rock gods?" *Rolling Stone*, June 16, 2015, available at https://www.rollingstone.com/music/music-news/rush-neil-peart-geddy-lee-alex-lifeson-59586/, last accessed May 24, 2020.
29   *Id.*
30   Andy Greene, "Neil Peart on Rush's New LP and Being a 'Bleeding Heart Libertarian': 'Too much attention and hoopla doesn't agree with my temperament,'" *Rolling Stone*, June 12, 2012, available at https://www.rollingstone.com/music/music-news/neil-peart-rush-new-lp-248712/, last accessed May 24, 2020; *see also* Donna Halper, interview with the author, February 11, 2020 (Appendix B).
31   *The Collected Works of G.K. Chesterton, Vol. 34:Illustrated London News, 1926-1928* (Ignatius Press, 1991), at 409.
32   Non-American readers: Please forgive any inaccuracies in this statement. However,

bath. These are the Republican and Democrat parties, and they are the only game in town. Every once in a while, a third-party candidate makes some hay—most notably oil magnate Ross Perot in the 1992 and 1996 presidential elections[33]—but various other ideologies are more like factions within the individual parties than separate parties themselves.

Further, while the definition of left-wing is pretty consistent worldwide, being on the political right means something different in America than it does in most other nations. Here in the U.S., as we move from the mainstream political left to the mainstream political right, the biggest issue dividing the ends of the spectrum is the degree to which the government intervenes in the economy and other aspects of people's lives. There's also the issue of taxes. A Democrat is *generally* more likely to support higher taxes as well as more regulations on businesses, while a Republican is *generally* more likely to support lower taxes and fewer regulations. These are *economic* differences. There are also a whole host of *social* differences, including being pro- or anti-abortion, pro- or anti-open borders, pro- or anti-firearm ownership, and so on. Plus, we can get into differing philosophies of Constitutional interpretation, from the left-wing perspective of interpreting it more permissively so as to *expand* governmental power, to the right-wing perspective of interpreting it narrowly so as to *limit* governmental power.

On many, many other issues and theories of government, though, left and right generally agree, but the simple version is that Democrats are generally *socially and fiscally liberal* and

---

this is book doesn't purport to dive deeply into various systems of government, so I'm going to leave this definition as-is.

33 Michael Levy, "United States presidential election of 1992," Brittanica.com, available at https://www.britannica.com/event/United-States-presidential-election-of-1992, last accessed May 26, 2020. Running as an independent, Ross Perot won nearly 19 percent of the popular vote, the highest of any third-party candidate since Theodore Roosevelt ran as a third-party candidate in 1912, but no electoral vote. Some Republicans blame Perot for siphoning too many votes away from George H.W. Bush, resulting in Bill Clinton's victory (*see, e.g.* Eliza Collins, "Did Perot Spoil 1992 Election for Bush? It's Complicated: Supporters of the then-president believe the independent candidate's effort denied them a second term, but some experts disagree," *Wall Street Journal*, July 10, 2019, available at https://www.wsj.com/articles/did-perot-spoil-1992-election-for-bush-its-complicated-11562714375, last accessed May 26, 2020).

Republicans are generally *socially and fiscally conservative.* And put another way, "Liberals favor government action to promote equality, whereas conservatives favor government action to promote order."[34]

This is a broad-brush description intended to set the stage for our discussion of libertarianism and, eventually, how it relates to Rush fans. You'll notice that the preceding paragraph doesn't have many footnotes. That's because my definitions are *very* broad and are close enough to accurate—what my high school music teacher used to call "good enough for rock n' roll"—for our purposes. There's also the twin facts that (a) this isn't a book about politics and (b) I'm starting to feel like I'm in law school, so let's move on.

So what does libertarianism entail? The Institute for Humane Studies (IHS) at George Mason University offers a comprehensive, succinct definition that's suitable for our purposes:

> The libertarian perspective is that peace, prosperity, and social harmony are fostered by "as much liberty as possible" and "as little government as necessary."
>
> With a long intellectual tradition spanning hundreds of years, libertarian ideas of individual rights, economic liberty, and limited government have contributed to history-changing movements like abolition, women's suffrage, and the civil rights movement.
>
> Libertarian is not a single viewpoint, but includes a wide variety of perspectives. Libertarians can range from market anarchists to advocates of a limited welfare state, but they are all united by

---

[34] The Institute for Humane Studies, "What Is Libertarian?" available at https://theihs.org/who-we-are/what-is-libertarian/, last accessed May 27, 2020.

a belief in personal liberty, economic freedom, and a skepticism of government power.[35]

Among the historical figures the IHS describes as libertarians are Rand; economists Friedrich Hayek, Milton Friedman, and Ludwig von Mises; writers Rose Wilder Lane and Isabel Paterson; philosopher John Locke; and American founding fathers Thomas Jefferson and James Madison.

Libertarians consider themselves a third option or party, but in my opinion libertarianism is more appropriately viewed as a *subset* of both the American left and the American right, being *socially liberal* and *fiscally conservative*, which is how Donna Halper described Neil's political beliefs at the time to me.[36]

Thank you for indulging me in this miniature civics lesson. But it's important for our discussion as to whether Rush appeals primarily to those who, like Neil Peart, are of a libertarian bent.

Scanning political publications, there is a strong case that this is so. Not everyone who listened to "2112" developed a libertarian perspective, but lots of fans, including Skid Row frontman Sebastian Bach, were at least inspired to *read* Ayn Rand:

> I was into the story [of "2112"], you know? I read the back and it was dedicated to The Fountainhead, the book, and I went right out and bought The Fountainhead and read it. I mean not too many bands make a twelve-year-old go out and buy The Fountainhead by Ayn Rand. "God damn, this rock band has got me all fired up about literature!"[37]

---

35   *Id.*
36   Donna Halper, interview with the author, February 11, 2020 (Appendix B) ("[Neil's] views at one time, and we used to argue about this, his views aligned very heavily with what we might call conservatives in many ways. He was always socially liberal, but I'm saying . . . his ideology was much more fiscally conservative, you know, the virtue of selfishness.").
37   *Rush: Beyond the Lighted Stage* (Documentary, 2010).

Bach is more of a dyed-in-the-wool Democrat[38] despite being both a Rush fan and one who has read Ayn Rand's work, but for others, Rush's lyrics and overall ethos represented a gateway into libertarianism. Scott Bullock of *Liberty* magazine interviewed Peart for the September 1997 issue, citing "promoting human freedom" among the things that endears Rush so much to its fans,[39] further perpetuating the stereotype that Rush fans are of a libertarian bent: "Peart's lyrics were a surprising change of pace, and unique in the annals of rock. At that time most rock lyrics fit into one of three categories: collectivist, left-wing political songs, maudlin singer-songwriter fare, or macabre heavy-metal posing."[40]

Bullock, obviously a fan of the band, sees Rand's influence all over Rush's oeuvre, from *Fly By Night* all the way up to the then-new *Test For Echo*. "'Tom Sawyer,'" writes Bullock, "contains perhaps the most Randian nugget in all Rush songs: 'His mind is not for rent/To any god or government.'"[41]

Writer and libertarian political activist Matt Kibbe shared a comprehensive, even-handed, and rather touching excerpt from his 2014 book *Don't Hurt People and Don't Take Their Stuff: A Libertarian Manifesto* in the pages of libertarian publication *Reason* that detailed how the *2112* album, and Rush in general, helped set him on his political course:

---

38 *See, e.g.*, Scott Munro, "Sebastian Bach: I would do a better job than Donald Trump," *Classic Rock*, July 11, 2019, available at https://www.loudersound.com/news/sebastian-bach-i-would-do-a-better-job-than-donald-trump, last accessed May 27, 2020; "Sebastian Bach: 'Anyone Is Smarter' Than Who We Have As President Now," *Blabbermouth.Net*, February 25, 2020, available at https://www.blabbermouth.net/news/sebastian-bach-anyone-is-smarter-than-who-we-have-as-president-now/, last accessed May 27, 2020 ("Last August, Bach lambasted Trump, Senate Majority Leader Mitch McConnell, Vice President Mike Pence and other Republican leaders for their inaction on gun regulation. A month earlier, Bach made headlines when he said that he "would do a better job" running the county than Trump. In a 2018 interview with TheRecord.com, Sebastian revealed that he voted for Hilary Clinton in the 2016 U.S. presidential election.")
39 Scott Bullock, "A Rebel and a Drummer," *Liberty*, September 1997, at 37 ("As Bill Banasiewicz said in *Visions*, his biography of Rush, the main interest of the group throughout its career, in addition to making great music, has been in promoting human freedom.").
40 *Id.*
41 *Id.*

In 1977, I bought my first Rush album. I was 13. The title of the disc was 2112, and the foldout jacket had a very cool and ominous red star on the cover. As soon as I got it home from the store, I carefully placed that vinyl record onto the felt-padded turntable of my parents' old Motorola console stereo.

The moment I dropped that stylus, and that needle caught the groove, I became obsessed with Rush like only thirteen-year-old boys can get obsessed. I turned up the volume as loud as I thought I could get away with, and I rocked.

Mom shut that jam session down real fast. So I turned down the stereo, sat down, and began to read the liner notes inside the album cover jacket instead. The text inside the cover read, "With acknowledgement to the genius of Ayn Rand." What an odd name, I thought. Who is Ayn Rand?[42]

Much like Sebastian Bach, the album's dedication set Kibbe on his way to seeking out Rand's novels. Unlike Bach, Rand's philosophy stuck with Kibbe. But as he reveals in his book, the band's struggle with their record label and refusal to conform to what it wanted the band to be resonated just as much. Was Rush's "willingness to stand on principle when the easier path was compromise"[43] a *result* of libertarian philosophy, or did libertarian philosophy appeal to Rush *because* of this willingness? You be the judge, but I think the latter is the case. Geddy Lee seems to agree with me: "You can say what you want about

---

42   Matt Kibbe, "'You Can't Have Freedom for Free': On Rush, Ayn Rand, and Not Compromising," *Reason*, April 22, 2014, available at https://reason.com/2014/04/22/matt-kibbe-book-excerpt-rush-and-aynrand/, last accessed May 27, 2020.
43   *Id.*

Ayn Rand and all the other implications of her work, but her artistic manifesto, for lack of a better term, was the one that struck home with us . . . It's about creative freedom. It's about believing in yourself."[44]

Kibbe wasn't the only one we would consider right-wing or Republican who took a liking to Rush. Here's Kyle Smith's tribute to Peart in the pages of venerable conservative publication, the *National Review*:

> He also labeled himself a libertarian and in youth dabbled in Ayn Randism, naming Rush's 1975 song "Anthem" for her 1937 novel Anthem, which was among George Orwell's influences for 1984, and crediting Rand in the liner notes for her influence on the 1976 Rush album 2112. What teen boy didn't also flirt with Rand? To persist with a Rand fixation is not the mark of a healthy mind, though. When asked in 2012 (again in Rolling Stone) if Rand's words still spoke to him, he said, "Oh, no. That was 40 years ago."[45]

"Many libertarians born into Generation X, your author included, are undying Rush fans,"[46] says Jeff Deist of Mises.org in his August 1, 2018 review of Peart's book *Far and Wide*. And as seen in Deist's review and most other discussions of Rush and Peart specifically, Ayn Rand features prominently:

> Those themes came courtesy of Peart, who wrote the band's lyrics and contributed heavily

---

44 *Id.*, quoting Geddy Lee's interview in *Rush: 2112 and Moving Pictures (Classic Albums)*, (Documentary, 2010).

45 Kyle Smith, "Farewell to Rock's Greatest Drummer (and Randian)," *National Review*, February 10, 2020, available at https://www.nationalreview.com/corner/remembering-rush-drummer-neil-peart-rocks-greatest-drummer-and-randian/, last accessed May 27, 2020.

46 Jeff Deist, "Neil Peart's Bleeding Heart," Mises.org, August 1, 2018, available at https://mises.org/wire/neil-pearts-bleeding-heart, last accessed May 27, 2020.

to arrangements. He is considered one of the all-time greats among drummers, both technically and stylistically, in stark contrast to time-keeping drummers who stay in the background. Known as a onetime fan of Ayn Rand (hence Anthem), Peart's rationalist and freethinker views were on full display in the band's early catalog. They even thanked Ayn Rand in the liner notes to the album 2112—only to be called "junior fascists" by some in the press.[47]

One of the best libertarian takes I have read comes from Steven Horowitz, writing for Libartarianism.org. In my opinion, Horowitz nails Peart more than any other writer I've read:

> I think this point also explains the much-discussed connection between Neil and Ayn Rand. For all of the ink spilled about this, it's all more simple than many think. The real Rand influence on Neil was The Fountainhead and not Atlas Shrugged. In fact, all three members read and liked The Fountainhead. That book's emphasis on artistic excellence and integrity and the values one brings to a career and to a life, and its ultimate vindication of those who pursue those values, explains much more about Neil's lyrics, his excellence at his craft, and the band's career path than anything else Rand ever wrote. Generation after generation keeps rediscovering Rand, and The Fountainhead is still taught in some high school American Literature courses (it's where I read it first). The reasons for that parallel the reasons why Rush's music will live on, similarly walking the shore of the mainstream: those are timeless, universal hu-

---

47 *Id.*

man values and ones that particularly appeal to youths who are trying to figure it all out. Very little of Rand's influence on Neil was explicitly political. That influence shows up in the themes of excellence, integrity, and honesty, and the drive to be the best you that you can be.

In the end, I don't think Neil was really much of a libertarian, nor are the bulk of his lyrics accurately described that way. The term that best describes them, as I have argued elsewhere, is "individualist." That term encompasses the values discussed above and the broad political themes that do appear from time to time in his lyrics. One need not be a libertarian to appreciate Neil's lyrics, as evidenced by my numerous leftist friends who are fans. But one does need, at some level I think, to believe that those values matter. Their music would be a hard listen otherwise.[48]

I'm going to give Horowitz the last word here, since Rand's emphasis on *individualism* appears to have been a greater influence on Peart than her economic philosophies. And anyway, Peart himself would walk away from both Rand and the "libertarian" label.

BLEEDING-HEART LIBERTARIAN

For some Rush fans, as Christopher J. McDonald puts it in *Rush, Rock Music, and the Middle Class*, "the individualist theme was

---

48 Steven Horowitz, "Everybody Got to Elevate from the Norm: The Enduring Appeal of Neil Peart and Rush," Libertarianism.org, January 15, 2020, available at https://www.libertarianism.org/columns/everybody-got-elevate-norm-enduring-appeal-neil-peart-rush, last accessed May 27, 2020. Horowitz also makes several trenchant observations about Rush's fan base being mostly white and mostly male (*see* Chapter III: Boys and Girls Together).

one of the less attractive aspects of the band."[49] For Peart, it seems like *economic* individualism was where he drew the line between his own beliefs and a full-blown libertarian stance. Back in 1997, Peart was describing himself as a "left-wing libertarian" based on his perception that the right was becoming too censorious,[50] although he noted a creeping left-wing streak of totalitarianism as well.[51] And Peart did express his belief that some sort of social safety net was needed for the less-fortunate,[52] a far cry from "begging hands and bleeding hearts" that will "only cry out for more"!

But people change, as Donna Halper notes: "[D]o you eat the same foods you ate thirty years ago? Do you wear the same clothes you wore thirty years ago?"[53] Peart himself noted to Bullock that it was Rand's dismissal of the "Woodstock generation" that first made him realize that Objectivism might not be the one true philosophy for him: "I realized there were certain elements of her thinking and work that were affirming for me, and others that weren't. That's an important thing for any young idealist to discover—that you are still your own person."[54] Peart also cites the hardening and division among the more hardcore Randians, which also turned him off from her philosophies.[55] As Donna Halper explains:

> So he [Neil] said, I took what I could from Ayn Rand and then it was time for the next thing. He said, that's the thing, you know? It's time to just look at these philosophies, look at them and then decide, is this still the right philosophy for me? If it is, hang on to it. If it isn't walk

---

49   Christopher J. McDonald, *Rush, Rock Music, and the Middle Class: Dreaming in Middletown (Profiles in Popular Music)* (Indiana University Press, 2009), at 99.
50   Bullock, "A Rebel and a Drummer," at 46.
51   *Id.*
52   *Id.*, at 39.
53   Donna Halper, interview with the author, February 11, 2020 (Appendix B).
54   Bullock, "A Rebel and a Drummer," at 39.
55   *Id.*, at 39, 46.

away and don't be ashamed. If you choose not to decide you still have made a choice.[56]

There is no shame in change, and Peart's evolving perspective naturally found its way into Rush's music. Not too many Rush songs dealt explicitly with politics, although the Peart that wrote "The Larger Bowl (A Pantoum)" in 2007 is of a very different mind than the Peart who wrote "Anthem" in 1975 and "Something for Nothing" in 1976 . . . but then again, so is the Peart who wrote globalist anthem "Territories" in 1985. "[A]s time went on," Halper notes, "the more he [Peart] got out there, the more he talked to people, the more he realized—he said this to me—he said, 'You know the playing field just isn't level.'"[57]

A perusal of Rush lyrics shows this change to be relatively gradual. By the time you get to a song like "Between the Wheels" from 1984's *Grace Under Pressure*, you're not surprised that Peart is anti-war and weary of USA/USSR Cold War tensions. "Territories" from 1985's *Power Windows* likewise doesn't feel out-of-the blue. 1987's *Hold Your Fire* features tracks such as "Turn The Page" and "Second Nature" which take more world-weary stances about politics, and yet "Show Don't Tell" from 1989's *Presto* finds Peart back in his full-throated, independent-minded glory.

Similarly, while the lamentations about global inequality on "Half the World" from 1996's *Test for Echo* are neither too on-the-nose nor blame-casting, they are markedly different from the pent-up anger cast—albeit obliquely—at radical Islam in "Peaceable Kingdom" from 2002's *Vapor Trails*. This anger is continued on "The Way the Wind Blows" from 2007's *Snakes & Arrows*, which lets no religious extremists off the hook regardless of their faith.

So yes, Rush did sing about politics, but in typical Rush fashion, something as divisive as politics becomes, in Peart's hands, universal.

56   Donna Halper, interview with the author, February 11, 2020 (Appendix B).
57   *Id.*

Which leads us to Peart's 2015 assertion to *Rolling Stone* that Rand Paul—and, presumably, most other Republicans—hates "women and brown people."[58] First, note that in 2012, Peart's tone was not quite so strident:

> Libertarianism as I understood it was very good and pure and we're all going to be successful and generous to the less fortunate and it was, to me, not dark or cynical. But then I soon saw, of course, the way that it gets twisted by the flaws of humanity. And that's when I evolve now into . . . a bleeding heart Libertarian. That'll do.[59]

Very different from three years later, where Peart engages in his a rather out-of-character smear of Senator Paul, as well as a "no true Scotsman" argument[60] about Christians: "'For a person of my sensibility, you're only left with the Democratic party,' says Peart, who also calls George W. Bush 'an instrument of evil.' 'If you're a compassionate person at all. The whole healthcare thing—denying mercy to suffering people? What? This is Christian?'"[61]

This dovetails nicely with our discussion about the religiosity, or lack thereof, of Rush fans, but first, it's worth discussing Barry Miles's incendiary interview with the band.

---

58 Hiatt, "From Rush With Love: Is this the end of the road for the geek-rock gods?" *Rolling Stone*, June 16, 2015.
59 Andy Greene, "Neil Peart on Rush's New LP and Being a 'Bleeding Heart Libertarian'" *Rolling Stone*, June 12, 2012.
60 Also called an "appeal to purity," a "no true Scotsman" fallacy is where "one's belief is rendered unfalsifiable because no matter how compelling the evidence is, one simply shifts the goalposts so that it wouldn't apply to a supposedly 'true' example. This kind of post-rationalization is a way of avoiding valid criticisms of one's argument." "No True Scotsman," *Your Logical Fallacy Is*, available at https://yourlogicalfallacyis.com/no-true-scotsman, last accessed May 31, 2020.
61 Hiatt, "From Rush With Love: Is this the end of the road for the geek-rock gods?" *Rolling Stone*, June 16, 2015.

DAMNED IF YOU DO . . .

Politically, it is a fact of life that you can never please everybody. And the band, and Neil in particular, did displease many as they backed away from libertarianism. "[S]ome of the Republicans were furious," says Donna Halper, "and he didn't care. And, you know, not that he didn't care about Republicans. But he never saw himself as the voice of the Republicans, or the voice of the Democrats."[62] Or libertarians, for that matter.

Jeff Deist of Mises.org called Peart's statement about Rand Paul "bizarre."[63] Writing in *Reason*, Matt Welch posits that some Rush fans will be "distressed" to learn that Peart would now only consider voting Democrat because of "health care and compassion."[64] And Brian Doherty, writing for the same publication, calls Peart an "I'm really a good guy, stop riding my ass" Rand recanter, who distanced himself from Rand for less-than intellectual reasons: "'Outgrew [Ayn Rand]' is the closest thing to an explanation, and there is no explanation at all for his reasoning that libertarianoid Rand Paul (whose name is no relation to Ms. Rand's) is anti-woman and anti-brown people, or what about his [Peart's] 'sensibility' matches the Democrats . . ."[65]

Doherty cites Bullock's 1997 interview in *Liberty*, particularly Peart's description of the backlash the band faced from the music press in the 1970s, and comes upon a rather uncharitable conclusion: "That [backlash] seems like a smoking gun: Peart's aversion to crediting Rand much now seems largely based on exactly the phenomenon Barbara Branden fingered: public pressure."[66]

---

62 Donna Halper, interview with the author, February 11, 2020 (Appendix B).
63 Deist, "Neil Peart's Bleeding Heart," Mises.org, August 1, 2018.
64 Matt Welch, "Neil Peart: Rand Paul 'hates women and brown people': Rush's famously Ayn Rand-inspired drummer/lyricist will only vote Democrat, because health care and compassion," *Reason*, July 16, 2015, available at https://reason.com/2015/06/16/neil-peart-rand-paul-hates-women-and-bro/, last accessed May 31, 2020.
65 Brian Doherty, "4 Prominent Ayn Rand Recanters: Sometimes famous people admit they admire Ayn Rand. And then sometimes they recant. Why?" *Reason*, August 3, 2015, available at https://reason.com/2015/08/03/4-prominent-ayn-rand-recant/?itm_source=parsely-api, last accessed May 31, 2020.
66 *Id.*

But what was the source of this backlash? To answer this question, we need to go back to 1978, when Barry Miles of the *New Musical Express* interviewed the band after catching them in concert at London's Hammersmith Odeon.

Miles is obviously on the political left. This is not a normative statement and is neither good nor bad. It is just a fact, one that's important to note because it influences his view of Rush. And his view isn't pretty. Amidst debating Neil Peart about Peart's wholehearted embrace of Ayn Rand's philosophy—both personal *and* economic at the time—Miles throws in *bon mots* about Peart being, shall we say, *fond of thrusting his right arm into the air*:

> So now I understood the freedom he was talking about. Freedom for employers and those with money to do what they like, and freedom for the workers to quit (and starve) or not. Work makes free. Didn't I remember that idea from somewhere? "Work Makes Free." Oh yes—it was written over the main gateway to Auschwitz concentration camp . . .[67]

As you can see, Godwin's Law[68] is not a phenomenon of the 21st century. Naturally, Geddy Lee, the Jewish son of Holocaust survivors, especially found the whole insinuation shockingly insulting and distasteful.

As a point-counterpoint discussion arguing the merits of laissez-faire capitalism versus a more interventionist government, the interview is fine, if completely orthogonal to rock and roll, but it's easy to see how it did nothing to endear Rush to the

---

67 Barry Miles, "Is everybody feelin' all RIGHT (Geddit . . . ?), *New Musical Express*, March 4, 1978, available at https://www.theguardian.com/music/2015/may/13/rush-nme-interview-1978-rocks-backpages, last accessed May 6, 2020.

68 Put forth by American attorney Mike Godwin in 1990, "*Godwin's law* is the proposition that the longer an internet argument goes on, the higher the probability becomes that something or someone will be compared to Adolf Hitler." Dictionary.com, available at https://www.dictionary.com/e/memes/godwins-law/, last accessed June 2, 2020. Obviously, Attorney Godwin's law existed before the Internet; he was just the first to define it.

music press. Quite the opposite! Take this exchange, appropriately enough, about healthcare:

> I went back to the national health question and grumbled: Suppose I was an orphan and I was sick. I'd like to think that I would get free medical care.
>
> "At whose expense?"
>
> At the state's expense.
>
> "The state? Well, where does the state get this marvellous magic money?"
>
> Tax.
>
> "Exactly. Well, maybe I don't wanna pay tax. There's the Salvation Army and all those voluntary organisations. Don't you think all those could look after those welfare systems where they are necessary? I'm not talking about the dole or all those kind of things which are abused, obviously.
>
> "Are you aware of the medical care that the people who work at IBM get, for instance? I think that you'll find that they get taken care of very satisfactorily."
>
> Oh God, sell your soul to the company. I hope none of you went to the Rush concert on dole money. That wouldn't fit in with Rush's philosophy at all.[69]

---

[69] Barry Miles, "Is everybody feelin' all RIGHT (Geddit . . . ?), *New Musical Express*, March 4, 1978, available at https://www.theguardian.com/music/2015/may/13/rush-nme-interview-1978-rocks-backpages, last accessed May 6, 2020.

People change their minds, and Neil's mind changed a lot between 1978 and 2015. And I'm not trying to catch Neil in a "gotcha!" type of trap—which would be especially gauche considering he is not alive to defend himself. But it is interesting that, contra Peart's later assertions that he really only bought in to Rand's *personal* philosophies about artistic freedom, his wholesale embrace of Rand's *economic* philosophies is interesting.

In any event, Miles did not like what he heard from Rush: "Rush would like to return to the survival-of-the-fittest jungle law, where the fittest is of course the one with the most money,"[70] he opines. And further, it's all there, hiding in plain sight:

> The thing is, these guys are advocating this stuff on stage and on record, and no one even questions it. No one is on their case. All the classic hallmarks of the right-wing are there: the pseudo-religious language (compare their lyrics to the Ayn Rand quote at the head of this article), which extends right down to calling the touring crew—road masters instead of road managers. The use of a quasi-mystical symbol—the naked man confronting the red star of socialism (at least I suppose that's what it's supposed to be). It's all there.[71]

The interview is worth reading in its entirety. One can only imagine what Geddy Lee (who only chimes in briefly) and Alex Lifeson (who is silent during the political portion of the interview) were thinking. But it seems that, by going head-to-head with Barry Miles, Neil Peart and Rush solidified their libertarian bona fides to the legions of fans who were, as conventional wisdom goes, emboldened by Rush's message of individualism and freedom from the state whether writers at the *New Musical Express* and other publications liked it or not.

70 *Id.*
71 *Id.*

That's a part of this band's appeal, after all: marching to the beat of your own highly skilled and complicated drummer.

YOU CAN CALL THEM FAITHLESS

It's no secret that Rush are atheists. For some, like Jillian Maryonovich, this is a part of the band's appeal.[72] That said, only a few Rush songs deal with religion at all, and most obliquely. "Freewill" comes to mind, as does "Roll the Bones," which expresses Neil's belief in the randomness of the universe. I suppose "The Temples of Syrinx" and the overall plot of "2112" is a slight jab at oppressive mysticism; so is "BU2B," although that song is ambiguous enough to be about either *Clockwork Angels*'s Watchmaker character or organized religion in general. In fact, the only direct reference to atheism is in "Faithless" from 2007's *Snakes & Arrows*; that album also features a stab at religious fanaticism of all stripes in "The Way the Wind Blows."

And yet *Test for Echo*'s "Totem" expresses a rather uplifting, if theologically muddled, view of spiritual ecumenism. However, in "Resist" from the same album Peart absolutely nails one aspect of religious worship:

> You can surrender
> Without a prayer
> But never really pray
> Pray without surrender

I don't need to repeat that Neil was an observant, compassionate, and intelligent man. This spills over to fans as well. In Donna Halper's words, "I can honestly say I have never lost a friend . . . over Rush, because Rush brings people together, and it always has."[73]

Still, all three members *are* irreligious, and the question is, does this attract a certain type of fan to the band? When asked in

---

72 *See* Chapter III: Boys and Girls Together, footnote 35.
73 Donna Halper, interview with the author, February 11, 2020 (Appendix B).

2016 if he believed in God, Alex Lifeson's answer was straightforward:

> No. When I was younger I did. My mother is not super-religious but she has a belief. My father was the total opposite. He thought religion was a crock. In my early teens I started to question it all. I had friends who were Jesus freaks, others were just very spiritual, and we had these great long discussions about these things. But as I get older it just becomes a less and less sensible thing to think about.[74]

Geddy Lee calls himself a "cultural Jew" who "loves [his] Jewish sense of humor" but is "not a practitioner."[75] He elaborated to *Heeb* magazine in 2009:

> I consider myself a Jew as a race, but not so much as a religion. I'm not down with religion at all. I'm a Jewish atheist, if that's possible . . . I celebrate the holidays in the sense that my family gets together for the holidays and I like being a part of that. So I observe the "getting together" aspect.[76]

And Neil Peart . . . as the voice of the band in a way that even Geddy Lee is not, his religious beliefs are already apparent to any listener able to understand the English language.

74 Paul Elliot, "Alex Lifeson on God, police brutality and 'disco biscuits,'" *Classic Rock*, October 13, 2016, available at https://www.loudersound.com/features/interview-alex-lifeson-on-god-police-brutality-and-disco-biscuits, last accessed May 22, 2020.
75 "Rush Frontman Geddy Lee—Any Extreme Religious Behavior Is Bad, Whether It Be Middle East Or the Middle West," *BraveWords*, July 9, 2007, available at http://bravewords.com/news/rush-frontman-geddy-lee-any-extreme-religious-behavior-is-bad-whether-it-be-middle-east-or-the-middle-west, last accessed June 2, 2020.
76 Arye Dworken, "A Show Of Hands, Rock Heavyweight Geddy Lee," *Heeb*, Spring 2009 (The Music Issue, #20), available at http://www.2112.net/powerwindows/transcripts/20090320heeb.htm, last accessed June 2, 2020.

The interesting thing, if I may be self-indulgent for a moment,[77] is that as a practicing Greek Orthodox Christian, I have never found any of Rush's songs about religion offensive even if I disagree with them. That was one of the aspects of their genius—and I do not use that word lightly. Still, I did often wonder if being religious put me in a minority of Rush fans.

I spoke with Rush fan, friend of Alex Lifeson, and Orthodox Church of America Metropolitan Tikhon and asked him if he ever found Rush's stance on religion off-putting:

> Your question is a very good one and one that I have wrestled with throughout my years of listening to Rush. My initial response is that, in terms of lyrical content, there are no Rush songs that, as a Christian, I don't care for or feel offended by. Neil was pretty open throughout his career about where he stood in terms of religion in general and I believe that Alex and Geddy fundamentally share his outlook. Those positions were never an obstacle to my appreciation of their music.
>
> Nevertheless, if I were to isolate one song or album, I would say that one of the more challenging albums for me to listen to is Snakes & Arrows. Although Neil's thoughts on religion are found in some form in many of his lyrics, that album comes across to me as the heaviest in terms of a negative view of religion ("Armor and Sword," "Faithless," "The Way the Wind Blows"). At the same time, even those lyrics do not target any particular religious group or specific beliefs. Rather, they point out the sometimes irrational behavior of extremists (religious and non-religious) and speak (rather

---

77 And of course I can; this is *my book*!

pessimistically) about the human condition as a whole. In that light, I do not disagree with his sentiments, since I understand, from the perspective of the Orthodox Church and the Holy Scriptures, the dangers of such extremism. However, I would take a more optimistic approach to the human condition he describes.

I think that Neil is often targeting "sham religiosity" as opposed to any particular religious beliefs. You can see this even in his travel books, where he likes to take note of the church signs, some of which he approves of, others not. So he is careful in his assessment of things, even if he disagrees with them.

I also think it could be argued that Neil is never criticizing directly as much as identifying certain unhealthy human behaviors or attitudes that he has observed. He then articulates those in the form of lyrics as a way to allow the listener to make his own evaluation or decision. For example, in the song "Roll the Bones," he raises the question of the suffering of innocent children in the context of faith which is "cold as ice" but frames it as a question, "If there's some immortal power/To control the dice?" While it's pretty clear where he himself stands on that question, there is a sense that he is genuinely asking the listener to consider that question for himself.

In a more personal way, I think I have never felt offended or oppressed by Neil's lyrics because I have gone through phases of similar questioning in my own journey. I first started listening to Rush when Permanent Waves was released in 1980 and, of course the two songs with the most active rotation on the radio were "The Spirit of Radio" and "Freewill." Musically, I was drawn more to the melody and infectious energy of "The Spirit of Radio," but intellectually, I was very intrigued by the lyrics of "Freewill." At the time, I was wrestling with a lot of "deep" questions (such as the question of suffering an the existence of God) and considered myself something of an agnostic or an atheist. Although I was raised in the Episcopal Church and was going to church regularly, there was a lot going on in my own mind and so the lyrics of "Freewill" resonated with me.

In particular, I was struck by the line: "If you choose not to decide, you still have made a choice." I can't say that that line, or even any lyrics from Neil, ever "influenced me" in a direct way. But I do think that there were elements of those lyrics, or fragments of thoughts and ideas, that I connected with and still connect with. I could even say that there are certain ideas that are clearly "Christian" or maybe even "Orthodox," even if Neil never intended them to taken in such a way. As an example, the song "Nobody's Hero" has the line: "Hero – is the voice of reason, against the howling mob/ Hero – is the pride of purpose in the unrewarding job." Although Neil may have had religious fanatics in mind as part of the "howling mob," the importance of reason is important in Christianity (Christ as the "logos," the rational worship we offer in the liturgy, etc.). Likewise, the idea of perseverance in an unrewarding job is very ascetical and recalls the desert fathers who often spent their entire lives weaving baskets as they entered deeply into prayer of the heart.

Ultimately, I think Neil was searching throughout his life for "the real relation, the underlying theme." For me, those are found in Christ and the Church but for him they are found elsewhere. But the fact that he was searching for answers to those questions reveal him to be a genuinely human person looking for honesty and integrity, which is what we should all strive for.[78]

I think His Eminence really dialed down into the essence of why Rush's views on religion were far more nuanced than most other atheistic rock bands. Neil Peart never set out to insult believers. He raised questions and presented his own perspective, and this perspective got Metropolitan Tikhon to think about his own faith and moved him towards Orthodoxy. What a fascinating story!

So there's one religious Rush fan. I know of *at least* one other: Author Roxane Salonen. Shortly after Neil's passing, Salonen wrote a poignant, widely syndicated piece titled "Did Rush's Neil Peart reach the pearly gates?" Far from being insulting or patronizing, Salonen ponders the ultimate final resting place of an unbeliever's soul in a thoughtful fashion Peart would likely approve of:

> [A]t times, the words also troubled me. In "Roll the Bones," Peart asks, and answers: "Why are we here? Because we're here. Roll the bones." We're just arbitrary outcomes, he was suggesting, not God's purposeful choices. The rest of the lyrics are much more poignant, but these sum up the self-admitting, non-religious mindset of the group.

---

78 Metropolitan Tikhon, interview with the author, August 15 – September 15, 2020 (Appendix D).

In a documentary on the band we watched together later that evening, we remembered the triumphs and tribulations the group experienced and endured. But as Peart, who'd tragically just lost his first wife and daughter, trekked cross-country on his motorcycle to heal, he seemed unable to pinpoint the divine hand in this restorative process.

And when the band talked about their emotional backstage embrace before the concert that launched their comeback after that dark time, realizing the "impossibility" of that moment, I couldn't help but wonder if they recognized God's grace, which makes the impossible possible.

We can only see what we can see, however, and I believe we'll be surprised at the guest list of the eternal gathering in heaven. I'm hoping I'll be on it, along with those I love. Certainly, my own life is the only one for which I'm fully culpable. But stories like Rush's leave me restless. Theirs is an inspiring tale of grit and talent, of overcoming hard pasts and enlivening the lives of many. And while I appreciate their musical talent and energy, I worry at witnessing their worldly success without a nod to God, who brings all blessing.

I don't believe our lives are randomly calculated like a roll of the dice. But God is merciful, and if there's a musical show in heaven needing a drummer, it's possible that, in God's providence, Peart's bones will not just roll, but rise. I pray that it might be so.[79]

---

79   Roxane Salonen, "Did Rush's Neil Peart reach the pearly gates?" February 17, 2020,

It's a good question, one I would imagine any thinking Christian would ask themselves. Fan Collin Christopher feels the same way; a Catholic, Collin states that he hopes Neil is "drumming and writing music in heaven."[80] And like Salonen, I too pray that Neil has found peace in death; just as importantly, I pray that his family and friends have found peace as well.

It's getting dusty in here . . . let's turn to the survey results.

SOME LIGHT DINNER-TABLE CONVERSATION

They hypothesis I had going into writing this book was that I would find the ranks of Rush fans to be staffed mostly with libertarian or right-leaning atheists and agnostics. For the purpose of getting into the actual survey results, I've made a few simplifications that I think will help us parse the data without our eyes glazing over.

For political affiliation, I grouped respondents into five broad buckets: right, which encompasses responses such as "conservative," "right," "Republican," and "right-leaning"; left, which encompasses responses such as "liberal," "left," "Democrat," and "left-leaning"; libertarian which encompasses responses such as "libertarian," and so on; and "independent/center/none," which is even more self-explanatory than the other three. Lastly, I have a catch-all "other" category for those which I truly could not find a place for.

598 of the 664 Rush fans who filled out the survey answered the question of political affiliation. I was expecting to find that most Rush fans were libertarian, as the stereotype went, but I learned that Rush fans skew heavily leftward, with 223 of the 598, or 37.2%, on the left-side of the political spectrum. This includes those who answered "Left," "Center-left," "Left-lean-

---

available at https://www.grandforksherald.com/lifestyle/faith/4953901-Salonen-Did-Rush%E2%80%99s-Neil-Peart-reach-the-pearly-gates, last accessed June 2, 2020.
80 Collin Christopher, response to author's survey, May 30, 2020 (Appendix A).

ing," "Liberal," "Democrat," "Socialist," "Progressive," "Far left," and "Hard left."

The second most represented category wasn't libertarian, but right, with 142, or 23.7%, falling on the right side of the spectrum. This included those who answered "Right," "Republican," "Conservative," "Traditional," "Center-right," "Right-leaning," "Far-right," "Reactionary," and "Right-wing."

Those of no particular party or who identified as "Independent," "Centrist," "Moderate," and "they all suck" made up 125, or 20.9% of respondents, revealing that some one-fifth of all Rush fans find politics and political parties utterly distasteful.

Surprisingly, and bucking the stereotype, Libertarian Rush fans came in fourth place, comprising 101, or 16.8% of Rush fans who answered this survey. I honestly expected Libertarians to make up at least forty, and likely fifty, percent of Rush fans, but this was not the case.

I suppose if you take the Libertarian faction and the Independent/None faction as one, or group the Libertarian and conservative factions together, you get results closer to my expectations, but the fact remains that most Rush fans are on the political left. This is especially interesting seeing as how it's those on the *right* and *Libertarian* sides who tend to write about Rush in political terms.

Last but not least, there were nine responses who did not fit into any of the four other categories: 2 anarchists,[81] and 1 each of Unitarian, New World Man, Catholic Nationalist, Freewill, Humanitarian, Monarchist, and "Love and peace to everyone. Save the planet."

Now on to that *other* thing polite people are not supposed to discuss at the dinner table: Religion. I put responses into two broad categories, "religious" and "non-religious," and then subdivided them further into categories like "Christian," individual Christian denominations, "Jewish," "Muslim," "Hindu," "pagan," "Wiccan," "non-denominational," etc., and then "atheist," "agnostic," and the like. I'm also putting "joke" answers,

---

81 Neither of whom were *the* Anarchist.

as well as "lapsed," "raised but not practicing," etc., into the "non-religious" category.

The results were somewhat surprising. Of the 508 who answered the question, 251, or 49.4% of Rush fans who responded, are religious, and 257, or 50.6% of Rush fans who responded, are non-religious.[82] 511 fans actually *provided* answers, but three must've read the question as "region," as I got the answers "Eastern US," "Western Florida," and "Ohio";[83] therefore, I did not count these three, giving me the total of 508.

Now, I'm not a mathematician, but 49.4% is not 50%, but it's close enough to conclude that, at least in my limited sampling, half of Rush fans are religious and half are not. This is *far* different than the 70/30 split I expected.

Of the religious, Christians comprise the largest portion at 212, or 84.4% of the 251 religious Rush fans. "Christian" is a broad category though, which can be further broken down by denomination.

Catholic: By far, the largest single denomination respondents belonged to was the Catholic Church, with 65, or 30.6% of those who indicated denomination, represented.

Orthodox: 6 Rush fans, or 2.8% of Christians who responded, are Orthodox Christians,[84] either Greek Orthodox specifically, or Eastern Orthodox.

Anglican/Church of England: There were also 5, or 2.3% of Rush fans who responded, being Anglicans.

Protestant: By "Protestant," I mean non-Catholic, non-Anglican, non-Orthodox, and non-Mormon, Christians. Twelve respondents indicated that they were Protestants, but rolling the specific denominations into this number, 47 respondents, or 22.1% of respondents, are Protestant. This can be further broken down as follows: General Protestant (12, or 5.6%), Baptist (10, or 4.7%), Lutheran (6, or 2.8%), Methodist (6, or 2.8%), Episcopalian (3, or 1.4%), Presbyterian (2, or 0.9%), Born Again

---

82   Rush fan survey (Appendix A).
83   Maybe some people really take their particular part of the world that seriously. I don't know.
84   Represent!

(2, or 0.9%), and 1, or 0.4% each of United Church of Canada, Charismatic/Pentecostal, Christian Spiritist, Evangelical, Reformed Christian, and Denominational Christian.

Mormon: 7 respondents, or 3.3% of Christian Rush fans, belong to the Church of Jesus Christ of Latter-Day Saints.

Non-Denominational: I separated out those who specified that they were non-denominational from those who answered "Christian"; now, the non-denominational Christians were included in the 212 number for overall Christian respondents, but 18, or 8.4% of Christian respondents pointed out that they were not a part of any particular church.

Jewish: 11 Rush fans who answered that they were religious, or 4.3%, identified as Jewish.

Muslim: Rounding out the Abrahamic faiths, 2, or 0.7% of religious Rush fans who responded to the survey are Muslim.

Buddhist: 4, or 1.5% of respondents, identified as Buddhists.

Spiritual: Another 4, or 1.5% of Rush fans, indicated that they were spiritual, but not religious.

Rounding out our survey, 2, or 0.7% of respondents, identified as Faithful, and another 2 (0.7%) as Taoist, while there were 1, or 0.3% each, who identified as Pagan, Wiccan, Druid, Holistic, Zen-influenced, being interested in Eastern religions/enlightenment, Earth-centered, Animist, and Gnostic.

Among 257 Rush fans who identified as not being religious, 126, or 49% stated either "None" or "N/A" to the question. For those who specified, 43, or 16.7% were Atheists and 42, or 16.3% were Agnostics. 19, or 7.3% of respondents, stated that they were raised in a particular faith but are either non-practicing, lapsed, or "recovering." Five, or 1.9%, indicated their religion as "Freewill," which I kept as a separate category since it's delightfully Rush-related. Rounding out the non-religious, there were 1, or 0.3% of Rush fans, who responded with answers including "Open mind," "be cool to one another," "Philosophy," "The Red Star," "Recording music, "Rush," "The Force," "Jedi," and lastly "The OG of fake news."

I understand that discussing religion, like politics, is uncomfortable for some, and I greatly appreciate everyone who responded to this question while respecting those who did not. The only purpose behind my making this inquiry was to show that Rush fans come in all varieties and are nowhere as monolithic as popularly assumed. The roughly fifty-fifty split between Rush fans being religious and being non-religious was the most surprising thing I discovered while writing this book.

To be fair, this is only really surprising if we believe the popular conception of Rush fans being libertarian atheists to be true. I guess Donna Halper was right when she told me that "the people that love this band are in many cases conservatives, liberals, libertarians, atheists, agnostics, Jews, Christians, Muslims, shall I go on?"[85] And if anybody would know about Rush fans, it's Halper:

> One of the fascinating things to me as a media historian is that there are very few bands that have brought together such a diverse coalition of fans, right across the spectrum, all united around the kinds of lyrics that Neil created.[86]

"Rush brings people together" indeed.

---

85   Donna Halper, interview with the author, February 11, 2020 (Appendix B).
86   *Id.*

FAN PROFILE: TOM DRISCOLL

Name: Tom Driscoll a.k.a. RUSHDUDE2112
Location: Texas
Age: 56
Gender: Male
Occupation: Corporate Schmuck, and Amateur Musicologist

My introduction to RUSH began in 1979 . . . I'm catching a ride to school with my friend, Robert Wood, who pops *All The World's A Stage* into the 8-track player of his Ford Granada. Suddenly the car fills with the opening notes of "Bastille Day," and then a voice unlike any other I've ever heard immediately has me hooked (my musical diet up to this point primarily consisted of KISS and Boston records)! Side One of *ATWAS* is still one of my all-time favorite bodies of music—right behind Side One of the *2112* album!

I immediately purchase and devour the entire *ATWAS* double album. Everything about these songs, the album, the band, and the way it was recorded is bigger and better than what I've experienced before! The album packaging alone was freaking awesome . . . a trifold cover with awesome live photos of the band. Wait, there's only 3 guys in this band making all of those wonderful rocking sounds? And what's up with that beautifully shining massive drum kit prominently featured on the front cover? (Later in life, I would learn that awesome drum kit was named "Chromey," and I actually played the restored version of Chromey in 2012!) To top it all off, I'm reading the credits inside of the *ATWAS* album and I find a "thank you" to Joe Anthony and Lou Roney of San Antonio's 99.5 KISS Radio. This is the rock radio station that I grew up listening to! The planets were aligning, and everything musically seemed to make sense to me now!

Footnote: Despite living in different cities, Robert Wood and I still share our appreciation of all things RUSH. Last year,

I was finally able to properly "thank" Robert for introducing me to RUSH's music by having Geddy Lee dedicate a copy of the *Big Beautiful Book of Bass* to
    Robert!

MY ABRIDGED HISTORY WITH RUSH - THE SOUNDTRACK OF MY LIFE

1979
ATWAS playing on an 8-track player changes my entire world.

1980
My first live RUSH show! San Antonio, TX on the Permanent Waves Tour with opener Max Webster. Unexpected highlight of the show: "Jacob's Ladder" live really grabbed my attention in a way that playing just the album had not accomplished. Unfortunately, it would be 35 years before I saw RUSH perform this song live again!

While everyone was crazy about "The Spirit of Radio," "Freewill" is the one that really stood out to me on *Permanent Waves*. The lyrics really resonated with me, and empowered me to become an independent thinker.

1981
My second RUSH live show! San Antonio, TX on the Moving Pictures Tour with Max Webster opening again. I didn't really "get" Max Webster as a band at that time. Over the years, I've really come to appreciate the contributions of Kim Mitchell and Pye Dubois.

1982
Damn, I was not able to attend the live show for the Subdivisions Tour. Still bothers me that I did not see "Countdown" performed live!

1984 - 1986

While many RUSH fans were bonkers about the *Grace Under Pressure* and *Power Windows* albums, I was NOT! This is the only period of my life where I "checked out" of the RUSH Camp temporarily. Too many keyboards and synthesized drums, and not enough guitars!

1987

Hearing "Force Ten" and "Time Stand Still" on the radio piqued my curiosity about RUSH again. About a week before the *Hold Your Fire* concert in San Antonio, TX, a friend offers to sell me his extra 7th row seat. Heck yeah, I'm going to the show! Opening act was Tommy Shaw and his solo band! While the RUSH setlist was heavily stacked from the "synth" albums, the live performances gave me a new appreciation for these songs. The icing on the cake was the kickass encore consisting of "2112: Overture/The Temples of Syrinx," "La Villa Strangiato," and "In the Mood"! I am back in the RUSH Camp!

1989 - 1990

Presto! The early start of the return to more guitars! At this point, I've graduated from college, and I'm out in the working world. My friend, Danny, and I caught the Presto Tour in Dallas, TX. This was Danny's first live RUSH show ever! Personal favorites of this tour were the return of "Freewill" and "Xanadu" to the setlist, and the emotionally-charged "The Pass." And of course, the performance of "Wipeout!" at the end of the RUSH encore!

1991 - 1992

Why are we here? To *Roll The Bones*! Love this album, and I had tickets to see the tour live in San Antonio, TX in Feb 1992 with Primus as the opener! However, I accepted a job promotion and relocation to Cleveland, OH in Jan 1992 and have to miss the San Antonio show. Even worse, RUSH had already played Cleveland (2 nights) in November 1991. While the relocation to Cleveland was important to my professional career, I still regret not seeing this tour in person.

1993 - 1994

I've relocated (again) for work, I now live in Kansas City, and I have a fiancée (who of course likes The Holy Triumvirate)! Our first RUSH live show together is the Counterparts Tour in April 1994 in Kansas City. ALL of the *Counterparts* songs are amazing—so glad that we saw "Cold Fire," "Nobody's Hero," and "Double Agent" performed live!

1996 - 1997

After a 3 year wait, *Test For Echo* is released! There's this new thing called the "internet" where you can read updates about the new album and find out all of the tour dates! In June 1997, my wife and
I enjoyed "An Evening with RUSH" at the Sandstone Amphitheater outside of Kansas City. At the last minute, I scored a 5th row floor seat right in front of Alex, my first concert ticket purchased from a ticket broker; money well spent! No opening act, two sets of killer RUSH songs, the COMPLETE "2112" performance, and the jaw dropping return of "Natural Science"! We are treated to the first appearance of a household appliance on the stage . . . a harbinger of things to come.

1998 - 2001

The longest and most heart-wrenching period in RUSH history. For a period of time, all fans lived with the possibility that Neil might be completely done with drumming, and, in turn, RUSH might be over. Thankfully, the Ghost Rider returned!

2002

THE RETURN OF RUSH! The band roars back with the album and tour that all fans had been hoping for—"One Little Victory," indeed! Through my job, I'm able to coordinate a business trip to the NY/NJ area, and catch the 9th stop on the Vapor Trails Tour at the PNC Bank Arts Center in Holmdel, NJ. I got goosebumps (and a little emotional) when The Three Stooges intro and "Tom Sawyer" began. This is the precise moment when I decided to not take any chances, and try to begin seeing as many RUSH live shows as I reasonably could arrange and afford! It was so good to have the thrills and sonic sensations of live RUSH back in my life and ringing ears. Oh and don't forget, that the band brought back the classic "Working Man" as the concert closer! My wife and I were able to catch the Vapor Trails Tour in both Dallas (August 2002) and New York's Madison Square Garden (Oct 2002)!

2004

One of my biggest RUSH regrets is missing the R30 Tour. We were in the process of selling a home, and buying another. Boy, did we have our priorities mixed up! The R30 Overture alone is one of the best musical pieces ever played by RUSH!

2007 - 2008

RUSH works with Nick Raskulinecz and delivers one of their best albums with *Snakes & Arrows*. "Far Cry" is everything a RUSH fan wants and more! Once again, I am able to catch the live show early in the tour at the PNC Bank Arts Center in July 2007. "Entre Nous" and "Circumstances" are played on this first leg—mind blowing! This tour also sees the welcome return of "Witch Hunt" and "A Passage to Bangkok" to the setlist. My wife and I caught the 2nd leg of this tour together in Austin, TX in April 2008. Thankfully I was able to catch this tour for a 3rd and final show in St. Paul, MN at the Xcel Energy Center in May 2008! A new challenge on my RUSH Bucket List has arisen: attending the opening night of a RUSH Tour!

CHAPTER V: THE FREEDOM OF MUSIC

"I don't know that you can really appreciate this band if you haven't seen them live." [1]

MAKING YOUR VOICE HEARD

The first time I saw Rush live was on July 12, 2002. The concert was at the Tweeter Center in Mansfield, Massachusetts, a town about 40 miles south of Boston. Mansfield is best known for being near Foxborough, home of the New England Patriots, but the Tweeter Center happens to be one of the best live music venues I have ever been to. It's an outdoor amphitheater that can hold just under 20,000 concertgoers, and the acoustics are excellent. There's nothing like heading to the Tweeter Center on a beautiful summer night to see some live music, the opening

---

1 Jim Ladd, KLOS Radio DJ, *Rush: 2112 and Moving Pictures (Classic Albums)*, (Documentary, 2010).

chords filling the air with the sun bright in the sky, night gently falling as the show goes on in that soft, New England way we only get to enjoy for about two months each year. For this Rush fan, it was the perfect place to see them.

It's not called the Tweeter Center anymore. And it didn't *used* to be called that either. In 1997, when I saw my first ever rock concert, The Who, a few months shy of my sixteenth birthday, it was still called the Great Woods Center for the Performing Arts. It became the Tweeter Center in 1999, named after a Boston-based electronics retail chain. Those Tweeter stores are all gone now, and in 2008 the Tweeter Center became the Comcast Center. Now, it's called the Xfinity Center, as it has been since 2013. The name of the place doesn't matter, though. The important thing in 2002 was that Rush was back. And as someone who didn't *start* listening to the band until *after* Neil's tragedies and their subsequent hiatus, I had thought I'd never get to see them live.[2]

All of us fans would have understood had the band packed it up for good, but we were gifted with *Vapor Trails* in 2002. It is a chaotic album, loud, strident, and heavy, some songs laden with melancholy and others bursting with pure joy.[3]

And it's different! *Vapor Trails* has so many layers of guitars, bass, and vocals, and sounds so unlike anything the band had produced before or would again. Alex Lifeson focuses on dense chord work and tone clusters while largely eschewing traditional guitar solos. Geddy Lee adopted this new strumming technique full of double-stops and bass chords. And Neil Peart . . . well, the opening drum salvo to lead-off track "One Little Victory" tells you all you need to know about his playing on the album. And there really weren't any keyboards. Given the uncharacteristic amount of overdubs for Rush, I sincerely wondered how they'd pull off the songs from *Vapor Trails* live.

---

2 Fun fact: Three songs from 1997's live album *Different Stages* were recorded at Great Woods: "Animate," "Leave That Thing Alone," and "2112."
3 "It's funny. I was just talking to Neil about *Vapor Trails* the other day. He says when he listens to it now he hears anger and confusion. For me, I don't hear that. I hear passion." Geddy Lee in Vinay Menon, *Rush: An Oral History* (Toronto Star Newspapers Limited, 2013), at 43.

So my older brother Drew and I, along with my best friends Tom, Pete, and Phil, hopped into my mom's Ford Expedition and drove down from central New Hampshire to Mansfield, to catch the show. I was twenty years old. It was a beautiful summer day, and I felt so glad to be young and alive. Good times.

I quickly learned that Rush shows are like a party where thousands of your friends showed up. One thing that struck me about the fans in attendance was that they seemed to know every single song inside and out. People sang along the entire set, not missing a word. And the air drumming. Oh Lord, the air drumming.

Rush and air drumming have a long and storied history. We all know the stereotype of the Rush fan furiously playing along with Neil. "Neil's the most air-drummed-to drummer of all time," Peart's friend, The Police's stickman Stewart Copeland told *Rolling Stone* in 2015.[4] "Rush concert a workout for air drummers," reads the *Hollywood Reporter*'s review of Rush's stop in Irvine, California on their Time Machine Tour in 2010: "Arguably the greatest rock drummer alive, he astounds with his speed, stamina and technique. Indeed, the legions of air drummers in the large crowd created a mini-maelstrom as they tried to keep up."[5] And "[w]ho can resist air-drumming when Rush comes on the radio?" asked Nicolas Grizzle of *Drum!* Magazine.[6] Certainly not Peter Zirpolo of the Baltimore Ravens' marching band, who was caught on camera in 2018 absolutely crushing Peart's part on "Tom Sawyer" on his imaginary drum set in a viral video.[7] And perhaps the high-water mark of mass

---

4   Brian Hiatt, "Neil Peart, Rush Drummer Who Set a New Standard for Rock Virtuosity, Dead at 67
Hall of Fame drummer and lyricist succumbs to brain cancer," *Rolling Stone*, January 10, 2020, available at https://www.rollingstone.com/music/music-news/neil-peart-rush-obituary-936221/, last accessed June 7, 2020.

5   Erik Pedersen, "Rush concert a workout for air drummers," *Hollywood Reporter*, August 16, 2010, available at https://www.reuters.com/article/us-music-rush/rush-concert-a-workout-for-air-drummers-idUSTRE67G04W20100817, last accessed June 7, 2020.

6   Nicolas Grizzle, "Remembering Neil Peart, 1952-2020," *Drum!*, January 10, 2020, available at https://drummagazine.com/remembering-neil-peart-1952-2020/, last accessed July 7, 2020.

7   Liam Daniel Pierce, "Air Drummer at Ravens Game Absolutely Nails Rush's 'Tom Sawyer': The man, a drummer in the Ravens' marching band, knows his Rush, knows it real

acceptance air-drumming to Rush was a Volkswagen commercial from 2012 featuring a buttoned-up business man rocking out to "Fly By Night" in his car when he thought nobody could see him.[8]

Spoiler: they can.

So I had been told, in person and on-line, about the air-drumming extravaganzas that Rush concerts turned into, and while I refrained from doing *too* much air drumming of my own, I had to watch the people around me—mostly men, mostly white, and mostly middle-aged (this is not a dig, just a part of this book's ongoing taxonomical effort. Also, it's New England, which is overwhelmingly white)—nail every nuance of Neil's playing on their ethereal sets.

I mean, the first song they played was "Tom Sawyer." Something like 15,000 grown men nailed the drum breaks along with Neil. And I still laugh every time I hear the song "Bravado," because during the concert, after Geddy sang the first line "If we burn our wings, flying too close to the sun," I looked to my right and some guy a few rows down, hunched over in ecstasy that may or may not have been chemically enhanced, mimed Neil's delicate little "one-e-and-a-*two*!" cymbal fill with a grimace of intense concentration plastered on his face.

It was awesome.

Another enduring memory: Some guy in front of us was not-so-secretly recording the show on circa-2002 technology. To verify if any bootleg we'd later find was this guy's, my brother and my buddy Phil kept cupping their hands around their mouths and yelling "Beef curtains!"[9] at the top of their lungs whenever the band was through playing a song. To date, no bootlegs have been discovered to feature this vital contribution to Rush's live concert history. Hey, it seemed funny at the time.

---

well," *Vice*, September 12, 2018, available at https://www.vice.com/en_us/article/kz5aav/air-drummer-at-ravens-game-absolutely-nails-rushs-tom-sawyer, last accessed June 7, 2020.
8   *See, e.g.,* https://www.youtube.com/watch?v=EGls1vVq0Dg.
9   "Beef curtains" is slang for a certain type of . . . oh, I'm not going to write it in this book. If you really want to see what it means, check out Urban Dictionary. Listen: we were all in our early twenties and we thought this sort of thing was the height of comedy.

The important thing was that the show was fantastic, a great mix of old songs and new. It was heavy on the hits, as befitting this being somewhat of a "comeback" tour, but there were a few surprises as well: Geddy and Alex emerging onstage with acoustic guitars after Neil's solo for an achingly pretty version of "Resist," and "Between Sun and Moon" being played live on tour for the first time. I did see Rush again, in 2004 on the R30 tour and in 2007 for the *Snakes & Arrows* tour, but that first concert experience was truly magical.

ALL THE WORLD'S INDEED A STAGE

Rush were a prodigious live act, performing 2,281 concerts between 1974 and 2015.[10] Their high water mark came in 1975, where they played a staggering 185 shows, but that torrid pace of over one-hundred shows per year continued through to the end of 1981. In that 1974-1981 span, Rush averaged 142 concerts per year. They would never play over 100 concerts a year, the highest post-1981 mark being 80 concerts in 1984.

Geddy Lee recalled the amount of shows differently, claiming in an interview in a 1978 interview that the band averaged 200 concerts per year, or maybe more.[11] Journalist Vinay Menon writes that after *2112* the band "practically lived on the road for the next few years, sometimes playing more than 260 nights a year."[12]

I hate disagreeing with Geddy Lee's memory or Vinay Menon's journalistic integrity, but I couldn't find anything corroborating these numbers. What matters is that Rush's intense touring schedule was killing them. In that same 1978 interview, Lee states the band will keep up that pace "as long as we're still standing." Years later, Lee recalled that the band was burning

---

10   *See, e.g.,* Setlist.fm, available at https://www.setlist.fm/stats/rush-13d6dd1d.html, last accessed June 7, 2020.
11   *Rush: Beyond the Lighted Stage* (Documentary, 2010).
12   Vinay Menon, *Rush: An Oral History* (Toronto Star Newspapers Limited, 2013), at 27.

out at that time, "getting fried and getting stupid."[13] The insane touring pace slowed to something more manageable, and the band's physical and mental health recovered. But clearly, Rush lived to play live, and the fans enthusiastically responded.

There was such a demand for this band, and it is a stereotype of Rush fans that the devoted will see the band multiple times per tour. Both the *Beyond the Lighted Stage* and *Time Stand Still* documentaries speak to such fans who, some attending over 100 total shows, including some fans like George Summers of Scotland and Martin Urionaguena of Argentina.[14]

Although Rush don't jam or deviate much from the recorded version while playing a concert, they are still a sight to behold. "I mean, these are three guys that make all this extraordinary music and you have to be at such a high technical level to pull that off," says KLOS DJ Jim Ladd. "It's hard enough in the studio, but live to pull that off says everything about them."[15] Such is Geddy, Alex, and Neil's skill that even the most difficult passages are played effortlessly and flawlessly live—I'll never forget seeing them play "YYZ" back in 2002, or the tricky, odd-time instrumental break in "Mission" on the *Snakes & Arrows* tour. Simply stunning.

It's interesting to note that, unlike other bands with massive live followings like The Grateful Dead, Pearl Jam, and Phish, Rush doesn't offer ever-changing setlists and extended improvisations. Generally speaking, what you hear on record is what you will hear live. And yet, Rush fans will still catch the band every tour, and some fans nearly every show.

I asked Ed Stenger his thoughts on this phenomenon, and he offered a simple, albeit brilliant, explanation: *they're just really, really good*, and it's impressive to see:

> Just the fact that they put on a good show and especially once they hit the big time in the eighties, they really took the time to put on a . . .

13 *Id.*
14 *See Rush: Time Stand Still* (Documentary, 2016).
15 *Rush: 2112 and Moving Pictures (Classic Albums)*, (Documentary, 2010).

spectacle for the fans too. Backdrop videos, the props and everything. They always talk about that one thing they learned from Kiss, touring with Kiss was that part of it. They brought it up multiple times in interviews, but they go back to that, to touring with Kiss and seeing how they did that, learning from that, and always thinking they always want to put on a good show. [T]hey're consistent. That's another thing, you know you're going to get a good show. They don't put on a bad show.[16]

The Rush/Kiss connection is an important point. Rush opened for Kiss in 1974 and 1975, and the two bands became quite close. As recently as 2018, Kiss guitarist and vocalist Paul Stanley called Rush the "most exciting" opening act they ever played with.[17]

This admiration was a two-way street, however, with Rush learning a lot from the Demon, the Starchild, the Spaceman, and the Catman about performing live:

> Regardless of what you want to say about Kiss musically or otherwise, there was no harder-working band than Kiss, and there was no band more determined to put on a spectacular show and give people their money's worth than Kiss. That was a great thing to see as an opening act.[18]

I concur wholeheartedly with Geddy here. I am personally not a fan of Kiss—I have nothing *against* them; they just don't

---

16 Ed Stenger, interview with the author, May 19, 2020 (Appendix C).
17 "PAUL STANLEY Says RUSH Was 'Most Exciting' Opening Band KISS Has Ever Had," *Blabbermouth.Net*, November 8, 2018, available at https://www.blabbermouth.net/news/paul-stanley-says-rush-was-most-exciting-opening-band-kiss-has-ever-had/, last accessed June 8, 2020.
18 *Rush: Beyond the Lighted Stage* (Documentary, 2010).

move the needle for me—but I respect the hell out of their work ethic and dedication to putting on a *show*.

ANOTHER EXAMPLE OF HOW RUSH BRINGS PEOPLE TOGETHER

Another self-indulgent aside:

My 12th grade physics teacher—and no, I'm not going to use her real name, so let's call her Mrs. Smith—was originally from Canada, complete with the accent and everything. She was a really nice lady, and a total nerd. A Trekkie, she had some *Star Trek* posters hanging around the classroom and on Halloween wore a perfect replica *Star Trek: The Next Generation* uniform to class. She also always found ways to tie sci-fi books and movies into the science she was teaching us, going so far as to have our final project be to take a sci-fi movie and examine whether the physics involved in it are realistic or not, and why.

Oh, and our class consisted of 22 boys and two girls.

We weren't *bad*, us boys, but the hormonal one-sidedness led to some *hilarious* exchanges, like when my buddy Tom, with whom I went to the Rush concert with in 2002, got sent to a table in the back of the room for talking too much. "Sit back there, Tom," Mrs. Smith said, pointing to the rear of the classroom. "Go to Siberia."

The next time she called on Tom, he didn't answer. "Tom! I'm talking to you!" Mrs. Smith called out, growing increasingly more agitated.

"What?" Tom called back. "I can't hear you! I'm in *Siberia*!"

We bought her flowers at the end of the school year. She was a good sport. And the final project I filmed with Tom and our other friends Dan and Jamie about *The Matrix* was so funny we had the class nearly peeing themselves.

Man, we had some *funny* projects, exploring the physics of *Mortal Kombat* complete with a mock fight between me and

Dan to demonstrate how Liu Kang's signature bicycle kick goes completely against the laws of physics, only for Dan to perform said maneuver by lying on the hood of Jamie's car and flailing his legs as Jamie drove slowly towards me.

During that fight, I also attacked Dan with a plunger. Yup, this is what your tax dollars go towards funding at public schools.

Anyway, *another* project we did about lighting actually has something to do with Rush.[19]

Our unit was about electricity, so we decided to write and videotape a performance of a song about lightning. I say "write" even though all we did was make our own lightning-themed lyrics to Vanilla Ice's "Ice Ice Baby" called "Lightning Baby" and have Dan rap, Tom as the DJ scratching a copy of R&B singer Johnny Kemp's 1986 debut album that we found at our local music store for like a dollar on my father's old turntable, me on bass and playing the hi-hat with my foot because Jamie couldn't keep the beat on the drums, and my sister filming us in lieu of our buddy Andy who couldn't be there.

It was pretty funny, and at the end I hopped on the drum set and played my own version of Neil's *Exit . . . Stage Left* solo on the drums just for the hell of it.

Everybody in our class loved the drum solo; I have to say I did a pretty good approximation of it. "Reminds me of some concerts I've been to," Mrs. Smith commented.

"Yeah? Like Rush?" I said.

"Ha ha, another Canada joke," Mrs. Smith replied. We had a history of poking fun at our neighbors to the north, and though Mrs. Smith didn't seem to mind, I'm sure it got old after a while.

"No, seriously, I love Rush," I replied.

Mrs. Smith didn't believe me. She thought I was pulling her leg. Other friends of mine told her that no, Alex was serious, he has all of their albums, and so on.

"I'll wear my t-shirt tomorrow," I told her, as a way of proving my devotion.

---

19 You are a *very* patient reader, and I appreciate it greatly.

"I saw Rush open for Kiss in 1975," Mrs. Smith said. That definitely piqued my interest. "How were they?" I asked.

"I don't remember," she said. "I just remember the drum solo."

EVEN THE COOL KIDS GET IT

Rush's live prowess is not lost on the hipsters and the cool kids, at least not anymore in the twenty-first century when it's suddenly acceptable to admit that you like Rush. In 2015, music writer Nathan Carson of *Vice* wrote a one-hundred percent sincere article (with a lot of swears) called "You're An Idiot If You Don't Think Rush Is The Best Live Band in the World." In it, Carson makes note of Rush's instrumental skill, that they both play the hits *and* dig deep into their back catalog, have a sense of humor, and put on a flat-out great show:

> After four decades of touring, Rush knows how to "mach schau." Now I'm not going to argue that Geddy is as viscerally compelling a performer as, say, Nick Cave. But he knows that. And Nick is not playing three instruments while he's climbing down into the crowd to get groped by the plebes. So what Rush does—aside from playing extremely complex music with only three musicians—is employ a highly sophisticated light show. Lasers, pyrotechnics, explosive charges and synchronized video make for a stage performance every bit as visually engaging as anything conjured by Tool or Muse.[20]

---

20 Nathan Carson, "You're An Idiot If You Don't Think Rush Is the Best Live Band in the World
A suite in eight parts," *Vice*, August 9, 2015, available at https://www.vice.com/en_us/article/6wqgp4/youre-an-idiot-if-you-dont-think-rush-is-the-best-live-band-in-the-world,

The visual spectacle is not lost on fans, and rock purists aside, it's one of the reasons to drop a lot of money on concert tickets instead of listening to the far cheaper record, tape, CD, or digital download in the comfort of your own home. Pink Floyd famously put on high-tech spectacles because of their admitted lack of on-stage charisma and technical chops. While Rush is far more animated than Pink Floyd ever were, they still realized that they were only three guys on a big stage, and the folks in the cheap seats deserved to get as much of a show as the front-row crowd.

Naturally, I wanted to know if Rush fans are truly this rabid, or if the documentaries and interviews cherry picked fans to make a point. We'll get into the results of my survey later in this chapter, but needless to say this is a decidedly innocuous stereotype about Rush fans, especially compared to the others like being nerdy, or somehow exclusionary based upon race and gender. However, the jury is still out on whether Rush fans also enjoyed shouting mild vulgarities in the hopes they'd be picked up in some bootlegger's concert recording.

YOUR FAVORITE MUSICIAN'S FAVORITE BAND

For "[a]ll the best players [growing up]," says Nine Inch Nails mastermind Trent Reznor, "I quickly learned, the language was Rush."[21] Kirk Hammett of Metallica—one of the most influential guitarists in the world of metal, had this to say about Alex Lifeson's playing on "La Villa Strangiato":

> That one kind of slow, open solo that Alex plays, the way he built that up had a huge impression on me because he was creating a mood by playing very, very sparsely and just slowly

last accessed June 8, 2020.
21   *Rush: Beyond the Lighted Stage* (Documentary, 2010).

amping up the intensity. I just thought that was the greatest thing in terms of lead guitar dynamics and phrasings. I see them as the high priests of conceptual metal. Big influence. Huge.[22]

High praise coming from the man who spawned a legion of imitators himself by reinventing the metal solo, adding a classic-rock flair with heavy use of a wah-wah pedal to complement the genre's typical two-handed tapping and speedy phrasing.

Hammett and Tool drummer Danny Carey make observations similar to famous Los Angeles Jim Ladd, having been blown away that such a full and powerful sound was created by only three guys. Dream Theater drummer Mike Portnoy and Pantera stickman Vinnie Paul were similarly influenced by "La Villa Strangiato." It was "probably the hardest song I ever learned how to play," says Paul. Portnoy calls the song the "benchmark of drumming."[23]

Smashing Pumpkins leader Billy Corgan had a similar revelation upon hearing "2112":

> The first thing that struck you was the level of musicianship was just insane . . . There was a moment in my life . . . that I actually knew how to play the entire side. I knew how to play "2112" all the way down. I knew every note, every moment. And I think back now, I think "How long did I have to fucking learn that?" I must've sat in the bedroom for a year to learn that fuckin' song.[24]

This meticulousness shows in Corgan's playing. He brought highly technical and inventive guitar soloing to the burgeoning alternative rock scene of the late 80s and early 90s to the forefront at a level equal to those of the late 60s and 70s. And Cor-

22 *Id.*
23 *Id.*
24 *Id.*

gan's bandmate, drummer Jimmy Chamberlain, viewed Rush's music in a similar light: "If you could learn those songs, that was a stepping stone to just about everything you needed to know. If you could play those songs with some proficiency, you could play pretty much anything else."[25]

It's unsurprising, then, that so many famous musicians are Rush fans, and that so many Rush fans are musicians, right? I mean, they'd *have* to be, since instrumental prowess is one of this band's main selling points.

And they'd *have* to be good at their instruments since the music is so damned complicated: "We're super nerdy like that. We've always been over-rehearsers," Geddy Lee explains in *Rush: Time Stand Still* about their preparations for their final tour in 2015. "The songs are complicated, and if we don't get to the point where you can do it without thinking, then it's not good because then if something happens during a show or something goes wrong, you can just deal with it much more easily if it's ingrained." You don't get as good as Rush if you don't dedicate heavy time and effort to honing your craft.

This can be heard not only on live recordings, but by listening to Rush's albums in chronological order. As good a guitarist as Alex Lifeson was from the get-go, it's impossible *not* to realize that his playing gets better with each successive album; not just his speed and technique, but the new sounds and styles he is able to wrangle out of his humble six string. "[H]earing him play live, on stage," says Carson, "you'll get the sort of shivers up your neck that you'd expect from David Gilmour."[26] Geddy Lee's bass work undergirds the band, playing quick, complex figures that are as challenging to play as any other bassist can spit out[27]—while handling vocals, keyboards, and bass-pedal duties—and sometimes, as on "Xanadu," guitar as well. And who can forget Neil Peart's rededication to his craft by taking

---

25 *Id.*
26 Carson, "You're An Idiot If You Don't Think Rush Is the Best Live Band in the World," *Vice*, August 9, 2015.
27 As a bassist who cut his teeth learning Rush parts, I say this from experience. Some of his parts are *tough*. "Turn the Page" in particular. And Geddy Lee sang while playing it!

lessons with drum legend Freddie Gruber in the mid-1990s?[28] These guys were serious about their musicianship from the beginning of their career through to the end of their final tour, always pushing themselves and getting better . . . and maintaining that level of proficiency into their sixties. As Peart has said, "I could play Charlie Watts's drum parts at 75, but not Neil Peart's drum parts."[29]

LONELY LERXST

There's a popular internet meme that shows a picture of Rush circa 2002 or so. The caption underneath reads "How Alex Lifeson Sees Rush." Below this is the same image, except with a black square over Alex Lifeson's face and the caption "How Everyone Else Sees Rush." It's funny because, for as great a guitarist as he is (and he *is* one of the best), Lifeson is arguably the *worst* musician in Rush,[30] or at least he's *perceived* that way:

> A lot of it has to do with Geddy being the singer and fronting the band. He's the face of the band. The singer always is. Then Neil is such a huge presence and he writes the lyrics. The lyrics are a big part of Rush too so you get those two things, the face of Rush and the mind of Rush essentially in Geddy and Neil. Then there's Alex. Naturally, he's the odd man out.

I agree with Stenger. In any other band, Alex Lifeson would be *the* centerpiece, the guy everyone's talking about. In Rush,

---

28   *See, e.g.,* William F. Miller, "The Reinvention of Neil Peart," *Modern Drummer*, November 1996, available at http://www.2112.net/powerwindows/transcripts/19961100moderndrummer.htm, last accessed June 8, 2020.
29   *Rush: Time Stand Still* (Documentary, 2016). And that's no knock on Charlie Watts; his playing style was perfect for The Rolling Stones, but it wouldn't have worked for Rush.
30   "He's a great guitarist, but of the three of them he's probably the worst musician, but he's still a great guitarist. There's so many good guitarists and Alex is definitely up there." Ed Stenger, interview with the author, May 19, 2020 (Appendix C).

he's third out of three. To use a sports metaphor, Alex Lifeson being in a band with Geddy Lee and Neil Peart is like adding Larry Bird to a basketball team that already has Michael Jordan and Magic Johnson. Sure, he's *Larry freaking Bird*, but come on—you've already got Magic and Michael.[31]

"He's the glue that holds that band together," Stenger says of Lifeson,[32] and that's the highest compliment you can give a guitarist. Unlike so many other shredders who love the spotlight, Lifeson is content to play *exactly* what the song needs, nothing more and nothing less. Sometimes this includes lots of solos and fast, prominent parts. Other times, like much of Rush's output from *Signals* through *Hold Your Fire*, that includes filling in the spaces left by the keyboards, bass, and drums, stepping out with the occasional solo or monster riff. In that era, for every "The Big Money" or "The Analog Kid," where the guitar is front and center, you have two or three songs like "Red Sector A," "Mission," "Manhattan Project," or "Losing It."

"Alex Lifeson Is The Unsung Hero Of Rush," PROG Magazine proclaimed in 1987:

> Neil Peart is frequently described as rock's greatest living drummer. Geddy Lee is revered as a virtuoso of the bass. But Lifeson remains hugely underrated as a guitarist.
>
> "That's never bothered me," Alex says. "Neil really is the greatest drummer! And Geddy is an amazing bass player. But for me, it's better to be an important part of the union than to be a standout.

---

[31] I have to mention the hilarious, unscripted scene in *Beyond the Lighted Stage* where Alex and Geddy are eating lunch at a deli. A waitress comes out asking for Geddy to sign some autographs for the cooks in the back, completely oblivious to the fact that Alex is, in fact, also in the band. Odd man out indeed.

[32] Ed Stenger, interview with the author, May 19, 2020 (Appendix C).

"In terms of a musical unit, I always thought that somebody's got to hold the ground."[33]

The ability to put ego aside and do what the band *needs*, despite having the chops to overplay, is the most compelling part of Lifeson's skillset. So yes, Lerxst is the overlooked member of Rush, but that in no way detracts from his brilliance.

ABSOLUTE WIZARDS

Does this dedication to their instruments appeal to the same type of fan who is also obsessive about other "nerdy" pursuits? Is Geddy, Alex, and Neil's mastery of their respective instruments what primarily attract people to Rush and not the music themselves? "If you know a drummer, they're probably a Rush fan," as Ed Stenger puts it,[34] but you could say the same about guitarists and bassists regarding Lifeson and Lee. So are Rush fans by-and-large *musicians* as well as music *fans*?

We'll get to that shortly, but it bears repeating that Lifeson is obviously not the only one who is lauded as being a complete and absolute master of his instrument. I swear, I never thought I'd live to see the day when *Vice* magazine, of all publications, sang Rush's praises, but here we are:

> This one's a no-brainer. Guitar Player magazine has awarded Geddy Lee the Best Rock Bass award six times. He's also in their Hall of Fame. Drummer Neil Peart has been named Best Rock Drummer in Modern Drummer magazine NINE times. For my money though, the secret weapon is guitarist Alex Lifeson. He's been getting swept under the rug for decades, but hearing him play live, on stage, you'll get

---

33   *PROG Magazine (Limited Edition)*, Issue 35, April 2013, available at https://www.cygnus-x1.net/links/rush/prog-04.2013.php, last accessed June 8, 2020.

34   Ed Stenger, interview with the author, May 19, 2020 (Appendix C).

the sort of shivers up your neck that you'd expect from David Gilmour.

All three of these guys perform everything live. Any sampled sounds are triggered by whichever band member happens to have a free digit at that given millisecond. No guest musicians are on stage or behind a curtain. Geddy is playing bass with his hands, synth with his feet, and singing lead. Neil Peart often has two complete drum kits including tubular bells and an array of wood blocks, chimes, and more toms and cymbals than most mammals can count. It's absolutely nuts and you can watch endless YouTube videos and concert DVDs to affirm that no member of Rush is ever fucking around or phoning it in.[35]

And it's so true. I have little to add to this save the fact that you can meet musicians who don't even like Rush's *music*, but they absolutely love and respect Geddy, Alex, and Neil *as musicians*. This kind of universal respect is rare.

Musicians as diverse as Tim Commerford of Rage Against the Machine, Billy Corgan of Smashing Pumpkins, Dave Grohl and Taylor Hawkins of the Foo Fighters, Vinnie Paul of Pantera, and Mike Portnoy and John Petrucci of Dream Theater extol Rush's musicianship. Indeed, Rush inspired a whole generation of rock musicians with their melding of progressive rock to heavy metal. As Hawkins explains, "If you liked Yes, and you liked Genesis for their complexity, yet you liked Black Sabbath for their power, then Rush was the perfect band for you."[36]

There are so, so many others that an entire book could be written about Rush's celebrity fans. But that's not why we're here. We're here to talk about *you*, the not-famous-but-still-im-

---

[35] Carson, You're An Idiot If You Don't Think Rush Is the Best Live Band in the World," *Vice*, August 9, 2015.
[36] *Rush: 2112 and Moving Pictures (Classic Albums)*, (Documentary, 2010).

portant Rush fan, to figure out what makes you tick, and why. So let's get to the survey.

Of the 660 respondents who answered the question, "Are you a musician," 354, or 53.6%, answered in the affirmative, leaving 306, or 46.3% of fans who responded as not being musicians. This a-little-more-than-half breakdown is what I expected based on personal experience: I have met plenty of Rush fans in my life, many *really* big fans, who don't play a thing.

Interestingly, some respondents *became* Rush fans by virtue of being musicians. "My friend Martin walked up to me and gave me a cassette dub of *Moving Pictures*," says lifelong fan Chris Bates. "He said 'You play bass. You'll like this.'"[37] Similarly, fan Bryan Benner got into Rush when his older sister's boyfriend told him "You are getting into drums, you should listen to Rush."[38] Jordyn T. also got into Rush while learning how to play drums.[39] "[I] [w]as starting drum lessons and someone showed me the drum solo on *A Show of Hands*," notes Reverend Kent Schaaf.[40]

Others were introduced to Rush *by* musicians. "My cousin introduced me to their [Rush's] music," responded one fan. "He is a drummer."[41]

Listen to Rush long enough, and hang out with other fans, and you're bound to pick up *some* knowledge of music. "I'm not a musician," Ed Stenger told me, but ". . . just from running this blog for so long, I picked up so many things from musicians about if you talk about Rush and what they add musically to the band."[42] But this could be said about many other bands as well. It's not as if Rush is the *only* band with really accomplished musicians, or that Rush are actually the certifiable *best* musicians ever (though one could make a *really* compelling argument that Neil Peart actually *was* the best rock drummer in history).

37 Chris Bates, response to author's survey, February 5, 2020 (Appendix A).
38 Bryan Benner, response to author's survey, February 5, 2020 (Appendix A).
39 Jordyn T., response to author's survey, February 5, 2020 (Appendix A).
40 Reverend Kent Schaff, response to author's survey, February 7, 2020 (Appendix A).
41 Name withheld by request, response to author's survey, February 5, 2020 (Appendix A).
42 Ed Stenger, interview with the author, May 19, 2020 (Appendix C).

Therefore, I'm not totally surprised that only 53.6% of fans surveyed are musicians. I don't know how that tracks with the general population, but that's not germane to the purposes of this book. The important thing is that we can say yes, *most* Rush fans are musicians, but not by a huge margin.

CONCERT HALL

So here we are, the final stop on our examination of the Rush fan type; our attempt to isolate and critically examine what commonalities exist between fans of this band. And this last one, the devotion of Rush fans to their live performances, is a fun one.

I asked 664 individual Rush fans if they had seen Rush in concert. 662 answered, with a whopping 625, or 94.4% of you, answering in the affirmative.[43] As far how many times fans have seen Rush, the numbers ranged from a low of one show to a high of 200.

Before we go further, a quick note about my methodology: Most of you kind souls who responded to my survey indicated a numerical value along with which tours you saw. However, some just said "Every tour since *Hemispheres*," or something like that; in these instances, I counted the tours using the list on Rush's official website. Some gave a range, like "12-14," so in all of these cases I used the higher number. Finally, anytime someone wrote "Too many to remember" or "A lot" or something like that, I picked the number 20. So forgive me if these aren't the *most* accurate numbers, but the gist of the survey still stands.

One of the interesting results is that Rush fans saw the band in concert an average of 12 times. That's quite a devoted following, but in line with my predictions. Also, this high degree of concert attendance isn't surprising given Rush's phenomenal live shows. There really is something special about seeing three guys make such fantastic noise all by themselves without any

---

43   Rush fan survey (Appendix A).

touring musicians, save for the *Clockwork Angels* String Ensemble during the *Clockwork Angels* tour, and having either Ben Mink or Jonathan Dinklage play violin on "Losing It" during the R40 tour. Plus, the band's humor, sincerity, and authenticity come through on stage.

Rush's skill and dedication to the live performance has been noted for decades, sometimes grudgingly, by music critics who might not be fans of the band but could at least respect their talents. We saw this with Paul Rambali's 1977 concert review for *New Musical Express*,[44] complimenting both their technical abilities and the light show, but not so much the songs.

A similar take on live Rush, full of backhanded compliments, can be found in Peter Goddard's' June 12, 1976 review of Rush's residency at Toronto's Massey Hall for the *Toronto Star*: "Rush is not the most subtle of rock groups. True, its kind of basic,[45] thundering music has its following, with some 2,500 showing up last night, rushing the stage at one point and cheering every song."[46] He also, quite humorously, calls Rush's music unsophisticated and implies that the fans are too simple to want anything more than Rush's "basic" rock, concluding that the show "was probably the best performance it has given here—although that's like saying you've just seen the best train wreck of your life."[47]

The buzz would grow, though, and by the time the band was again playing in Canada that October, reports of steadily growing audiences were filling articles about Rush. "Reports of attendances in the Maritime region are inconsistent," wrote David Farrell in *Record Week*, "but overall, Rush appear to have generated a good bit of excitement."[48] "Nugent's Backup Group

---

44   *See* Chapter II: Superior Cynics.
45   Words fail me when I see Rush's music described as "basic." One wonders what other bands Goddard was comparing them to.
46   Peter Goddard, "Rock Trio Is A Threat To Old Massey Hall," *Toronto Star*, June 12, 1976, available at http://www.2112.net/powerwindows/transcripts/19760612torontostar.htm, last accessed June 10, 2020.
47   *Id. See also*, Steve Pond, Chapter III, footnote 4 ([I]it's hard not to be somewhat impressed by the fact that only three musicians can create such a massive, leaden sound.").
48   David Farrell, "Rush Tour Hit By Nationalist Backlash," *Record Week*, October 25, 1976, available at http://www.2112.net/powerwindows/transcripts/19761025recordweek.

Destined For Stardom," read another article, anticipating Rush's 1977 stop in Lubbock, Texas, in support of the Motor City Madman.[49]

By the time the 1980s rolled around, even the normally hostile British music press was at least acknowledging that Rush put on a great live show while also commenting on their work ethic. Two reviews of Rush's June 7, 1980 show at the Hammersmith Odeon in London are telling examples that the shift in perception about Rush was changing, albeit still filled with snarky asides about the band's music and fans. The first from Robin Smith of *Record Mirror*:

> When the Rush circus hits the roads it burns rubber for nine months or more—and the band have to build up the stamina of Olympic athletes, keeping their brains unclouded.
>
> The strange thing is that they don't need to work that hard anymore. After a series of mega platinum albums, they could well afford to go down with a severe attack of Zeppelinitus and stay off the road for a year or more.
>
> But Rush are fanatical workaholics and almost every year brings a full scale British tour with absolutely no signs of wear and tear. This time they might come away with a little profit, even though they've just forked out 20,000 dollars in air freighting charges before putting a foot on stage.

htm, last accessed June 10, 2020.
49 "Nugent's Backup Group Destined For Stardom," *Lubbock Avalanche-Journal*, January 9, 1977, available at http://www.2112.net/powerwindows/transcripts/19770109lubbockjournal.htm, last accessed June 10, 2020 ("When Ted Nugent brings his high energy brand of outrageous rock to the Lubbock Municipal Coliseum Jan. 19, one of the backup groups will be a Canadian rock band called Rush. However, many in the industry happen to feel this group may be headlining concerts themselves in a very short time.").

Rush are the true intellectuals of heavy metal, Yes meeting Motorhead down a dark and windy alley. Lots of crash, bang and dry ice to be sure, but just listen to those themes and lyrics.

If God had wanted a soundtrack when he gave Moses the Ten Commandments then he would have commissioned Rush to do it. Heroic themes stoked and fried by the constant pulse of life and the forces of nature.[50]

Note Smith's appreciation for the band's work ethic. I find it interesting that this aspect of Rush is appreciated both by fans and critics.

John Gill's review for *Sounds*, however, can almost be called glowing. Gill finds very little fault with the music itself; after commenting on the band seeming a bit uninspired at the beginning, likely due to technical problems, he notes that Rush started to come alive during "Xanadu." He also praised the "brightness, clarity and precision of the performance" of "Natural Science," their "self-assured, sophisticated" swagger during "Hemispheres" that retained their "underlying guignol[51] thrill," and the "savage beauty" of Peart's solo.[52] Show closer, the encore "La Villa Strangiato," Gill noted, was particularly impressive: "After two-and a quarter hours of non-stop fiery performance, they still manage to infuse it with freshness, style, complexity and adrenalin."[53]

The fan/critic split was noticed relatively early in the band's career. "Simply, Rush has never been appreciated by the crit-

50   Robin Smith, "Reeling Under A Million Bad Puns, Robin "Burger King" Smith Gives Rush What For: In The Coke Snorting, Pill Popping, Dope Polluted Eighties, Rush Are As Clean And Wholesome As Mom's Apple Pie," *Record Mirror*, June 14, 1980, available at http://www.2112.net/powerwindows/transcripts/19800614recordmirror.htm, last accessed June 10, 2020.
51   Great word!
52   John Gill, "Rush—Hammersmith Odeon Review," *Sounds*, June 14, 1980, available at http://www.2112.net/powerwindows/transcripts/19800614sounds.htm, last accessed June 10, 2020.
53   *Id.*

ics, and none of their albums qualify as 'critic's choices.' Their concerts are likewise either misconstrued, ignored or often misjudged by most critics, despite public reactions to the contrary," wrote Max Thaler in *Circus* in 1978.[54] But by the mid-80s, Rush had truly become a live juggernaut, their stage shows and music wowing nearly everyone who attended and getting better and more refined as the years went on and the audiences grew:

> Whereas their last show was bombarded with technical effects beyond the saturation point, last night's Power Windows performance before 10,000 at Copps Coliseum was a breath of fresh air.
>
> The visual production of the concert was still mind-boggling. Songs about human behaviour, challenge, endurance and warfare were integrated with cynical cartoons, splices of video or a dynamic laser 'n light show.
>
> In fact, the cinematic value of Rush live is comparable to watching a musical Raiders of the Lost Ark—always adventurous.

So wrote Nick Krewen of the *Hamilton Spectator* on March 1, 1986.[55]

Fast forward to the early 1990s and we see journalists like Louise King of the *St. Louis Post-Dispatch* writing things like:

> Anyone fortunate enough to have seen Rush live can attest to the fact that the Canadian hard-rock trio's concerts are more than a mu-

---

54   Max Thaler, "Recognition Is Only Half The Fun: Rush Audiences Grow Quickly As Critics Slowly Catch On," *Circus*, January 5, 1978, available at http://www.2112.net/powerwindows/transcripts/19780105circus.htm, last accessed June 10, 2020.

55   Nick Krewen, "New Rush Show Like A Breath Of Fresh Air," *Hamilton Spectator*, March 1, 1986, available at http://www.2112.net/powerwindows/transcripts/19860301hamiltonspectator.htm, last accessed June 10, 2020.

sical happening; they're an audio and visual event that assaults the senses from all sides.

And based on the band's performance at The Arena Thursday night, it appears Rush has been able to maintain the spectacular nature of its stage show through the years without taking anything away from its thoughtful, intelligent, highly developed musical compositions.[56]

And it's only a small leap forward in time and space to see the encomiums given to the band today. With such a rich, vibrant, and high-quality concert history—and a bevy of fans who have been rushing to see them live for forty years—I think it would be fun to see what memories those fans who responded to my survey have from the multitude of shows they'd been to.

MAKING MEMORIES

I'll go first.

My enduring Rush concert memory speaks to this. At the July 12, 2002 show Alex Lifeson went into his traditional monologue during "La Villa Strangiato," his "meltdown" where he says whatever is on his mind. That night, he discussed how difficult it was for him to quit smoking. He's a funny guy, and utterly ridiculous. I remember him looking back at Neil afterwards, trying to get Neil to smile. The stoic Peart just sort of stares at Alex for a bit, and then, slowly, finally cracks an almost imperceptible smile before they launch back into the song.

Except watching a video of the performance on YouTube while writing this book, that moment *didn't happen* during "La Villa Strangiato" on July 12, 2002 at the then-Tweeter Center in Mansfield, Massachusetts. I couldn't find a video of "La Vil-

---

56 Louise King, "Rush Melds Showmanship, Great Music," *St. Louis Post-Dispatch*, November 8, 1991, available at http://www.2112.net/powerwindows/transcripts/19911108stlouispostdispatch.htm, last accessed June 10, 2020.

la Strangiato" at the August 12, 2004 show I went to confirm. Maybe this happened during "By-Tor and the Snow Dog" or some other song. The important thing, though is that it *did* happen, it was *funny*, and although I might be conflating a few of the shows I went to, I'll never forget the shared joy between performer and audience.

And I'm getting confused by just the *three* Rush concerts I have seen. I can't imagine how some of you who have seen over fifty keep them straight.

One final memory: When I saw Rush on June 27, 2007 on the *Snakes & Arrows* tour, near the end Geddy Lee came out with a video camera asked the crowd to wave and say "Hi, Canada!" because their Canadian fans were always asking him what the United States was like, and Geddy always told them us Americans were *really nice*. He wanted video proof, so we gave it to him.[57]

Enough about me. Here is but a sampling of some of the great Rush concert memories from you, the fans (all responses are available in Appendix A):

> All hold a special place in my heart, but I did have the opportunity to ride Neil's motorcycle from the dealer to his trailer backstage on the Time Machine tour. That will always be a pure moment of joy for me.
> – Bryan Benner

> So many. All the great tailgate times with friends, listening to soundchecks from outside the venue(s), drinking beers, freaking out over every single note . . . Watching balloons fall from the ceiling and being handed a free (!) t-shirt on the HYF [Hold Your Fire] tour stop in San Diego. Decking a guy for being drunk, rude, and bel-

---

[57] Fan Michael Perdue's favorite concert memory is also when Geddy pointed a camera at the crowd during a stop on the *Snakes & Arrows* tour. (Michael Perdue, response to author's survey, February 5, 2020) (Appendix A).

ligerent and watching him get escorted out by security (and not me!) on the Power Windows tour. Yelling "Hey!" during the "[2112] Overture." Screaming after "concert hall!" [during "The Spirit of Radio"]. Laughing during "blah blah blah" [at Rush's Rock and Roll Hall of Fame induction]. Laughing at Jan Wenner's reaction to the crowd's roar [also at the Hall of Fame induction]. The first time I heard "Bastille Day." Meeting Geddy. Getting to work on not one, but 4 (!) Rush-related books. Sharing beers with Kevin J. Anderson over dinner and discussing how much Neil meant to us. Getting an email from Neil telling me, "Good job!" on Clockwork Lives (the graphic novel). Getting the only copy of that same book that Neil ever signed, to me. Hearing the news that Neil had re-joined Geddy and Alex, and that Rush would be an entity again. Every concert from Power Windows on (Signals too, but I don't remember it and I missed GuP!), sometimes getting lucky enough to see them more than once on that tour. The final two shows. Neil sneaking out from behind the drum riser to surprise Al and Ged. Watching Beyond The Lighted Stage and Time Stand Still in a movie theatre with my wife, alternately laughing and crying, and her turning to me at the end of both and saying, "I finally get it." Working with Skip Daly, Eric Hansen, Pegi Cecconi, Patrick McLoughlin, Stewart Copeland, Les Claypool, Howard Ungerleider, and all the great Rush fans, roadies, family, and compatriots. Nothing but great memories—even the sad ones are ones I will hold on to. And I hope for many more, simply through the power of the words and the music.
– Mark Irwin

Moving Pictures . . . saw a guy get stabbed in the gut and some tripping chic[k] threw up on the seats in front of her.
– Marci Jo, fan

Besides the music and performance the fact that the women's restroom lines are shorter than the men's.
– Joyce L.

Crying on "Vital Signs," looking at Geddy Lee in the eyes and feeling like he was smiling at me . . . And finding out how "Peart' is pronounced.
– Sylvie Yeranotsian

Aw man. One time I was air drumm[ing] and ended up air drumming the same improvisational fill as Neil. Also just air drumming together with everyone . . . that doesn't happen at any other show. The smiles you give each other, and the pats on the back strangers would give you when you did a section right . . . the feeling of being in that crowd was just so special compared to other fan bases I'm in.
– David Stewart

At my first show I stood next to a guy who had been to over a hundred shows. He was air drumming the entire time. Other than that, watching them play "What You're Doing" and a few other older songs on the R40 tour ignited a passion for music that I thought I had lost in my 20s.
– David B., aka Dave2112

My older brother and I finally seeing a Rush concert together in 2002. I cried when they opened up the set with "Tom Sawyer." It was a moment I will never forget. Just seeing Neil back behind the kit after what happened to his wife and daughter . . . It made me appreciate these guys so much more and the dedication they put in every tour. Neil was bashing the crap out of his drums that night. I will never forget watching Neil break a set of sticks in half and throwing them to his tech behind the stage after "Ghost Rider."
– Tony V.

1. My first concert at Deeside Arena—we met the band after the concert and got autographs! 2. Neil sent his sticks out to my 12 year son at Newcastle UK in 2011. 3. Once saw Geddy with his daughter in Toronto and said "Hi." He was very nice and wished me well for my stay in the city! 4. Howard Ungerleider invited me to sit with him at the Clockwork Angels Concert in Indianapolis, a fantastic experience and unique insight for me (cost me a fortune to get there)!
– Mark R.

My friend and I decorated our tank tops with Rush logos and lyrics and wore them to the show. We got there and we were in the first uncovered section of an outdoor venue, and it started pouring, but we didn't care at all. As we walked in, someone from the stands shouted at us "Rush never looked so good!" and we laughed about it, but looking back, we were definitely some of the youngest people there, and we felt right at home.
- Jill M.

First one 1982! Signals tour at the Mecca in Milwaukee. I didn't sit down for the entire show. We were top row but dead center. We didn't care how far away we were. When the lights reflected off Alex's guitar it shine[d] all the back to us and we were in the spotlight of his guitar. It was unreal.

Another memory was Grace Under Pressure and when they started "Witch Hunt" the entire balcony vibrates from the low tone of the keyboard. Same show we ran to where they left the stage and as we were running Neil's towel hits my friend in the face. We were pissed because he wasn't even Rush fan.

Last memory, last tour United Center in Chicago, took my brother for his birthday, flew out from CT. Best seats of our lives. Front row stage right. As close as we could ever dream of as teens. Worth the money and thank god we were normal stoners growing up we would have never had jobs that would allow us that kind of seat. I say due to the positive influence of Rush.
– Todd Swift

My husband and I saw them at the MSG in the R40 tour, our first and only RUSH concert. We bought the tickets before even having the American visa, they were the perfect excuse to finally go to NY and their show was mind-blowing.
– Laura O.

Every show kicked ass! I think hearing them play "Mystic Rhythms" as the sun was going down at an outdoor show was pretty special.

The R30 overture was a huge surprise and an exciting way to kick off that show, too (remember, this was in the early 2000s when the internet was still young and you couldn't look up a band's setlist from the night before).
– Drew

The Clockworks Angels Tour blew me away. Not only did the addition of the mini-orchestra add a whole new dimension but that first act gave me a new appreciation for some of the mid-period, keyboard-oriented material that I didn't care for when it was first released.[58]
– W. Earl Brown

First concert 5.25.1975, Rush warmed up Kiss, I had NEVER heard of them at the time, and watched them in amazement. And the influence helped create my music career, and business for the next 30 years. Driving by their bus door 2.24.81 after the concert, and Alex was standing by the front door, I got to hand him the concert program, and got signatures from Alex, Geddy, and Neil. RIP Neil . . . Rock In Peace.
– Scott Johnson

Traveling to New Haven to see show with Primus opening, then seeing them the next night at Nassau Coliseum 9th row. I did see them front row on Time Machine Tour which is a favorite too. It was always great reviewing the setlist with friends while traveling back home after the show.
– Scott Hoelldobler

---

58   I concur with Earl; the Clockwork Angels Tour had a *killer* set list.

R40: Took my then 5 year old daughter (first rush show), my 10 year old daughter (second show) and my wife.
– Drew Golburgh

Arriving in a limo with a bunch of people including my ex-wife (not ex then) and woman in the car that desperately wanted to be my girlfriend. AWKWARD! And for the record I never cheated though looking back I wish I had. Also on that night I took my daughter to that concert and introduced her to Rush in a big way. That was on the Test for Echo tour. Laughing at my ex-wife and ex-friend because they both fell asleep at Counterparts and missed the whole concert so I made friends with a couple next me and had a great night anyway.
– Rick B.

Took my little brother to Roll the Bones I was 16/17 and he was 14—someone in the crowd passed him a joint at one point. He looked at me and goes "What do I do with this?" My reply? "Give it to me." Lol.
– Bri W.

I always loved the anticipation leading up to the beginning of the show, many of them opening with "[The] Spirit of Radio," which is one of my favorites. Hearing "La Villa Strangiato" live has to be one of my highlights, though—it's a masterpiece!"
– Chad

Favorite probably isn't the correct word, more appropriately would be powerful memory. My 23 year old son died in March of 2015. I had

been planning to take him to see Rush for the first time as we shared a love of music together. I decided to go to the show anyway (5/23/2015). Although I can't say that it is a happy memory, I found it to be somewhat therapeutic and I'm glad I went."
– Phil Mele, diehard fan

Finger high five from Alex. I was sitting close enough to get up to the stage and he was able to reach me. Other than that, being able to hear most of my faves performed live over the course of many tours.
– Brad Ebert

Nothing particularly noteworthy . . . no, wait . . . it was the Clockwork Angels Tour. It was my wife's third Rush concert. She's not really a fan—doesn't hate them, but never even heard of them until she met me. But when they played "Tom Sawyer", I turned to look at my wife and there she was, singing along and having fun. SO. DAMN. HOT.
– Craig K.

Favorite concert had to be 2013 CWA [Clockwork Angels] because 1) It was just a great show from one of my favorite LPs & 2) it was in my home town (Raleigh, NC at the time) so easy drive to and fro. However, I literally flew half way around the planet for the R40 show in Irvine—Kabul, Afghanistan to LAX—and was able to get 12th row center stage seats. Awesome! Best Rush memory!
– Marc J. Stansell, Huntersville, NC – life-long fan

First time seeing Rush March of 1985. Lee Civic Center Fort Meyers Florida. This was a 5 date little tour in Florida for reasons I'm not sure. Grace Under Pressure tour was finished. This show debuted 3 new songs from Power Windows. This was one of 5 dates in Florida. 2 shows in Miami, 2 shows in Lakeland and 1 show in Fort Meyers Florida. These shows debuted new songs form Power Windows.
– Gregory Brown, Longwood, Florida

Rocking out as the only two on our feet in the posh seats at The o2 in London to the MP album in its entirety on the Time Machine tour.
– Chris, a fan

Seeing them for the first time in over 10 years on the R30 tour in Birmingham with one of my oldest friends who got me into Rush back in the 70's. Sadly he passed away a few years later from cancer and never got to see them again. It brings back fantastic memories of my friend and always brings a tear to my eye when I think of that night.
– Andy

The stage getup for Clockwork tour just looked really interesting with all the steampunk stuff. Musically all concerts were fantastic.
– Marc Brennan

My first musical epiphany on December 10, 1977 Hollywood Sportitorium. They opened for Bob Seger. I absolutely could not get over that all that strange and different music was coming from just 3 guys. A Musical style I had never heard before. "Xanadu" trapped me for-

ever in the fandom of Rush and "2112" locked that cage and threw away the key.
– Dave L.

I heard "Natural Science" for the first time at the second leg of R30. It immediately became my favorite song.
– Karina Maloney

Each concert I saw was amazing but my favorite was in 2015. I took my family on vacation to Southern California for a couple of days, visited some museums and we had a great time as a family. Night of the concert, ordered room service for my high school-aged kids, then my wife and I saw the band at Irvine Meadows. It was a fantastic concert and thrilled that my wife left the concert as a new fan.
– Sam Jessup, a fan

The September 2010 Time Machine Tour show outside of Washington, D.C., was like stepping into a time machine for me. I had not seen the band in nearly 20 years, and so much of my life had changed across those two decades, from surviving a couple of combat tours in the U.S. Army to getting married and having kids and starting a new life. At the time, I was just grateful to be where I was, knowing how fragile life can be. With some understanding of how difficult the intervening years must have been for Neil and the band, it was a gift to have them back and touring again. I went to the show with my younger brother (who introduced me to Rush) and an Army buddy I served in Iraq with, and we had seats right in front of Geddy. Seeing the band on stage again, after so many hard-fought-and-won years, was a feeling so

familiar and comforting, like an arm around your shoulder from a favorite uncle. There they were, like they always had been, so reassuring and positive in every way. I remember Geddy looking right at us and smiling, as if to say, "Welcome back. It's OK." And it was.
– Peter Fitzgerald

Time Machine 2011. With both my brothers who have both passed away now.
– Kelly

Being blown away at my first rush concert at age 14. I was in awe by how these 3 guys could put out so much sound in their music and be so tight.
– Rick W.

There was an asshole in front of me and my buddies that wouldn't sit down and there was a young guy that came all the way from Japan behind us and asked him to sit down and he wouldn't so I made him sit down thought it was kinda ignorant.
– Jim Johnston

My 8-year-old daughter falling asleep during "2112." She will NEVER live it down.
– W. Lane Startin

Seeing them play "Cygnus X-1" the first time I saw them, the inflatable rabbits from the Presto tour, and the Clockwork Angels tour was amazing, with the string section playing with them. I really enjoyed the video they played during "Dreamline" as a tribute to Neil Armstrong.
– Ken Scott

A Rush-fan friend and I took our boyfriends (who had no clue who Rush was) to Pine Knob in 1979. We were completely geeked out and the guys were lost. Good times! Got together with a bunch of guys I worked with (30 years ago) in August to see Cinema Strangiato—their memories and recall of concerts was amazing!

– Anne

As you can see, these stories range from funny to poignant, and I'd love to highlight all of them. I've included all that I have permission to include in Appendix A, and I recommend reading through all of them. They're well worth your time and show just how fantastic and memorable a live act Rush truly was.

CHAPTER VI: HOW DO WE MAKE CONTACT WITH ONE ANOTHER?

"I have never lost a friend . . . over Rush." [1]

PROFILE OF A FAN

So here we are, at the end of our taxonomy of your average Rush fan, though I'm sure you've seen that Rush fans are anything but "average." As is the case with most fanbases, some Rush fan stereotypes are true (mostly male, mostly white), while others are not (mostly musicians, mostly atheists, mostly libertarian). But a desire to create a fan profile was only one reason why I wrote this book. One thing we know about Rush fans is that they *really* love this band, and that this band means a lot to them.

The next natural question is *why*?

Why do so many millions of us feel this kinship with three Canadian musicians—nice guys by all accounts—whom the majority of us have never met? Why did Neil's lyrics and the band's playing speak to us so deeply? And how, exactly, did the music of Rush affect our lives?

As with the concert memories we sampled in Chapter V, the fans who took my survey were incredibly open and generous in sharing their personal stories about what Rush means to them. We'll get into those later in the chapter, but first I want to examine the deep and heartfelt connection between Rush and what some have called the world's most dedicated fan base.[2]

DIFFERENT BUT THE SAME

The relationship between the band and its fans is one aspect of 2016's *Time Stand Still* documentary: "Rush had built their reputation the hard way: on the road. Their strange flavor and singular sound ignited a deep connection with their fans unlike anything else in modern music."[3] But it was more than just Rush's live prowess that forged this bond.[4] This book takes a further look at this phenomenon, and will offer my own conclusion based upon the evidence I've uncovered in my research and from the fans I queried as a part of this project.

There are other reasons speculated as to why fans identify so strongly with Rush. "Rush fans are sort of united behind the idea that the band has always been underappreciated, and it never really got its due," fan Jason Flynn told the Minneapolis *Star Tribune* in in 2013.[5] I can see this underdog, us-against-them

---

2   *See, e.g.,* Peter Noble of London's Noble PR in Steve Adams, "Canadian Icons Find Fans Everywhere: Loyal International Followers Wait Years Between Rush Tours," *Billboard*, May 15, 2004, available at https://books.google.com/books?id=1hAEAAAAM-BAJ&pg=PA42&lpg=PA42&dq=rush+world%27s+most+dedicated+fans&source=bl&ots=yNFjU512sL&sig=ACfU3U3q5bA9c4172-X55qQOoVVgd1NKI-g&hl=en&sa=X&ved=2ahUKEwj13u3_w_rpAhVzgXIEHbRrCssQ6AEwAnoE-CAkQAQ#v=onepage&q=rush%20world's%20most%20dedicated%20fans&f=false, last accessed June 15, 2020.
3   *Rush: Time Stand Still* (Documentary, 2016).
4   *See* Chapter V: The Freedom of Music.
5   Chris Riemenschneider, "Kiss', Rush's fairly fanatical fans: When Rush and Kiss hit the State Fair, they'll bring some of the nuttiest, most diehard -- we didn't say geeky -- fans in all of rock," *Star Tribune*, August 17, 2013, available at https://www.startribune.com/kiss-rush-s-fairly-fanatical-fans/101575683/, last accessed June 15, 2020.

aspect as a *part* of this bond—and I can relate. But I don't think it's the most *important* one.

Is it the band's integrity? As Brendan Babineaux put it in *Vie* magazine:

> Rush has consistently written music, not to satisfy a record company's idea of a hit record, but to remain loyal to the core of what Rush is: a band determined to stay true to themselves while relying on their core fan base to partake in the musical journey with them.[6]

Again, this is a huge part of the band's appeal, but there has to be something besides the band's stubborn refusal to bow to trends and to the bean-counters that keeps this fan base so loyal, some connection between the *music* and the *listener*. After all, how did this band who went from hard, complex prog to more accessible radio rock to keyboard-drenched pop and back again keep the fans along for the ride and even grow their fan base? "The fans have been behind this band with a devotion that's just inspiring," Donna Halper explains. "You know have generations of RUSH families. You have people turning their kids onto RUSH."[7] That's a remarkable feat for any band, but particularly astounding for one who has changed up their sound so much over the years.

This multi-generational aspect of Rush fandom is particularly interesting. I spoke to my longtime friend and former bandmate Marc Brennan, a drummer, about this.

> From my experience, I was able to learn drums for "Anthem" and "Bastille Day" by listening to my Dad's record album, then I was able to jam with him because he already learned guitar parts years earlier! It's a cool experience that fos-

---
6 Brendan Babineaux, "Rush: Caught In The Camera Eye," *Vie*, Fall 2011, available at http://viemagazine.com/article/rush/, last accessed June 15, 2020.
7 Vinay Menon, *Rush: An Oral History* (Toronto Star Newspapers Limited, 2013), at 49.

ters learning, bonding, and builds confidence.[8]

How cool is that?

Most rock groups who make such dramatic musical turns tend to *shed* the old fans as they pick up new ones, removing a lot of the fan continuity. Not Rush. It's astonishing to listen to *A Farewell to Kings*, released in 1977, and then *Hold Your Fire*, released a mere ten years later. "Is this the same band that did 'Xanadu'?" you might wonder after listening to a track like "Prime Mover." And equally as astonishing to realize yes it is. The *nucleus* is there. The Rush *sound* is there. But at the same time, it still sounds different.

There's more to the story here, and I think one particular profile in *Time Stand Still* crystallizes just why this band means so much to so many people.

EVERYDAY GLORY

"Everyday Glory," the final song on Rush's 1993 *Counterparts* album, is an anthemic, bittersweet, and ultimately hopeful song detailing the struggles of ordinary people who rise to the occasion and triumph over whatever hardships life throws at them:

> In the city where nobody smiles
> And nobody dreams
> In the city where desperation
> Drives the bored to extremes
> Just one spark of decency
> Against a starless night
> One glow of hope and dignity
> A child can follow the light

For Scottish Rush fan George Summers, the song became a rallying cry as he recovered from a horrific car accident that

---

8   Marc Brennan, interview with the author, September 28 – October 9 (Appendix E).

should have killed him; though he survived, he was told he would never walk again:

> There's obviously songs which mean an awful lot to me, while I was in the hospital. "Everyday Glory," just rising up and being able to do stuff again. The one that perhaps says the most is "Rise from where you've been, from the ashes." It sounds awfully dramatic. But you know, I was dead.[9]

The 1998 car accident—a 90-foot plunge—killed George's friend who was driving. His legs shattered, his back fractured, his spine punctured, on fire, and drowned, George spent six months alone recuperating far from home. "So what's going to inspire you then?" he asks. "You listen to music."[10]

Alone, with doctors telling him he'd never walk again, George cranked up the Rush and thought to himself "Yes I am." And he did. Though he walks with a cane, *he can walk*. And watching him speak in *Time Stand Still*, hearing the emotion in his voice, there is no doubt that Rush's music and Neil's lyrics played a huge part in his recovery.

> *Everyday people*
> *Everyday shame*
> *Everyday promise shot down in flames*
> *Everyday sunrise*
> *Another everyday story*
> *Rise from the ashes*
> *A blaze of everyday glory*

Who is George Summers but one everyday man in a situation that most certainly does *not* happen every day? Everyday victims can easily fall prey to despair—a massive detriment to any sort of physical recovery. But George's is an inspiring story,

---

9 George Summers in *Rush: Time Stand Still* (Documentary, 2016).
10 *Id.*

that of an everyman who refused to let his bad situation define him and instead defined himself by how he reacted to it, rising from the ashes to walk again.

It's really amazing, and many thanks to George for being brave enough to share it on camera. His story speaks to the power that art can have to affect our lives in a positive way. And George made it to see Rush on their final show, August 1 2015 in Los Angeles . . . the same day as his 1998 car accident.

These are the stories that warm the soul of any artist. This is the power of Rush. This is why fans have stuck with the band through thick and thin, through every stylistic shift and musical interlude, through every hiatus and on every tour. Some may say this is hokey, but Rush is truly a special band. I know for a fact that there are so many other wonderful, talented, and inspiring musicians, artists, and writers who have helped their fans through tough times. But the Rush phenomenon is one of the most special, and few single stories illustrate this as well as George's.

THE WORDSMITH

"If you've ever felt like an outsider," says Donna Halper, "if you've ever felt not understood, if you've ever felt different, if you've ever felt not taken seriously, there's a Rush lyric for you."[11] She's right, of course. It's impossible to downplay the prominent role Neil Peart's words play in the bond between Rush and their fans and the meaning their music has in fans' lives. Whether fair or not, a band's lyricist has as much, if not more, of an impact on the listener than most other members, even the lead singer.

Neil had a gift for taking complex thoughts, making them coherent, and writing them in a way that spoke to the listener directly. "Neil's lyrics, his specifically, seem to really speak to people . . . as if they were written for them," says Ed Stenger.[12] Peart's

---

11 Donna Halper, interview with the author, February 11, 2020 (Appendix B).
12 Ed Stenger, interview with the author, May 19, 2020 (Appendix C).

presence in the band was so massive that, although it was Geddy Lee singing, it really feels as though it's Neil Peart *speaking*.

We've already discussed in Chapter II how the song "Subdivisions" resonated with a wide swath of Rush fans, but other songs have had similar impacts. "Everyday Glory" is one, and another is "The Pass" from 1989's *Presto*. "The Pass" is Peart's paean to hope in the face of the burgeoning teenage suicide epidemic, and is especially poignant to anyone who has felt alone, misunderstood, and hopeless:

> *Proud swagger out of the schoolyard*
> *Waiting for the world's applause*
> *Rebel without a conscience*
> *Martyr without a cause*
>
> *Static on your frequency*
> *Electrical storm in your veins*
> *Raging at unreachable glory*
> *Straining at invisible chains*
>
> *And now you're trembling on a rocky ledge*
> *Staring down into a heartless sea*
> *Can't face life on a razor's edge*
> *Nothings what you thought it would be*
>
> *All of us get lost in the darkness*
> *Dreamers learn to steer by the stars*
> *All of us do time in the gutter*
> *Dreamers turn to look at the cars*
> *Turn around and turn around and turn around*
> *Turn around and walk the razor's edge*
> *Don't turn your back*
> *And slam the door on me*
>
> *It's not as if this barricade*
> *Blocks the only road*
> *It's not as if you're all alone*

In wanting to explode

Someone set a bad example
Made surrender seem all right
The act of a noble warrior
Who lost the will to fight

And now you're trembling on a rocky ledge
Staring down into a heartless sea
Done with life on a razor's edge
Nothings what you thought it would be

All of us get lost in the darkness
Dreamers learn to steer by the stars
All of us do time in the gutter
Dreamers turn to look at the cars
Turn around and turn around and turn around
Turn around and walk the razor's edge
Don't turn your back
And slam the door on me

No hero in your tragedy
No daring in your escape
No salutes for your surrender
Nothing noble in your fate
Christ, what have you done?

All of us get lost in the darkness
Dreamers learn to steer by the stars
All of us do time in the gutter
Dreamers turn to look at the cars
Turn around and turn around and turn around
Turn around and walk the razor's edge
Turn around and walk the razor's edge
Turn around and walk the razor's edge
Don't turn your back
And slam the door on me

As it has been said many times, Peart never condescends, he never lashes, and he never casts blame. Despite eschewing the cheap way of scoring lyrical points, Peart managed to make emotional connections with millions of listeners.

Yet Peart's lyrics would not have nearly the impact they do without the exquisite music written by Alex Lifeson and Geddy Lee. There is something profound about words set to music that makes them resonate more than they would on paper alone. This is not to discount poetry, but merely to highlight the powerful synergy that music and words can have together, even in an art form so often considered "low" like rock and roll. It's this marriage of music and lyrics,[13] the notes helping deliver the message, that makes songs like "The Pass" and "Everyday Glory" so powerful. As another famous Canadian, Marshall McLuhan famously put it, the medium *is* the message. And Rush's medium—kick-ass, intelligent rock n' roll—is the perfect medium for Peart's lyrical messages.

A DELICATE BALANCE

Neil Peart writes the words, but Geddy Lee has to sing them. "Look how many books he reads. Look at the words he uses," Lee recalls upon first getting to know Peart. "This guy is probably capable of writing lyrics."[14] And these lyrics are sometimes, in Lee's words, a "mouthful": "It was really stimulating, but really a mouthful to sing in the kind of rocking style that we were doing at that time."[15] Indeed, Peart's lyrics fundamentally changed the way Lee sang, and they also changed the way Lee viewed himself as a frontman singing words that he did not write himself:

---

13   For a great explanation of the synergy between Lee and Peart and how Geddy assists in the lyric-writing process, see the documentary *The Game of Snakes & Arrows* (2007) about the making of the album of the same name.
14   *Rush: Beyond the Lighted Stage* (Documentary, 2010).
15   *Id.*

> When Neil gives me a sheet of lyrics, he gives me complete license to use what I respond to, or not to use. And a lot of the songs on records . . . he might write a page and I'll only like four lines on a page. And I'll take those four lines and I'll be able to use them and make them meaningful. And it's not always that I don't like them. It's just what I can bring something them, what I feel I can use. So it has to be lyrics I strongly respond to. So I can take those four lines and I'll put them in a song and then I'll give him the song and then he'll rewrite a whole other song around those four lines . . . And he also has great sympathy for me as writer, as a melody writer, and as a vocalist. And he realizes that certain ways that he may be able to express a though will not translate vocally comfortably . . . The marriage of his thoughts and my feelings as a singer, I have to feel, I have to interpret those, so I have to believe them, and I have to believe them as if they were my thoughts.[16]

"I'll give Geddy a bunch of lyrics to go through," Neil Peart explains in *Rush: An Oral History*. "Sometimes he'll find one verse that he likes and I'll be happy as can be. And he'll say, 'Well, if I just had another one like this, or take these lines and switch them around,' I'm inspired by that, not threatened or humiliated by it. It's respectful and inspiring."[17]

Not every singer could make lines like "Begin the day with a friendly voice, a companion unobtrusive," "The slackjaw gaze of true profanity feels more like surrender than defeat," or "Energy is contagious, enthusiasm spreads/Tides respond to lunar gravitation, everything turns in synchronous relation" flow as

---

16 *The Game of Snakes & Arrows* (Documentary, 2007).
17 Vinay Menon, *Rush: An Oral History* (Toronto Star Newspapers Limited, 2013), at 37.

well as Geddy Lee does. The fact that Lee will only sing what resonates *with him* helps these sometimes verbose stanzas resonate with the listener, and that is truly a form of magic.

"The song says something to you," says Lee. "Your favorite songs say something to you, and they don't necessarily have to be the same thing that the writer intended as long as there's all that possibility."[18] Obviously, some songs, including Rush songs, have messages that are universally accepted; "The Pass" and "Subdivisions" are obvious examples. This directness helps explain why these songs, as well as those like "Everyday Glory," resonate so deeply with fans.

The two songs that helped Rush cement its status as a world-class rock band, "2112" and "Tom Sawyer," are also relatively direct in their exhortations to stand up for your beliefs against the weight of the masses, although the latter is couched in some more labyrinthine metaphors than most rebellious rock songs. It's telling that these two songs are perhaps Rush's most famous tunes, though this same message is also made explicitly clear in songs like "Anthem," "Something For Nothing," "Freewill," and "Show Don't Tell."

Yet Neil Peart's lyrical output doesn't exclusively focus on the theme of resistance to social norms and pressures. Songs like "Entre Nous," "Open Secrets," and "Presto" discuss love and relationships in mature and often quite beautiful language. "The Spirit of Radio" touches upon a communal aspect of modern life that any listener born between 1940 and 1990 can relate to. "Ghost Rider" explores how we heal from tragedy, while "One Little Victory" is a bracing anthem about the power of small steps. "The Big Money" takes a critical and even-handed look at the costs and benefits of massive wealth and power. "Superconductor" touches upon the phony nature of the entertainment business, and "Limelight" is perhaps the most insightful exploration of the concept of fame ever recorded by a rock group.

Needless to say, they lyrical content of Rush's songs covers a vast amount of ground; inevitable when you consider they've

---

18 *The Game of Snakes & Arrows* (Documentary, 2007).

recorded 40 years' worth of songs. But unlike some bands who tread the same sex, drugs, and rock n' roll ground, Peart continuously looked for new things to write about, and fresh angles to approach old tropes, with the same vigor that Lee and Lifeson pushed the boundaries of Rush's music.

Taken in isolation, Neil Peart's lyrics read like poetry; if you disagree, just read something like "Closer to the Heart" or "Losing It" and get back to me. On their own, absent any musical accompaniment, Peart's words are evocative and impactful, full of rich imagery, clever metaphors, and enough emotion to make a Romantic poet proud. But combined with the music, their impact is even stronger—the words graft themselves onto your brain in such a profound way that thorny stanzas like "Well-oiled leather, hot metal and oil, the scented country air," and "She's got a liquid-crystal compass, a picture book of the rivers under the Sahara" seem to roll off the tongue.

What is it about the power of words melded to music that is stronger than the sum of each individual part? This isn't a phenomenon unique to Rush's music, but given the high quality and sheer level of thought and deliberation that goes into Peart's lyrics, I think it's worth delving into this part of the Rush phenomenon and perhaps better understand *why* the music of this band is so important to so many people.

A BEAUTIFUL MARRIAGE

Music has a pulse, and it is this pulse, this physical aspect, which helps the music connect with the listener. However, as musicologist Daniel J. Levitin explains, "Music communicates to us emotionally through systematic violations of expectations."[19] Very often, the biggest impact in a piece of music, whether rock and roll, classical, or jazz, occurs when you *don't* get the thing you expected to get.

---

19 Daniel J. Levitin, *This Is Your Brain on Music: The Science of a Human Obsession* (Dutton, 2006), at 168.

These violations can occur in any domain—the domain of pitch, timbre, contour, rhythm, tempo, and so on—but occur they must. Music is organized sound, but the organization has to involve some element of the unexpected or itis emotionally flat and robotic. Too much organization may technically still be music, but it would be music that no one wants to listen to. Scales, for example, are organized, but most parents get sick of hearing their children play them after five minutes.[20]

It's interesting that one of the criticisms historically lobbied at Rush is that their music is too "technical" (whatever that means) or too "robotic"; it's almost as if the ones making these comments haven't really ever *listened* to it. In fact, I would argue that it's this violation of expectations that makes so much of Rush's music exciting and memorable in songs like "La Villa Strangiato," "YYZ," "Headlong Flight," and "2112" to name a few.

Here are a few more dramatic examples: Most rock and pop songs have choruses that ramp up the speed, intensity, volume, or all three. With this in mind, think about songs like "The Analog Kid" and "Ghost of a Chance." They have what I like to call "reverse-choruses" in that they become more spacious and *slower* than the verses. They stick in your memory because they are so different than what happened before and what happens after. This is an important aspect about music to remember: *Everything* depends upon the context in which it is played, what happens before any given note is played, and where things goes next. After all, taken in isolation, a note is just a note.

So that helps us with the musical portion. What about when the music is the delivery medium for lyrics? What does *this* marriage, the one between notes and words, do to our brain?

---

20 *Id.* at 168-169.

First, it's important to note that the human brain binds a piece of music—both the notes and the lyrics—to the brain *better* when the words and music are presented as a unified package as opposed to reading the lyrics while the melody is played or sung in the background.[21] We've already discussed the ways in which music can affect the listener's emotions, and there is ample literature to back this up.[22] But while "[m]usic has long been an effective way to communicate to the masses," it can't be stated enough that "lyrics have played a massive role," especially in the twentieth and twenty-first centuries where the overwhelming majority of popular music contains lyrics.[23]

The lyrics to a piece of music have been shown to affect the listener's mood, which in turn can affect their thoughts. This concept is axiomatic to most anyone reading this book, but there is scientific evidence to back up the anecdotal evidence. And one obvious, long-running concern is the possible *negative* effects song lyrics may on listeners:

> Another paper, published in 2003 in the Journal of Personality and Social Psychology, reported that music can incite aggressive thoughts and feelings. During five experiments with 75 female and 70 male college students, those who heard a violent song were shown to feel more hostile than those who heard a nonviolent song, from the same artist and style.

---

21 *See, e.g.,* Irene Alonso, Lila Davachi, Romaine, Lila Valabrègue, Virginie Lambrecq, Sophie Dupont, and Séverine Samsona, "Neural correlates of binding lyrics and melodies for the encoding of new songs," in *Neurolmage*, Volume 127, February 15, 2016, at 333-345; *see also* Dr. Victoria Williamson, "Brain binding of music and lyrics," *Music Psychology*, April 4, 206, available at https://musicpsychology.co.uk/brain-binding-of-music-and-lyrics/, last accessed June 17, 2020.
22 *See, e.g.,* Nina Avramova, "How music can change the way you feel and act," *CNN.com*, February 20, 2019, available at https://www.cnn.com/2019/02/08/health/music-brain-behavior-intl/index.html, last accessed June 17, 2020.
23 Patricia Fox Ransom, "Message in the Music: Do Lyrics Influence Well-Being?" University of Pennsylvania Scholarly Commons, 2015, at 11, available at https://www.semanticscholar.org/paper/Message-in-the-Music%3A-Do-Lyrics-Influence-Ransom/62f125035fa55c5b801f4dc951a320b2b5cbaa8f, last accessed June 17, 2020.

The study showed that violent songs led to more aggressive thoughts in three different measures: More aggressive interpretations when looking at ambiguous words, an increased speed with which people read aggressive compared to non-aggressive words and a greater proportion of people completing aggressive words when filling in blanks on forms given to them during the study.

One way to put these findings, say the authors, is that participants who listened to violent rock songs then interpret the meaning of ambiguous words such as "rock" and "stick" in an aggressive way.

The study adds that the outcomes of hostile thoughts could be short-lived. If the next song's lyrics are nonviolent or if some other nonviolent event occurs, the effects of violent lyrics will dissipate, states the paper.[24]

The idea that pop music, be it rock or hip-hop or whatever, can affect behavior is as controversial as the idea that things like video games can affect behavior. A detailed exploration of the truth or falsehood of these claims is beyond the scope of this book, but I think it's disingenuous to claim that music and lyrics, and music coupled with lyrics, has *no* discernable effect on the listener whatsoever. After all, if it didn't, then the responses I solicited from fans asking what Rush's music meant to them, and all of these stories about how Rush has helped people through hard times, would be nothing more than made-up nonsense with no rational reason to exist beyond the realm of

---

24 Nina Avramova, "How music can change the way you feel and act," *CNN.com*, February 20, 2019, available at https://www.cnn.com/2019/02/08/health/music-brain-behavior-intl/index.html, last accessed June 17, 2020.

an individual respondent's flight of fancy, and I therefore should not take *any* of these stories seriously.

I fundamentally reject that stance, both because it's unfair based upon my own experience, and also because I don't think anyone who responded to my survey is crazy.[25] Nor do I think the science explaining the link between music, music and lyrics, and mood is somehow bogus or flawed. In fact, based upon what I've seen as a layman *and what I've experienced as a musician*, I find it quite compelling.

Patricia Fox Ransom's paper on the relatively under-studied relationship between lyrics and mood nails a few key points that pertain to Neil's lyrics. "[S]ad song lyrics," writes Ransom, "can sometimes bring about pleasant feelings. This happens when a listener feels understood by an artist."[26] This is no different from Donna Halper's assertion that "If you've ever felt like an outsider, if you've ever felt not understood, if you've ever felt different, if you've ever felt not taken seriously, there's a Rush lyric for you."[27] Fan Phil Mele relates: "As a lonely disenfranchised adolescent, I would read the lyrics to their songs and somewhere along the way I realized there were other people that thought about the things that I thought about."[28]

Ransom, however, does not stop at sad songs; indeed, the focus of her paper is on lyrics' ability to influence *positive* well-being. Music *can* influence a listener's mood or well-being without the listener's consent,[29] but I think it's safe to say that most people listen to Rush of their own free will, absent an older sibling or a parent "torturing" you by playing Rush in the car or somewhere else. So there's something about this music and the accompanying words that makes people want to keep listening, again and again, for decades.

Could it be that it makes them *feel good*? Or to put it more precisely, could it be that it gives the listener *meaning*? The na-

25 For the record, though, *I* might be the crazy one for trying to write a book like this.
26 Ransom, "Message in the Music" at 12.
27 Donna Halper, interview with the author, February 11, 2020 (Appendix B).
28 Phil Mele, response to author's survey, February 9, 2020 (Appendix A).
29 Ransom, "Message in the Music," at 14.

scent research into the power of lyrics suggests that lyrics, similar to religious worship and other spiritual practices, can give people meaning and thus increase their well-being: "When individuals understand where they find meaning in their own lives they understand a little more about themselves. This self-understanding is important for many reasons. It may provide clarity into who we are and how we make decisions. The more meaning you have in your life the higher your well-being."[30]

It's a fascinating area of research, and even though I am nowhere near being considered an expert, or even particularly well-versed in it, I think Ransom is on to something. Art affects people's moods—this is why we like it. And Rush tends to be a very positive, upbeat band with an empowering message that never casts aspersions or blame on others . . . or the listener. "Songs like 'Subdivisions,' 'Losing It,' and 'The Pass' have helped me realize that I'm not alone in dealing with certain things that affect me (such as depression, anxiety, and feeling like I don't fit in with any social groups)," says fan David S. "Just knowing that I'm not the only one who deals with this sort of stuff, and to listen to lyrics on these topics by my favorite band of all time, means the world to me."[31]

In a sharp contrast to *Blender* calling Neil Peart the second-worst lyricist in rock history,[32] none other than *SPIN* magazine eulogized Peart by highlighting his five most powerful lyrics, in writer Christa Titus's opinion, "five songs in which his [Peart's] writing succinctly captured the wonders of the human condition—a state of being that, despite his own darkest moments, he embraced with optimism."[33] These are, from five to one, "Mystic Rhythms," "Resist," "Subdivisions," "The Pass," and "Bravado."

What's striking in light of the research we have just discussed is not the songs Titus chose for her top five, but the lan-

---

30 *Id.* at 15 (citations omitted).
31 David S., response to author's survey, February 5, 2020 (Appendix A).
32 *See* Chapter III: Boys and Girls Together.
33 Christa Titus, "Remembering 5 of Neil Peart's Most Powerful Song Lyrics," *SPIN*, January 17, 2020, available at https://www.spin.com/2020/01/neil-peart-rush-powerful-song-lyrics/, last accessed June 18, 2020.

guage she uses in describing their impact. Here, for example, is a portion of her take on "The Pass":

> Peart avoids clichéd platitudes that can make emotional suffering worse by recognizing the legitimacy of one's problems when he points out, "All of us get lost in the darkness ... all of us do time in the gutter" (another Wilde reference). He acknowledges adolescents' malleable spirits ("Someone set a bad example/made surrender seem all right"), but he also de-romanticizes the fatal act by declaring, "No hero in your tragedy/no daring in your escape/no salutes for your surrender/nothing noble in your fate." While the track is resolute and—by Rush norms—sparse, Lifeson's defiant guitar solo and the finale signal the dogged hope that the narrator holds for the future.[34]

Peart, Titus notes, "recognizes the legitimacy" of teenagers' problems, echoing Ransom's assertion that sad songs can elicit positive emotions when the listener feels as though the lyricist understands them.

As an aside, "The Pass" shows up in survey responses quite a bit, and understandably so. For example, Professor Christy Tondeur cites *Presto* as her favorite album because "'The Pass' helped me through family suicide attempts. It's my emotional favorite."[35]

Likewise with "Subdivisions": Titus keys in on Peart's recognition and understanding of the teenage mindset:

> If you're a suburban kid with your creature comforts met, you're likely expected to have few complaints. Peart captures the disquiet

---

34 *Id.*
35 Professor Cristy Tondeur, response to author's survey, February 5, 2020 (Appendix A).

that lingers in the psyche of those who others assume live a carefree life. It's not only peer pressure that high schoolers struggle with "in the basement bars/in the backs of cars"; it's the discontent with the expectation to follow paths predetermined by authority figures.[36]

And with regards to "Bravado," "what matters is that you just go for it; the swagger you earn is for your tenacity, not grasping the prize."[37] What a bracing and encouraging message set to some of Rush's most gorgeous music.

I think I have shown that the deep connection Rush fans feel with the band's music and the meaning they derive from it is because these songs help *give* people meaning in their lives, and on balance provide listeners with an overwhelming sense of *positive* emotion. There are no angsty, angry diatribes blaming parents or women or men or society. There are only epic tales of adventure and discovery, celebrations of life and nature and all it has to offer, and above all the idea that *you* are in control of your life, that what *you* think and feel matters, and that *you* can make a difference on a large scale and small . . . and sometimes those small victories are the greatest ones of all.

SPEAK TO ME

One of the questions I asked in my survey was "What does Rush's music mean to you?" I asked this not to pry—well, maybe a *little*—but to drill down into *why* Rush fans are so passionate. As with the section on fans' concert memories in Chapter V, now is the perfect time to let the fans speak for themselves (all responses are in Appendix A). Here is a selection of some of the great responses fans were so generous in providing. In these stories, you'll find many examples of the concepts discussed in

---

36 Christa Titus, "Remembering 5 of Neil Peart's Most Powerful Song Lyrics," *SPIN*, January 17, 2020.
37 *Id.*

this chapter, as well as the previous five, and as I'm sure you will note, prove that I wasn't totally off my rocker in trying to explain why this band means so much to so many people:

> Rush's music, and Neil's accompanied lyrics and books, have honestly helped save my life numerous times over. I was really depressed starting when I was 11 or 12 up until I started playing bass guitar at 15 years old. From the beginning of becoming a musician, I continually challenged myself as I quickly grew bored with playing Top 40 hits and other popular music from the 80s and 90s that I had been exposed to at that point.
>
> After a few months of obsessing over *Moving Pictures* and prior Rush albums, I decided to just buy them all in chronological order a few at a time, as I had just gotten my first job and had my own disposable income. Seeing how much this band had progressed and changed their sound really inspired me musically.
>
> By the time I was 17 a little album dropped in my lap called *Presto*. I thought it sounded very empty, tinny, and the lyrics didn't really connect with me well at first. And then I got to "The Pass." I still, to this day, and maybe even more so since Neil's passing, get emotional and simultaneous goosebumps when I hear this song. I researched the meaning behind it and found it was about teenage suicide. A concept that, I was all too familiar with, as an acquaintance in high school had recently committed suicide. The fact Neil challenged the virtue or point of suicide on a literal level, rather than just pandering to the other common talking

points about suicide, has honestly helped me break that thought in my brain. I have rarely contemplated suicide in my life since hearing this song.

It was shortly after I had caught up to current with Rush, at that time *Test for Echo* was their last album and *Vapor Trails* had just been announced, that I wanted more! I had purchased the majority of their discography via Amazon, and they had recommended a book of his that was recently released called *Ghost Rider: Travels on the Healing Road*. And it blew me away. I read the entire book in one weekend, reading for hours and hours at a time. Even now, after dozens of times reading it, I read it in a similar fashion each time. I cannot accurately summarize how much that book has meant to me. For tragedy strikes us all in one form or another, and Neil's humility, honesty, quest for meaning, and brutal honesty are amazing.

Since that book, Rush has released a few more albums, which I also love, Neil has written a few more books, and I have been fortunate to see them live twice, when many of my friends who share my passion for Rush have not been fortunate to see them at all. I will forever treasure seeing them on their farewell tour.

And as I find myself in the wake of Neil's departure from this earth as obsessed with their music at 34 that I was at 17, it is a humbling reminder of so many things he wrote and said about life, and living it to the fullest. Suddenly, he is gone from our lives, but there is a level of

respect and bliss that I now recognize from the mark he left upon this world.
— David B., aka Dave2112

The great thing about Rush is that they did their own thing, and were successful at it. They wrote music that may not appeal to everyone, but they still filled big arenas and sold lots of albums. The music is just so interesting, there's so much going on. And they had the talent that others couldn't even approach.
— Donne Puckle

It's a soundtrack to my adult life. I'm proud that in 1985 when I bought Power Windows my friends ridiculed me because they were into New Wave and punk rock and they thought I was an old dinosaur. Throughout these decades I would burn out on Rush and not play them for a year or two and then they come out with a new album and blow me away I would dive into the new stuff and then pull out my old Rush music and play it all over again. There are tears rolling down my cheeks right now because I'll never get to do that again. Rush has always been there; it's always been a part of my life. I would drive along in the car and Neil Peart lyrics could help me think of something beyond myself. Rush effectively has become a part of who I am. I'll always have the history but it's sad to think I'm not going to get any more lyrics or music from Neil Peart.
— Steven Patri, super fan

Music that has inspired me to expand my horizons, my perspective on where music can go and where it can take you. Makes me feel com-

fortable to embrace my inner nerd and celebrate it out loud. They definitely inspired me to practice like a maniac to be as superior on my instrument as the three of them were. Maybe Rush was never a "cool" band but they made a home for weirdos and outcasts to be cool.
– Andy Taylor

Timeline of my life. I came to California to be a professional drummer because of my Rush influences. Life went a different way and has been great. I like to think Rush helped me get to where I am.
– Mike M.

Everything. It's why I started playing music. Rush is that cornerstone in my life that makes me feel complete and if I never found Rush, I don't think I would of found anything to replace it.
– J. Rhodes

Honestly, it means the world to me. Rush were always there for me, and always will be. I would have literally ended my life in High School, but for some reason "Everyday Glory" (lyrics and music) kept me fighting another day.
– Rob Mallory

Awareness of humanity, killer musicians who don't conform to the norm.
– Kent Schaaf

Believe in yourself. BE yourself, it's OK to be different because there are others just like you.
– JZ

This is difficult to answer. I could say "everything," but that's not quite right. "Everything" is my family, my wife and kids. I'll paraphrase what I said about this on my blog:

The music you love passes the barriers of reason and memory and goes straight into the core of your being. And I LOVE that music. The music Rush made tapped into my brain and went straight to my heart. It's literally part of me. That's why it hit so hard when Neal Peart died. I don't actually know anyone in the band, and they never knew me—but their songs had a window into my soul. It sounds overwrought to say it like that, but it's the truth.

– Ing

It has been my saving grace, my Foundation and something that kept me going even in the darkest, loneliest times. I have always touted their integrity and talent.

Friends I have not seen in years will tell me "Every time I hear a RUSH song, I think of you." That means a lot to me. One other thought/fanism: when I worked at a local radio station, WCCC in Hartford, I even went by the on air name "David Rush!"

– Dave B.

Lots of things, but I'll mention three:

1. Rush music forms the basis for my own approach to songwriting. I think in their "language" when I write riffs, melodies, and lyrics, almost to the point where I have to make a conscious effort not to plagiarize the band.

2. Most of their songs are so familiar to me now, like dear friends. They bring me comfort and consolation and I know them by heart. And yet, I consistently discover new things about them. It's such a wonderful thought, that I will never stop listening to them, and they will never cease to find new ways to inspire me.

3. At the risk of sounding pretentious, I am a synesthete, which means that my different senses overlap in weird ways. Among other things, I can see music. When I listen to any Rush song, what I see is a unique and sublime tapestry of beautiful shapes, colors and textures. I just love to completely lose myself in that experience every now and then."
– Ossian C.

My words to Neil have always been, "Thank you for giving voice to that which my soul knew but for which it had no words." Geddy has said, live, "thanks for keeping us company." I say, "thanks for keeping me company, for being the soundtrack of my life and the voice of rationalism and encouragement."
– Library Liz

Being a musician, I always hear the music first and the lyrics follow. With RUSH, once I get

to the lyrics, I discover the depth of the stories portrayed by Neil Peart. I even started reading books by authors that had a big influence on Neil; in particular, Ayn Rand.
– Ray "Stix" Dalli

Rush got me through all of the dark times I can remember. When I was depressed, I could find songs that would remind me there was more to life than what I was feeling in that moment. I met some of my best friends because we had Rush in common. Neil's drumming inspired me to be a better musician and his lyrics inspired me to be a better person.
– Derek G.

It's meant the world. I had told a few close friends that had been long time Rush fans with me (attended the GUP and PoW shows together) that although it didn't register at the time, many of life's most important lessons had their greatest impact when taught through lyrics and prose. My parents were great and they taught me all the important lessons I needed, but they never really sank in until I heard them in a lyric or read an example in a story.

Neil's lyrics so often illuminated ideas and feelings that I had felt, but never really articulated. When I heard the lyrics to "Subdivisions," that song was specifically about me at that exact moment in time (and many like me). There are so many songs like that in the Rush catalog—"Freewill," "Witch Hunt," "Hemispheres," "The Analog Kid," "Bravado," "Roll the Bones," "Faithless," the list goes on and on.

I've always thought of Rush as closer to family than just a band. We share very similar upbringings, ethics, senses of humor, and it's on so many levels that I feel a connection. I would want to be their friends if they were just regular guys at work and not members of this band. I think it's the consistency of their philosophies, characters, and just their personalities that makes them stand the test of time. Rush has been one of the longest and most reliable sources of joy, wonder, inspiration, and delight in my entire life and I'm forever grateful for their music and words.
– Darren Hightower

Going to concerts with friends and being a part of something that the mainstream didn't understand.
– Ben W.

Their music felt to me to be aimed at people who did not fit in with others when I started listening to them. See lyrics of "Subdivisions." Thanks to my older brother[38] for introducing me to Rush when we went to a KISS concert and Rush was the opening act.
–Scott W.

It's the music of a lifetime. I almost can't remember them not being a part in my world. My two brothers are no longer here but I have so many memories and our appreciation for the band that we shared lives on every time I hear anything from the massive Rush catalogue. I could read Neil's books or the stories from his

---

38   *Lots* of fans got introduced to Rush by older brothers; see the complete survey responses in Appendix A.

website over and over and still get something out of them. I think that will always be true.
– Kelly

My older brother was a drummer, so I liked them for Neil's drumming and Alex's guitar playing. I just loved everything about their sound.
– Ken Scott

I still vividly remember the day I was walking home from primary school and heard "The Spirit of Radio" blaring from somebody's car. WHAT WAS THAT?! It was my first rock and roll, the first time I heard a driving 4/4 time, wah-wah guitar. That was the sound of escape, freedom... everything that was good. Not long after my brother and I had a Moving Pictures cassette that kept wearing out and had to be bought over and over again. Signals was the first album I ever bought brand new. I remember poring over the lyrics, playing it over and over again. The album got a bad rap, but I still like it a lot—you just had to listen a bit harder for the guitars, but they are superb. Grace Under Pressure was my first concert. Power Windows my second. And they were/are decent guys. I ran into Geddy Lee at Bloor Cinema in Toronto when I was in university there. Once at an airport check in. He was acting like anyone else. He and Alex Lifeson are lifelong friends and they act like it. I know a former neighbor of Alex Lifeson's—he was a great neighbor. Stuff like that sets them above. I have to confess that I drifted from their music in the later years. The tricky time signatures, the somewhat nutty ar-

rangements. But they did way too much to influence me to ever let them go.
– Andrew D.

Musically there is a weird dichotomy. On the one hand, it's famous for being so difficult for real musicians to play. On the other hand, there's been no other band where I'm able to hear each of the 3 instruments so distinctly, which (as a non-musician) makes it the easiest band in the world to play air guitar, whiffle bat bass, or steering wheel drums. And lyrically, it's just so reliably thought-provoking that even a song or album that doesn't have much appeal musically is worth paying attention to.
– Rocky McDonald

I associate Rush's music with the last hurrah of my youthful idealism. For me, their music made up a great deal of the soundtrack of those segue years between young and full adulthood.
– C. Carrasco

Pretty much everything . . . How to live your life, appreciate reading books, someone is always on your side.
– Vince Benard

I like they continuously challenged themselves and didn't make easy music. I appreciate their dedication to their craft.
– J. Wright

As a young teenager they were my little secret, I had the Starman from 2112 embroidered on the back of my denim jacket and people would ask what it was, but occasionally you'd pass

someone else wearing a Rush badge, and you'd just have a kind of silent exchange with each other, a little smile of acknowledgement—"nobody knows what we know."
– Kirka

Again, I'll paste over some things I wrote at the time of Neil's passing. There's no concise answer here.

"[C]ountless great memories and friendships developed around Rush and Peart. As this 'internet' and 'newsgroups' thing developed, so too did friendships with people from across the globe who seemingly had little else in common apart from an affinity for this band. Some of those online friendships evolved into valued real-life friendships that persist to this day. We've met up in several cities to catch concerts and over the years have seen each other through the ups and downs of life—from personal and professional triumph to break-ups and serious illness—all the while surrounded by constant, irreverent, sometimes brilliant, and sometimes just plain stupid humor. Probably not unlike the band themselves.

"Closer to home, my brother and I, along with other friends and eventually spouses (God bless 'em!) and kids, enjoyed numerous shows. I was fortunate enough to see a few of those from either the front row, or very near it—and let me tell you that watching Peart do his thing from that close is unforgettable. I was close enough to hear his kit as it sounded on stage and could distinguish it from the arena's amplified PA audio. The man was a force. It wasn't just virtuosic. It was downright athletic. Every impact was like a precision guided smart-bomb.

"Popular music has never had, and likely never will have, a better voice for human freedom and progress than Neil Peart and Rush. Over a 40-year span of writing, the styles and quality evolved tremendously, but from 1975 to 2015 there were consistent ideas present. Career spanning themes of the individual's triumph over the collective (as visually expressed by the famous 2112 Starman logo) are pervasive, as are a skepticism of governmental and religious authority, a sympathetic look at non-conformity, along with celebrations of personal fortitude and artistic integrity. Other topics touched on with an intelligence rarely heard in a rock context were the nature of heroism, the embracing of the randomness and uncertainty of our fates, environmental concerns, mindless nationalism, censorship and bigotry, teen suicide, the Cold War and the fall of the Iron Curtain, religious fanaticism and terrorism, the rise of the atomic age, coping with personal tragedy and grief ... hardly the usual rock-n-roll fodder. Even when Peart got political, it was always written in such a way as to be timeless, and not nailed down directly to whatever events of the day prompted it. Songs like "Territories" and "Witch Hunt" are as perfectly applicable to today's world as they were in the 1980s. I'd be lying if I said that his work did not impact my early-adulthood process of sorting out my own worldviews, and though I doubt we'd see everything the same (what two adults do?!), I would not object if someone applied his self-described 'bleeding heart libertarian' label to me.

So thanks, Neil Peart. Drummer, lyricist, travel writer, wanderer, observer of the human condition . . . You were, and will likely remain, and huge part of my life's soundtrack and some of my favorite memories."
– Mike B.

Rush is one of the strongest bonds I have with my husband. I can think of almost every milestone in my relationship and pick a RUSH song for that moment. They were with us when we were planning our life together and they have also given us strength during the hard times.

We have Neil's words engraved on our wedding rings, and we used his words when we can't find how to say it ourselves, RUSH lyrics are our secret code.
– Laura O.

That's a tough question to answer. Like many fans, the Rush songs really strike an emotional chord with me. So, I guess it really depends on the song.

For example, "The Pass" always chokes me up because of its connection with suicide. As someone who has considered committing suicide in the past, I tend to play it whenever I am down, as a reminder.

I also find songs like "Something for Nothing," "Stick It Out," and "Cut to the Chase" to be very inspirational.
– Steve F.

RUSH music kept me sane and alive through middle school and high school. The lyrics combined with such complex musical arrangement was just addictive. What I loved was that they weren't love songs. The lyrics were specific yet vague and it was easy to see yourself in the Peart's imagination. I would put my headphones on, crank the music and disappear into the music.

I have never been a girl's girl. I had more I'm common with my guy friends and we would talk about Rush and even go to concerts together. I also never felt out of place being one of the rare female obsessed RUSH fans.

One of the best parts of a Rush concert, if you are a female fan, are the nonexistent lines for the bathroom!
– Professor Cristy Tondeur

Rush's music means so much to me. Their music, is like a friendship. They are always there for me, regardless of what is going on in my life. I can always rely on those three guys to pull me up, bring me comfort, and hope. They have influenced my musical desires and beliefs, as well as my everyday beliefs. Rush is a way of life.
– Alec T.

Oh god. Can I say "everything"? I mean, not "everything" but . . .

Look. I'm not a musician. I can't tell you, musically, what makes their music so incredible and unique. I couldn't point out a 7/8 time signature if my life depended on it. But like I said before . . . Rush is what I listened to to NOT be sad. There is a vitality, an energy, to their music that resonates with me. Neil's lyrics inspire me. Alex's guitar SOARS like the most majestic eagle. Geddy's voice can give me goosebumps.

I was 14 when I got into them and I'll be 45 this summer. 30 years and though I've grown and changed—and Rush grew and changed in those same years—their music has spoken to me in every phase of my life. Songs that felt like my anthem when I was a teenager still have meaning for me today. A different meaning, but meaning nonetheless. Different lyrics stand out over time; understanding and interpretation shifts. But the songs are still here. Still . . . present.

The band has given me inspiration, support, contemplation, and joy. I first discovered them in one of the darkest periods of my life and they became a beacon of light that has remained bright for 30 years.

I'm not sure I can explain it better than that.

Thanks for letting me talk.
– Craig[39]

    As with the concert memories, I could read these stories forever. They are wonderful, inspirational, humorous, touching, and show just how much Rush and their music connected with listeners, and connect the listeners with each other. Though I only know a few of the respondents personally (Hi Drew! Hi Marc!)

---

[39] My pleasure, Craig. Thanks for taking the time to respond to my survey!

and am friends with a few others on-line (Hi Xavier! Hi Ing!), through writing this book I feel like I have actually gotten to *know* all of you. And I'm continually blown away by how many fans are thanking *me*, when it is *I* who should be thanking *you*.

I am well aware that there are other musical artists who have touched their fans' lives in similarly profound ways, but I also think—and like to think I've provided ample evidence in support of my position—that the Rush phenomenon is different. Fans are different in ethnicity, political bent, religious affiliation, occupation, education, and geography, but there *is* a Rush fan type, with attributes that bind us together through the music. Rush fans are nearly universally thoughtful, independent-minded, big-hearted, and curious. Though not all musicians, all respond to the music in similar ways. These stories are all unique, but the thread that runs through them is that *listening to Rush makes them feel good,* and it *makes them think.*

To Geddy Lee, Alex Lifeson, and Neil Peart, I imagine this is what kept them going for forty-plus years of songwriting, constant musical improvement, and physically and emotionally grueling touring. Theirs is a legacy of people whose lives have been *improved* by sheer dint of being Rush fans. And that, dear reader, is a special thing indeed, one that I don't think you find in all that many rock and roll bands.

I suppose now you may be wondering what Rush means to *me*, your humble author, and how I came to be a fan. I told you I would be a little self-indulgent earlier in this book, so I'd like to briefly discuss my path to Rush fandom and what this band means to me.

MY STORY, WHICH IS NOT ALL THAT IMPRESSIVE

I didn't have an "A-ha!" Rush moment like many fans did. I didn't hear them once and become hooked immediately. In fact, even though my father shared his love of rock and roll with my siblings and me, Rush was something of a joke.

See, my father is a *huge* fan of groups and artists like Led Zeppelin, the Allman Brothers Band, the Rolling Stones, Jimi Hendrix, The Who, David Bowie, The Doors, and The Beatles, but actively disliked Rush.

It wasn't just Geddy Lee's voice, although that was a part of it. My father was never into Pink Floyd either, so I think it's safe to say that prog rock was never his thing. Yes, Vanilla Fudge, ELP, Genesis, Frank Zappa[40] . . . you'd rarely, if ever, hear music by these groups emanating from my dad's stereo. Rush was frivolous, for lack of a better word. I remember laughing in the car when "Tom Sawyer" would come on, the famous keyboard part being a particular source of amusement.

Except . . . I kind of liked it. I liked when the guitar and bass started playing that riff. I liked the drums, the guitar solo, and the *energy*. I was probably twelve at the time, and already a big fan of noted Rush-fans Primus, but I never had the nerve to say, "Hey, you know, this is pretty cool."

I'd be exposed to Rush again shortly thereafter. I play bass and was in a band with some classmates in the eighth grade. Our singer/keyboardists had an older brother who was a wizard on the four-string, and was the first person I ever took lessons from. Anyway, at a party his brother threw that summer, our little band was invited to play for some hundred or so of his friends and family before *his* band of *really cool high-schoolers*. The show was in a huge outdoor field on their land in the wilds of rural New Hampshire. After we had played, my friend's brother put *Chronicles* on the PA and I remember being blown away by "Limelight."

"Who is this?" I asked my buddy.

"This? This is Rush. They're pretty cool."

"Yeah," I said, sort of staring off into space during Alex's guitar solo. I mean, the guitar solo is transcendent, but it was the sound of Geddy's bass that really hooked me.

---

40 Yes, I consider Zappa progressive. And don't get me started on Zappa, because I could write *another* whole book on my love for Frank Zappa.

Flash forward maybe a year later. I'm in high school now and waiting in the car with my mother in the parking lot at our elementary school for my little sister to be finished with some after-school project or other, and "Limelight" comes on again. My attention was galvanized on every note. *What was this strange, wonderful music?* I thought. But then my sister came out, the radio was turned off, and I thought nothing of it.

Flash forward another two years. I'm a junior in high school. The Internet just reached our small town. As an avid reader of *Bass Player* magazine, Geddy Lee always popped up in articles and mentions. I vividly recall one of their "Classic Album" profiles they stuck into each review section. That particular month, the re-review was of *Moving Pictures*. Just reading the descriptions of the songs rekindled my interest in Rush and made me want to buy this album at my earliest convenience.

Before I did that, though, I checked out some tracks from *Moving Pictures* and other albums on the Internet. *Test for Echo* had come out a year or so before, and on one Rush fan site that had a radio station playing a mix of Rush tracks I heard a snippet of "Time and Motion." The *heaviness* of it made me realize Rush was far more multifaceted than I had originally thought.

My music teacher in high school was a wonderful human guy. He was pretty young when I was in high school, in his early thirties, so I asked him about Rush. "Oh yeah, I think you'd like them, being a bass player" he said (that musician connection again!). So when I had the scratch, I bought myself a copy of *Moving Pictures* and eagerly played it on the massive stereo system in my room I had inherited from my father. Or maybe I listened to it on the car stereo—either way, I knew I *had* to hear this album, and somehow deep down I knew I'd love it.

That was my "A-ha!" moment, I guess. Listening to "Tom Sawyer" from start to finish and reading along with the lyrics the way I used to whenever I'd get a new album. My first thought: "Holy cow, this Neil Peart guy really *is* as good as all the music magazines say!" Second: "Geddy Lee's voice isn't nearly as bad as everyone's been telling me," and third, "This sounds like the music of the future."

I vividly recall turning up the volume at the fadeout of "Tom Sawyer" so I could hear more of Neil's drums. Then Alex Lifeson's opening harmonic chimes of "Red Barchetta" tickled my ears and the song really transported me into another headspace. And when "YYZ" came on, and the song kicked into high gear, that was it. I was hooked. I devoted most of my allowance and money from chores and summer jobs to purchasing the rest of the Rush catalogue.

Interestingly, I think *Test for Echo* was the second album I got. My brother and my dad were out and about doing errands, and as per usual hanging out with dad inevitably included a trip to a music store to buy some CDs. Since I wasn't able to go along that time, my brother snagged *Test for Echo* for me, and I loved it.[41] "This is the same band?" I thought at first, before realizing "Oh yeah, this is the same band."

Different Stages was the next one I bought, and it was then that I learned about Neil's personal tragedies. Rush was over. "Oh well," I told myself. "He needs to do what's important. At least there are all these other albums for me to buy."

I remember sitting with my music teacher later that year the same diner I washed dishes at the previous summer to earn enough to buy my first real bass guitar.[42] We were having dinner before our All-State Band performance which happened to be in our town that year. I told him I had bought *Moving Pictures* and that Rush had quickly become my new favorite band.

"What I always liked about them," my music teacher told me (and I'm paraphrasing because it was twenty years ago) "is that their music is so highly orchestrated." That characterization really stuck with me. Every note, every drum hit, and every syllable was calculated for maximum impact. Despite Rush's technical wizardry, not a single note was wasted. *Everything served the song.*

41 On a similar trip with dad I was not a part of, my brother also snagged the *Chronicles* and *A Show of Hands* VHS tapes for me. Great guy, my brother.
42 It was an American standard Precision Bass. Sadly, I had to sell this along with *all of my other music gear* including a black Rickenbacker 4003S and a Geddy Lee Jazz Bass sometime in 2015 to cover my mortgage during a bout of unemployment caused by my return to school. Yes, I'm still bitter about it.

That made me understand the importance of melding technical ability and intentionality. What good is playing tons of notes if they're purposeless? Listening to Rush made me become, if I do say so myself, a really good bass player. I learned so many of their songs, and learning them helped me become a better player in general because there are so many techniques one picks up while playing Geddy's bass lines. And it made me feel really good about myself to pull off tricky passages like the solos in "YYZ" or the middle section of "Freewill." It felt like through their music, anything was possible.

And that's what Rush means to me: *possibilities*.

It wasn't just the musical possibilities either. The intellect and erudition of Neil's lyrics inspired me to make the music I wrote be less boneheaded and more thoughtful, more outside of the norm. The marriage of the lyrics and music, and the craftsmanship Rush displayed along with their instrumental virtuosity pushed me to make sure that everything *I* did was thoughtful and complete, not overdone and not half-baked. I like to think this spilled over into other endeavors as well.

And as with the fans who were kind enough to respond to my survey, Rush's music helped get me through hard times. "Subdivisions" and "The Pass" remain personal favorites. But so are "Show Don't Tell" and "Cut to the Chase" and "Anthem" and other songs about thinking for yourself. "2112" inspired me, like so many others, to read Ayn Rand.[43] Rush's lyrics gave me an appreciation of how literature can inspire rock music, which was awesome because I'm an avid reader. It felt like Rush gave me permission to be intelligent.

Cool, right?

Songs like "The Analog Kid," "Dreamline," and "Middletown Dreams" showed me I wasn't the only one who had to get out of my small town and make my way in the city. "Prime Mover" taught me it was okay to take sheer joy in being alive. "One Little Victory," "Ghost Rider," "Secret Touch," and the

---

[43] While I enjoyed *The Fountainhead* well enough and read *Anthem* and—you're not going to believe this—*every last word* of *Atlas Shrugged* (something I will *never* do again), I personally find the only book of hers to have any real *literary* merit to be her debut, *We the Living*.

other tracks on *Vapor Trails* showed me how we can get past personal tragedy one small step at a time. "Time Stand Still" and "Dog Years" made me that it was natural and normal to lament the passage of time. And most recently, songs on *Clockwork Angels* like "Headlong Flight" really celebrated life as a grand adventure—I was married with my first child when that album came out. And personal favorite "Wish Them Well" helped me get through some rough times when I was feeling lots of resentment in my life.

It's safe to say that what Rush means to me is unique, yet at the same time I can't help but see the commonalities between my experiences and the stories shared by all the lovely fans who participated in the writing of this book. I am an almost-forty white male American of one-hundred percent Greek descent, a devout Orthodox Christian who considers my politics somewhere between "bleeding-heart libertarian" and the traditional right, who is a musician and has seen Rush multiple times and who most definitely enjoys what are considered nerd hobbies. This puts me almost in the wheelhouse of your average Rush fan, yet what writing this book has taught me is that there is no such thing as an "average" Rush fan. We are truly a unique and special breed of music fans I would go as far as to call a *family*.

Thank you for indulging me in a little authorial self-insert, but more importantly, from the bottom of my heart, thank you for reading and for being a part of this book.

FAN PROFILE: ROB D.

Name: Rob D.
Location: Wilmington, Delaware
Age: 33 years old
Gender: Male
Occupation: Associate at an accounting firm and freelance musician

"I will be the first to admit that I developed my Rush fandom late. Very late. I had heard their 'radio hits' several times growing up, but I had other bands that I enjoyed listening to more in high school and college. When *Clockwork Angels* came out, I bought it and enjoyed it (especially "Headlong Flight," which would become one of my Top 5 favorite Rush songs), but I still didn't dive in completely. However, once the *Clockwork Angels Live* album was released, I distinctly remember playing that album over and over again. The setlist, the drum solos, the string ensemble, the musicianship—it all clicked. Whatever had been trying to get through to me for all those years, had finally broken through. I was in, hook, line, and sinker.

Growing up, I had a close family friend who was a Rush diehard. Even though he knew I enjoyed listening to rock music, he never tried to push me to dive deeper into Rush. I guess he must have known that I would get there eventually. When I finally got the chance to see the band in concert during the R40 Tour, I knew I had to go with him. Whatever logistics we had to go through, we would do it, so we could finally see a Rush concert together. Before the show, we had a Rush-themed meal (we dined on honeydew and By-Tor snowdogs, for example) and then made the 45-minute drive to the arena. As the fans know, the setlist for the R40 Tour was incredible, especially since we got to see 'Losing It' live, too. It was an incredible night, and I knew I was around my people. I distinctly remember chatting with fellow fans in between sets, and everyone was incredibly friendly. Rush fandom was alive and well, and I am honored to be a part of it.

It has been said many times before, but it's true—being a Rush fan (especially a die-hard) is like being a part of a secret society. A special bond that you share with the likes of Trey Parker, Matt Stone, Paul Rudd, the Trailer Park Boys, Eugene Levy, Peter Dinklage, Jason Segel, Jay Baruchel, as well as countless musicians who have been inspired by the band over the years. I love the moments when I'm talking music with people, and then halfway through the conversation, discover that we're both Rush fans. It's so much fun being a part of various current message boards, such as rushisaband.com, where superfans share new Rush references from *Jeopardy!*, *The Goldbergs*, *South Park*, *Family Guy*, etc. *Beyond the Lighted Stage* and *Time Stand Still* are staples in my library, proof that the Rush fandom is something extraordinary.

As I mentioned, once I fell in love with the band, I fell hard. I quickly bought every single CD and DVD in the discography. I added more and more vinyl albums to my record collection (I can tell that I'm dating myself already). Every new live album, every new box set, I had to have it. I bought every book related to the band. I even started buying Neil's books and DVDs, as well. For the first time in my life, I became an avid collector. I ran out of room on my coffee table for all the coffee table books, which caused lovely additional conversations with my wife. Every time I think my collection is in a great place, I see a picture of someone with a massive selection, and it just makes me smile. There's always more merchandise to obtain!

As aforementioned, "Headlong Flight" is one of my favorite Rush songs. I love how the song allows each member to showcase their talents—Geddy on the bass and vocals, Alex on guitar, and Neil on the drums (especially during the extended live drum solo). The fact that it rocks so hard is just icing on the cake. The song has everything a rock fan could want. Other favorites include the classic "Tom Sawyer" (just because it's obvious doesn't mean it's not correct), "Far Cry" off *Snakes & Arrows*, "Time Stand Still" and "Turn the Page" off *Hold Your Fire*

(I know a lot of fans don't love the synthesizer period, but this album spoke to me. And the United States Army Band's cover of "Time Stand Still" from this past February is absolutely gorgeous), "The Garden" (what a perfect song to end a career on), and "Working Man" and "Finding My Way" off of the debut (again, they are classics for a reason). Based on those songs, one can tell that my favorite albums are *Clockwork Angels*, *Moving Pictures*, *Rush*, and *Hold Your Fire*, as well as *2112* and *Fly By Night*.

I am fortunate to have a few Rush cover bands in my area that I've seen over the years (back when we had live concerts), and I also saw *Time Stand Still* when it was out in theaters. It's so awesome to hang out with local Rush fans, to enjoy the music together that we all love. Meeting Geddy during the *Big Beautiful Book of Bass* tour was a highlight of my life. I was understandably starstruck, but I wouldn't trade it for the world. I know I have a long way to go in my Rush fandom, but I can't wait to see where it takes me.

CHAPTER VII: A MEASURE OF LOVE AND RESPECT

". . . I feel so bad for his best friend, I feel so bad for his parents, and his little daughter who I met, and his wife, and for Geddy and Alex . . ." [1]

THE MEASURE OF A LIFE

This is it. The end. Not of the book—not yet. But the end of Rush. In some ways, this is the hardest chapter to write because the Rush story ended conclusively in Santa Monica, California on January 7, 2020 when Neil Ellwood Peart died of glioblastoma. Fans knew the band was done touring as of August 1, 2015. Large-scale tours, at least, but surely there'd be more albums, more *music*, and maybe a one-off show here and there. But with Neil's untimely death, the book of Rush as a continuing operation ended definitively, period, full-stop.

The band had been aware since 2015 that the end was nigh. In the *Time Stand Still* documentary, all three members of the band appear keenly aware that the R40 tour would be their last.

"The beginning, there's so much hope and it's a clean slate and you just go for it," says Alex Lifeson. "The ending never feels like it's the right time to end. And for all the reasons that I'd like it to be over, which are almost exclusively physical things, in my heart and in my mind, I'm not ready. We haven't really known another life."[2]

"I don't think there is really an end," said Neil Peart. "I have no fear of the future, no regret—to the contrary. This is, to me, a fantastic thing we've done, and I feel great that I was able to sustain my prime for a long, long time and keep improving to the level that I wanted to get to." For Peart, the end of Rush almost seems a matter of pride; he sounds like many a professional athlete who walked away from the game before their skills deteriorated to the point they were unable to compete: "To go out on the top and not face the diminishing of your abilities; that's what I couldn't face."[3]

Geddy Lee notes that they were kids when they started Rush, and that the band gave them their identity. "If all that is true, then you'd have to say that ending is harder than beginning, because the beginning is a place you've escaped to that's been a warm and nurturing environment for over forty years. And walking away from that is not so fun."[4]

Given the close bond between Geddy, Alex, and Neil, and their respect for each other not just as musicians and friends, but as *men*, it's no wonder that there were no attempts to somehow continue on without Neil after the drum master's retirement.

Neil was as irreplaceable to Rush as Keith Moon was to The Who and John Bonham was to Led Zeppelin. But more than a musical loss to the other members of the band, Geddy and Alex lost a *friend*, or a "soul brother" as Rush's official statement called Neil.

2   *Rush: Time Stand Still* (Documentary, 2016).
3   *Id.*
4   *Id.*

The statement in question was simple and direct:

> It is with broken hearts and the deepest sadness that we must share the terrible news that on Tuesday our friend, soul brother and band mate of over 45 years, Neil, has lost his incredibly brave three and a half year battle with brain cancer (Glioblastoma). We ask that friends, fans, and media alike understandably respect the family's need for privacy and peace at this extremely painful and difficult time. Those wishing to express their condolences can choose a cancer research group or charity of their choice and make a donation in Neil Peart's name.
>
> Rest in peace brother.
>
> Neil Peart September 12, 1952 – January 7, 2020[5]

Fans, of course, were sensitive to the fact that Geddy and Alex making new music really wasn't important anymore. Interestingly, after Neil's retirement there had been speculation about what Geddy and Alex would do musically, *if* they could, without Neil. A 2018 article in *Rolling Stones* asks, somewhat provocatively, "Could There Be Life For Rush Without Neil Peart?" and outlines three possibilities: Get a new drummer, change the band's name, or have Geddy Lee go solo.[6] "If

---

5 *See, e.g.,* "Geddy Lee and Alex Lifeson Issue Statement on the Death of Neil Peart," MetalSucks.com, January 10, 2020, available at https://www.metalsucks.net/2020/01/10/geddy-lee-and-alex-lifeson-issue-statement-on-the-death-of-neil-peart/, last accessed June 19, 2020.

6 Andy Greene, "Could There Be Life For Rush Without Neil Peart? We outline three ways in which the music of Rush could continue to exist on the concert circuit now that their legendary drummer is retired," *Rolling Stone*, October 23, 2018, available at https://www.rollingstone.com/music/music-news/could-rush-continue-after-neil-peart-745690/, last accessed June 19, 2020.

Journey can play stadiums without Steve Perry," author Andy Greene posits, "Rush can certainly carry on without Peart."[7] The band might have been over as a touring concern, but it wasn't as though they never saw each other. In fact, as Donna Halper mentioned, the online rumor that they stopped speaking with each other after Neil's retirement was a complete fabrication.[8] "We're very close—I was just talking to Alex this morning," Geddy Lee told *Bass Guitar* magazine two months before Peart's death:[9]

> We try to get together regularly. I was just in LA three weeks ago, visiting Neil. You know, when the band ended, everybody had a different sort of response to that last show, so it took a little bit of time for everyone to sort it out in their own brains, how we were gonna move forward. At the end we just decided that the most important thing is that friends are friends. That's what comes first, so that's the way it's remained.[10]

Remember: These three guys shared a deep bond, and were not just coworkers. Their association with each other didn't suddenly end when the band did. And while they may have been tossing the idea of doing something without Neil around before Peart's death,[11] or at least saying as much during interviews,

---

7 *Id.*

8 Donna Halper, interview with the author, February 11, 2020 (Appendix B).

9 Ellen O'Reilly, "Geddy Lee: Progressively Minded, Forward Thinking," *Bass Guitar*, Issue 175, November 2019, available at http://www.2112.net/powerwindows/transcripts/20191100bassguitar.htm, last accessed June 22, 2020.

10 *Id.*

11 *See, e.g.*, Ryan Reed, "Geddy Lee on Rush's Prog-Rock Opus 'Hemispheres': 'We Had to Raise Our Game': The bassist reflects on writing side-long 'mini rock operas,' singing in awkward keys and Alex Lifeson's mysterious 'bedroom accident'—and offers an update on the state of Rush," *Rolling Stone*, October 22, 2018, available at https://www.rollingstone.com/music/music-news/rush-geddy-lee-interview-prog-rock-hemispheres-738828/, last accessed June 19, 2020 ("I would say there's no chance of seeing Rush on tour again as Alex, Geddy, Neil. But would you see one of us or two of us or three of us? That's possible.").

this possibility appeared to have been put to bed as recently as March of 2019, where Alex Lifeson finally seemed to come to terms with the end of Rush:

> "It wasn't until a year later (after the final gig) that I started to feel better about it all. I realised we'd gone out on a high note."
>
> ...
>
> Reflecting more upon that final concert, Alex called it a "very powerful" experience, explaining: "I remember looking around the whole arena and trying to take it all in. The lighting. The crowd. The people around me. It was very emotional for us.
>
> "I loved the way we presented those shows, starting with 'Clockwork Angels' and then working our way back to the very beginning. But had we done a typical-length tour of about 80 dates, I think I would have been more satisfied with it."
>
> Asked if he has since come to terms with Rush being over, Alex said: "Yes, I think so. I don't want to be in a band and tour any more. I don't feel the need to carry on with what I did for almost half a century. I'm fine with it now. And I'm as busy as I would ever want to be."[12]

A May 31, 2020 interview with Alex Lifeson on *Talkin' Golf with Ann Liguori* puts the pain of Neil's loss into words, and is

---

[12] Scott Colothan, "Alex Lifeson says he's finally come to terms with Rush's demise," *Planet Rock*, March 15, 2019, available at https://planetradio.co.uk/planet-rock/news/rock-news/alex-lifeson-say-hes-finally-come-to-terms-with-rushs-demise/, last accessed June 19, 2020.

one of the few lengthy statements either Geddy or Alex have made since Neil's passing:

> It's been very difficult. After Neil passed in January I've played very little guitar. I don't feel inspired and motivated. It was the same thing when [Neil's] daughter died in a car accident in 1997. I didn't really play for about a year. I just don't feel it in my heart right now. Every time I pick up a guitar I just aimlessly kind of mess around with it and put it down. Normally I would pick up a guitar and I would play for a couple of hours without even being aware that I'm spending that much time. So I know it will come back . . . I don't know if the motivation is there for [Geddy and I] to do anything right now. We're certainly proud of our track record and we still love music. But it's different now . . .[13]

Alex's sorrow is evident just reading his words. It is encouraging that fans are overwhelmingly respectful of this and haven't been filling the Internet with calls for Geddy Lee and Alex Lifeson to soldier on, as though the two of them really owe the fans anything more than the forty years of fantastic music and concerts they've been given! Speaking on the Bob Cesca show, Donna Halper put it best: "In fairness, Neil gave us a 45 year musical album."[14]

---

13   Alex Lifeson, *Talkin' Golf with Ann Liguori*, WFAN (New York), May 31, 2020, available at https://omny.fm/shows/wfanam-on-demand/talking-golf-with-ann-liguori-8, last accessed June 19, 2020, excerpt from RushIsABand.com, available at https://www.rush-isaband.com/blog/2020/05/31/5442/Alex-Lifeson-talks-golf-Rush-and-Neil-Peart-with-Ann-Liguori-in-new-radio-interview/, last accessed June 19, 2020.

14   Donna Halper, *The Bob Cesca Show Interview: Donna Halper on Neil Peart*, January 22, 2020, available at http://www.bobcesca.com/the-bob-cesca-show-interview-donna-halper-on-neil-peart-1-22-20/

IT'S LIKE WE KNEW HIM

People die all the time. The year 2020 was a difficult one for me personally, as I lost a great-aunt shortly after New Year's and a great-uncle about a month later. They both lived full lives, thank God—my great-aunt was a few months shy of 96, and my great-uncle was nearly 90—and neither of them suffered too much, but their passings were still difficult.

Celebrities die all the time, too. Sometimes their passing hits fans pretty hard. Prince and David Bowie, two musicians I admire greatly, both died in 2016. I was saddened, as it meant that neither man would be producing any new music, but aside from listening to them a bit more in tribute, I did not feel a sadness deeper than what any thinking, feeling person experiences upon learning of someone's death. You express your sadness, say some prayers, and get on with your life. This is not to sound callous, but it is a truth about human beings. After all, if we mourned greatly at the death of every single person on Earth, we would have precious little emotional energy for much of anything else.

And besides, in 2016 my mother-in-law passed away at the age of 57. This was where the bulk of my emotional and spiritual—as well as physical—energy was directed that year. No offense to Messrs. Bowie and Prince, but their deaths did not affect me one fraction of an iota as much as hers did.

So why am I writing a book about Rush and devoting an entire chapter to Neil Peart's passing?

Because Neil's death *felt* different to me than David Bowie's and Prince's and every musician and celebrity death I've ever been made aware of. Did Neil's passing affect me as deeply as my great-aunt's or my great-uncle's, both of whom also died in 2020? Good Lord, no. But it *did* feel like I knew him, and I *did* feel sadness. Real sadness.

Your next question may be: "Why aren't you writing a book about your great-aunt or your great-uncle?" To which I answer: "Because the deep sorrow and sadness I felt at their deaths was *normal.* I knew them. They were family! They were both huge, tangible parts of my life. I knew them personally for my whole life! I never met Neil Peart once. *That* is why I am writing this." If this sounds gauche or uncaring towards my deceased family members, I apologize. That is not my intent and if it is the impression I am giving, I am truly sorry. But—and this is important—scanning the Internet after Neil's death to see other fan reactions, and speaking with family and friends of mine who were likewise huge Rush fans, I learned that *I was not alone in feeling this.*

The celebrity encomiums and tributes are unsurprising. It is only natural that Neil's peers and personal friends, many of whom were also famous musicians or actors, would be absolutely gutted by his death.[15] These are touching, but are not particularly striking and are not what this chapter, or this entire book, are about. I am more interested in the *fans'* reaction, since as I discovered, I wasn't the only fan to feel this way.

"It felt like a friend had died," Ed Stenger told me:[16]

> I don't know exactly why that is compared to other artists why it's different. It's hard to say from being such a big Rush fan and being such a fan of Neil in particular, it's easy for me to see why it affected me so much . . . I'm not sure why everybody else felt the same way. I didn't expect everybody else to feel as affected as me, but they were.[17]

I commented to Ed about this outpouring of genuine grief from the fans despite Peart being such a private individual. Ed opined that it likely came from Neil's position as Rush's lyricist

---

15   *See, e.g.,* Gab Ginsburg, "Musicians React to Rush Drummer Neil Peart's Death: 'His Influence and Music Will Live On,'" *Billboard*, January 10, 2020, available at https://www.billboard.com/articles/columns/rock/8547797/neil-peart-dies-rush-drummer-dead-musicians-react#:~:text=Rush%20drummer%20and%20lyricist%20Neil,the%20news%20via%20social%20media., last accessed June 22, 2020.
16   Ed Stenger, interview with the author, May 19, 2020 (Appendix C).
17   *Id.*

and the window his words in Rush's songs, as well as in his multiple novels, gave people into his mind:

> He was a very real. He was a real guy. He was what you saw. He didn't try to be something that he wasn't . . . He was a unique dude. He's someone you can definitely identify with and he's a nice guy too. Like I said, from reading all of the stuff he wrote and his lyrics and everything, you just get a good feeling about him and the way he thinks.

I can't help but think about how un-rockstar-like Peart was. There's a lovely moment in the *Time Stand Still* documentary where Peart is showing the cameraman how he plans his motorcycle routes between shows, and he is positively giddy like a young boy about the prospect of seeing some hidden parts of the United States. *This* is what Peart got excited about: Not booze, not drugs, not strip clubs, but travel. I mean, the guy was an avid *birdwatcher*, for crying out loud.[18]

"I was devastated. I cried myself to sleep that night," was fan Lindsey E.'s reaction to Peart's death.[19] "I withdrew and processed it while listening to the music he created," said fan Steven S.[20] Tony V. "cried like no tomorrow. It felt like the death of a family member. I am still trying to hold back tears whenever I hear 'The Garden.'"[21] But it is UK Comedy writer Trevor Rudge who perhaps puts my own, and many other fans', feelings into words succinctly and perfectly: "I have never been so affected by the death of someone I never met. The feeling of sadness, loss, unfairness is greater than I have felt, even for peo-

---

18 *See, e.g.,* Donna Halper, The Bob Cesca Show Interview: Donna Halper on Neil Peart, January 22, 2020, available at http://www.bobcesca.com/the-bob-cesca-show-interview-donna-halper-on-neil-peart-1-22-20/.
19 Lindsey E., response to author's survey, February 5, 2020 (Appendix A).
20 Steven S., response to author's survey, February 5, 2020 (Appendix A).
21 Tony V., response to author's survey, February 5, 2020 (Appendix A).

ple I have known personally . . . Neil deserved his retirement, he deserved longer."[22]

RITUALS AND REVERENCE

Medium is a popular Internet blogging platform—named, perhaps, after Marshall McLuhan's famous statement?[23] My brother sent me a well-written piece called "Nobody's Hero" by a gentleman named Steven Weber, penned after Peart's death. Weber's article resonated because he put into words so much of what I was feeling:

> Shortly after learning of Neil's death all I could say to myself was, "This is not what was supposed to happen." A sentiment that would be echoed by all who knew him and fans filling social media posts with their grief. He deserved his second chance.
>
> Now, in a dramatic twist of irony we find ourselves the Ghost Riders. Once again drawing from Neil's words and his experience with loss and grief spilled into written pages and song lyrics to soothe our own little baby souls.[24]

Weber touches on an important point about the fan reaction to Peart's death: the man had been through so much already; didn't he deserve a break?

Neil did have a second chance, though. He married photographer Carrie Nuttall in 2000 and had a daughter, Olivia, in 2009. In a January 12, 2020 post on her blog, Donna Halper

---

22   Trevor Rudge, response to author's survey, February 5, 2020 (Appendix A).
23   *See* Chapter VI: How Do We Make Contact With One Another? And no: as far as I can tell, McLuhan was not the inspiration for the platform's name.
24   Steven Weber, "Nobody's Hero," Medium.com, January 16, 2020, available at https://medium.com/@pHSteve/nobodys-hero-d2775dfda119, last accessed June 22, 2020.

comments upon this aspect of Peart's personality, his optimism and his belief in second chances:

> Whether I saw him in person or not, Neil remained a presence in my life—through his amazing lyrics, and through the privilege of watching him play. He was such a gifted drummer, and widely admired by his fellow musicians in other bands. And I kept up with his life—the tragic loss of his wife and daughter, his time away from the band, his eventual return... And then, one night in September 2010, when I had come to see the band perform in Boston, out of nowhere, he asked to see me. We hugged, like two old friends, and then we chatted about politics, about philosophy, about family, and yes, about "King Lear"—he still had the copy of the play he had borrowed from me, and as I posted to social media at the time, I was very moved to find he still had it, and it still meant something to him.
>
> And as he and I were saying goodbye, we were standing out in the hall and he remarked upon the lesson he took from "King Lear"—that it's not enough to say you love someone; you have to show it. And he remarked upon second chances—that he hadn't been there enough for his daughter Selena (he loved her, but by his own admission, he was on the road a lot); but he absolutely was going to be there for his daughter Olivia. It was a promise he kept.[25]

---

25 Donna Halper, "This Wasn't Supposed to Happen: Some Thoughts About the Death of Neil Peart," *Dialogue & Discourse: a Blog by Donna Halper,* January 12, 2020, available at https://dlhalperblog.blogspot.com/2020/01/this-wasnt-supposed-to-happen-some.html, last accessed June 22, 2020.

Halper knew Neil personally, but her sentiments echo those of fans who did not, which is part of why it is so interesting to read her words when thinking about fans' reactions. Halper was obviously a fan herself, though a fan from a much different and closer perspective than the rest of us. Her concluding paragraph in this tribute post could have been written by any of us:

> Neil Peart was an honorable, ethical human being. Despite being one of the music industry's greatest drummers, he was never arrogant. He treated drumming, and song-writing, as art forms, and he elevated both. He loved being a musician, and his lyrics resonated with so many fans. Neil was also a charitable person—but when he gave (which he often did), he never wanted to call attention to himself. He lived his life his way, never afraid to be himself, encouraging others to be themselves too. He left a large body of incredible music that will live on. And he left years of wonderful memories that his millions of fans will never forget. To think of a world without Neil in it breaks my heart. But I consider myself fortunate to have known him. May he rest in peace.[26]

There are dozens of other tributes on Medium written by fans feeling these same things. A two-part series by writer Claudio D'Andrea asks this exact same question: "What's hard is knowing how to grieve for someone you've known and not known your whole life. This is why his death has been so hard to process."[27] Through the course of his writing, D'Andrea wonders, "What about the grieving process for someone you've

---

26   *Id.*
27   Claudio D'Andrea, "Neil Ellwood Peart, 1952–2020: A remarkable treasure of a life," Medium.com, January 14, 2020, available at https://medium.com/cd-flotsam-jetsam/neil-ellwood-peart-1952-2020-a-remarkable-treasure-of-a-life-9f8f0bf02511, last accessed June 22, 2020.

never 'known'?"[28] and finds answers in the uniquely human process of *ritual*.

In his quest for closure, D'Andrea reached out to two friends of his, funeral professional and musician Scott "Sax" Webster, and Reverend Jim Evans of the United Church of Canada. Webster told D'Andrea that such feelings are normal:

> When we revere such strangers who impact us to our soul and to the core of heart and mind, I think we tend to hold these idols in higher regards than even sometimes our own loved ones because of the special bond or relationship we've cultivated through their craft.[29]

I see a lot of merit in this. After all, art is truly a magical and uniquely human thing that touches us on a level so deep, the only comparable thing is a religious experience (it is also no surprise, then, that so many religious practices incorporate music, art, and ritual). So this touches on the *why*, but what about the grieving process for someone you never knew, like, say, a celebrity musician?

Webster's suggestion is what many of us have been doing since we learned about Peart's death: *celebrate* the individual. Talk about them. Listen to their music![30] Sound advice—a great way to mourn someone you never met, and something that might also explain the *2,000 percent* increase in Rush's music sales following Peart's death.[31]

Reverend Evans has similar advice for D'Andrea and all other Rush fans coping with Peart's death. I'm reproducing a

---

28 Claudio D'Andrea, "Neil Ellwood Peart, 1952–2020, Pt. II: Grappling with the grief," Medium.com, January 25, 2020, available at https://medium.com/cd-flotsam-jetsam/neil-ellwood-peart-1952-2020-pt-ii-grappling-with-the-grief-32a84b4ae631, last accessed June 22, 2020.
29 Scott "Sax" Webster, quoted in *Id.*
30 *Id.*
31 Will Lavin, "Rush sales increase by over 2,000% following Neil Peart's death: That's a whole lot of love," *New Musical Express*, January 18, 2020, available at https://www.nme.com/news/music/rush-sales-increase-2000-percent-neil-peart-death-2598435, last accessed June 22, 2020.

large portion of it here since, in a demonstration of how we are all connected by such slender threads of commonality, I find that the Reverend's words speak volumes:

> Grief, Evans says, is "an individual expression of our humanity, and each and every one of us uses the places deep within ourselves to find the path to healing." He suggested my own healing may have already started when I put down my thoughts in the tribute I wrote.
>
> In his ministry, Evans says he presides at the funerals of many people he's never met. He hears about that person "through the voices of those who loved the deceased" and then reflects and finds "threads that express the meaning and purpose of the life of the deceased. I try to know the person through the stories that are shared with me."
>
> Evans says that it seems that I "knew" Peart in my own way. He was part of my own story and each of us is "known by other people in various ways.
>
> "Those closest to us know us one way (parents, partners, siblings, children) and the circle extends to friends, those we work with, and on it goes . . .
>
> "None of us is known by any one person in our entirety. We have many facets and sides, we show different faces."
>
> Some of us, Evans continues, "have deep insight into the core of our beings." Peart may be one of those unique individuals "who was

so aware of himself and at the same time was so giving of himself that he was able to share more of his true nature than most of us (often the artist is the one who does this in our world).

"Why would we grieve any less for those who impacted our lives through their art? Often it is the connection of art and music that bridges those places where we feel that someone truly knows and understands us."

Evans says he cried "deeply and profoundly" himself when he learned that CBC radio broadcaster and humorist Stuart McLean died in 2017.

"To grieve is not so much to profess a loss, as it is to understand love. The famous aphorism is true—we never cry if we never love. The only way to never experience sadness is to never experience love.

"So you love Neil Peart. You love what he gave to your life, how he influenced the garden that is your life.

"My suggestion is to not shy away from how you feel—and remember it is about you. This is your place, your story."

Evans acknowledges "the power of ritual as part of the healing process," saying that is one of the strengths of society through a church, religion and funerals. Not long ago, he continues, a "whole integrated machine" sprung into action when someone died in a community: Friends and neighbours offered food, visited family and participated in the ritual of a funeral service.

Evans says he believes in the power of ritual to help us grieve—not necessarily traditional funerals, but actions and processes in which we honour and celebrate those who touched our lives. Like Webster and my Twitter friend Tony Sollazzo also suggested, it helps to hold a ritual around Peart with others who understand my feelings and relationship with the great drummer and his music.[32]

If you're still grappling with why the death of Neil Peart, whom you likely never met, affected and may still affect you so profoundly, I hope that reading this brings you some comfort. Not only are you *not* weird for mourning a stranger, you are normal in wanting some way to express your grief.

On that note, I suppose that this book is my own way of processing Peart's death. I have found myself connecting with Rush fans in a way I never have before. My time is limited and I spend most of it with my family or writing novels and not interacting with fan communities. However, perhaps it is high time I do *more* of the latter, since we all seem to be in the same boat.

This project, in large part, has been my own way of giving back to the band and to the fans, and my sincere hope is that in addition to being entertaining and informative, I have helped you to deal with your own feelings about why a rock band has meant so much to you in your life.

And if not, that's fine as well.

"There's people out there that are still grieving as if they knew him because . . . they felt like they did through his mu-

---

[32] Claudio D'Andrea, "Neil Ellwood Peart, 1952–2020, Pt. II: Grappling with the grief," Medium.com, January 25, 2020, available at https://medium.com/cd-flotsam-jetsam/neil-ellwood-peart-1952-2020-pt-ii-grappling-with-the-grief-32a84b4ae631, last accessed June 22, 2020.

sic," Donna Halper said on Bob Cesca's show. "I think the best thing that any of us could do is to honor him by being our best selves, by being true to our ethics, and by doing something out there that makes the world a better place and doing it in his memory."[33]

WHAT NEIL PEART MEANT TO ME

I received a text on January 10 at 4:11 p.m. from my brother, reading (and pardon the profanity): "Holy fuck dude just saw that Neil Peart died!!"

I looked it up and replied: "Oh my God he had brain cancer?"

We commiserated, wondering why we felt the way we did about the death of a man we never met. "Normally celebrity deaths I'm like 'it's sad but that's life,'" my brother texted later that day, "but with certain musicians who mean so much to me, it hurts."

I wholeheartedly agreed with him then, and I still do.

Rush always felt like *my* band. They wrote music and lyrics that spoke to *my* interests, not just as a musician but as a reader and enjoyer of the finer—and nerdier—things in life. That they weren't "cool" was a part of the appeal. Rush were the "World's Biggest Cult Band," as had been said by many over the years, and when you met a fellow Rush fan there was an immediate bond, as though you had found one of *your* people.

It may have been that I, like so many other fans, got into Rush as young man. In my case, I was seventeen, a time when one's personality is still forming and one is still seeking out and forging an identity. Rush helped me forge mine. They made it okay to think, to be interested in the world around you *and* the world inside you. In a way, Rush gave me permission to be myself both in high school and a broader American cultural milieu

---

[33] Donna Halper, *The Bob Cesca Show Interview: Donna Halper on Neil Peart*, January 22, 2020, available at http://www.bobcesca.com/the-bob-cesca-show-interview-donna-halper-on-neil-peart-1-22-20/

that seemed to *demand* you conform to the role outside forces want to place you in.

Perhaps it all sounds silly to those not in the know, but Rush armed me with the power to stand athwart trends and peer pressure and say, with a smile on my face and no malice in my heart, "No, I'm good. You do you thing over there. I'll be over here doing my own. If want to join me, great. If not, that's cool too." All I could do was wish them well.

It has been said by so many, but when Neil Peart died and Rush finally ended, it felt like a part of my childhood died. This is not to say Rush is child*ish*. Far from it! Rush's music over the years developed and matured, a reflection of Geddy, Alex, and Neil's much vaunted status as "regular guys." Let me just comment on how wild that is: Rush were rock stars who are loved by their fans for *not* being rock stars.

Their longevity and continuous ability to write and record new music—and *excellent* new music at that—made them a constant presence in my life. And suddenly . . . it was gone. There would be no more new music, no more Neil Peart lyrics to pour over, no more shows to attend. It's a fact of existence that everything, both good and bad, eventually comes to an end, but even with that understanding it's never fun when something good is gone from the world.

I never knew Neil Peart, but like countless fans the world over I *felt* like I did. That is a special thing for one man to have accomplished. I'm not trying to diminish Alex and Geddy's role in this, but they are still alive, thank God. It is Neil, the *brains* of the band, The Professor, the backbone of Rush's powerful sound, who has passed away, and this is why the outpouring of love is directed mostly his way.

I'm sure Geddy Lee and Alex Lifeson understand this, because from their few public statements upon the death of their soul-brother it is apparent that they feel the same way. And they *knew* the guy intimately. One can only imagine the depth of their hurt, and that of Neil's wife, daughter, parents, family, and friends. This band was their life for so long, and they made their wonderful, thoughtful music *together*, three friends against the odds. Rush, and Neil Peart, will continue to inspire countless other individuals for generations to come, and I think that is what hurts the most: the fact that there will be no more words of wisdom from Neil Ellwood Peart.

It sounds selfish, and I own that. But it's the truth. And I don't think Neil would want me or any other fan to express anything but the unvarnished truth about whatever it is we are talking about.

Godspeed, Mr. Peart, and thank you.

I HOPE YOU HEAR THIS, WHEREVER YOU ARE

"The Garden," the final song on Rush's final studio album, is beautiful beyond words. The words to the song take on a special poignancy now that Neil is gone:

> The measure of a life is a measure of love and respect
> So hard to earn, so easily burned
>
> In the fullness of time
> A garden to nurture and protect
> It's a measure of a life
>
> The treasure of a life
> Is a measure of love and respect
> The way you live, the gifts that you give
>
> In the fullness of time
> Is the only return that you expect

If Peart ever worried that he would not be loved or respected, those worries would be put to bed by the sheer fact that *literally nobody has had a single negative thing to say about him after his death.* How many public figures in the twenty-first century can you say that about? In fact, the only negative thing I can think of is the fact that people like me wish he were still alive to make more new music, a result of the love us fans have for the man.

The responses to my survey question, "How did you react to Neil Peart's death?" illustrate this beautifully, so now I think it is time once again to let the fans share their stories as a part of our ritual of mourning for a man that none of us knew:

> [Peart's death h]it me hard, cried, reflected on all he meant to me and my life. Such a huge influence. Here is what I wrote a day or so after . . .
>
> I started playing drums around 10 years old. My uncle gave me an old set of Ludwig drums, some Beatles, Queen and Led Zeppelin albums, a few pointers and off I went.
>
> About a year later a friend, Larry Dobrow, gave me a tape, knowing that I played and said I should hear this drummer. The song was "Tom Sawyer" by Rush. I played that tape over and over, I never heard a drummer like that and listened over and over again. It sounded like he had a hundred drums during that drum fill in the middle of the song.
>
> I soon started to learn more about Rush, this was 1981, so Rush had several albums out already. I remember getting a few and the one that stood out was their second live album Exit . . . Stage Left. I listened to that over and over again. The drum solo during "YYZ" was just amazing. So many great songs.

Around 1982 Rush had a new album out called Signals and I heard they were playing at Madison Square Garden. I begged my parents to get tickets. My Dad took me and Eric Becker, a good friend and neighbor who also got heavy into Rush in those days. Eric and I would go to so many Rush shows over the years. I don't think I can count how many times I've seen Rush live. In so many states and even in their hometown of Toronto. I never missed a tour since Signals. I'm so happy I got to take my kids to a few shows as well.

When I was 13 I remember seeing an ad for a live Rush video of Exit . . . Stage Left in a magazine, I got the form filled out, got a check from Mom and mailed off for a copy in Betamax format. We happened to have a player at home.

I watched that video from start to finish every single night. I fell asleep to that video so many nights.

I studied over and over everything Neil did in those videos. Just trying to unlock how he played those songs.

In that Exit . . . Stage Left concert video, Alex wore a red suit jacket, yellow leather tie and shiny red shoes. When I had to go a buy a suit for my Confirmation I begged my Mom to get that suit. We went to several stores looking for a red suit jacket. We finally found it, found the yellow tie and those shiny red shoes. I stood out like sore thumb in church that day but felt so cool wearing it.

Every time Rush had a new album, I was at the record store the day it came out, got it home and listened to it, read every lyric and the liner notes, over and over again. Rush was just about the only thing I listened to until my early to mid-twenties, I finally started to branch out a bit but most were so influenced by Rush it was only natural to listen to them as well.

During the Power Windows Tour I had to have a front row experience. I found a ticket broker and paid $105 for a front row seat. I was with our regular group of friends at that show but no one else would pay that much money for a ticket. Normal tickets had to be $20 or so back then, so I sat up there by myself. This was early 1986 so I was still only 15.

Alex, Geddy and Neil were and still are in some ways such a huge part of my life. My chest still hurts just thinking about this loss.

I'd dream about the day I'd get to meet Neil so many times. Try and play it out in my head, not to act like a fan but just get to talk and listen to him tell stories. For the longest time I wanted a BMW bike like Neil's in hopes to somehow cross paths on the road.

There has not been a bigger influence on my life than Neil Peart and Rush. I'm sad I'll never get to hear him play again. I'm sad I'll never get to read another story or book or lyric from him. I'm sad for his family who finally got him off the road and home only for him to be put through the hell cancer is.

Fuck cancer! Rest easy Neil, gone too soon but never will be forgotten.
– Rich M.

I cried and cried because his poetry spoke to me during all the important parts of my life. Each album holds some significance to me because I remember where I was in my life when I heard each album for the first time.

I also was so depressed because the hope of future Rush music was extinguished.
– Professor Cristy Tondeur

Very sad.

Never felt that way about someone I didn't know personally. I was 9 when John Lennon was murdered and that was a crushing blow.

But this was different.

Neil Peart was my mentor through my teens, my 20s, 30s to present day.

Even though as a drummer I discovered many bands and many great drummers over the years.

Neil will always be my favorite
– Ed Morrow

Shock. Had no idea he was so sick. Felt the worst for his daughter—I thought he'd retired (1) to be with the family and (2) 'cause he just didn't think he could do it to his standards anymore.
– Rob Leas, Rush fan for life

Believe it or not, I knew about it through a friend who happened to be at the hospital when he was diagnosed. I kept quiet for several years like a true Rush fan. When I heard he passed I felt like an important person in my life had left. It's interesting how Neil taught his fans so much. Because of his strong desire for privacy and his reasons for keeping his boundaries from fans, I understood that I actually didn't know him. He kept me in check with not grieving too much. It's true, I actually don't know him. Why should I feel such a loss? But either way, I did feel the loss. I had moments of tears. I've listened only to Rush since he passed and for some weird reason, the songs are hitting me differently now. More meaningful. More deep. I'm paying way more attention to his lyrics now and re-learning how amazing his lyrics are. He truly taught me how to live.

– Mark Baldwin

Nostalgically: My friends and I were all rush fans and admirers. Lying in bed with the headphones on. Wanting to become a writer—becoming a writer—had everything to do with the fascination his lyrics inspired.

– Kevin, a fan

My heart was crushed. I didn't know that he was even sick. I came home and sat by myself on the couch and cried sporadically. I told my wife I wasn't hungry and cancelled our date night, she said she was going to pick up dinner and I said I would eat sand. I was extremely sad.

– Mark in Gundo

Found out as I was leaving work the day. Sat in my car in a dark corner of a parking garage and cried.
– Michael Medwick

It's been about three weeks and it still hurts. I listened to every album and every live concert release in order. I'm reading Traveling Music, something I've had for years and never took the time to read it. I also wore all my concert shirts every day for a week.
– Richard Harwell

I never felt like that stranger was a long awaited friend, but I was (and still am) extremely sad. I never thought Rush would really be gone. I accepted that there wouldn't be any more tours, but I always thought they'd do a few shows in Vegas or Toronto or something.
– Frank Mahan, lifelong Rush fan

Very, VERY sad. First, utter shock and disbelief when I heard the news because it came out of the blue. Then a real sadness because of his incredible drumming and lyrics. Neil just seemed like a normal, down to earth guy who happened to be the greatest living drummer on the planet in one of the biggest bands of all time. Even though Rush had retired, it was comforting knowing that they were all alive and well. I also felt grief for his family, Geddy, Alex, and other friends who knew him.
– Drew

Initially shock/disbelief. Couldn't think straight the rest of the day. Haven't completely lost it

yet, but the tears will come. Mine just come slow.
– KatSkahnne

Shock and tears. Connected with a few people I hadn't spoken with in a while. Collective grief and continued recovery.
– Brent Rose

Stunned . . . utterly stunned. I felt like a favorite teacher had died.
– Jim Lake

Shock, sat down and cried, felt like I lost a member of the family
– Ken Ballinger

I'm still grieving but am much better now. I was shocked by the news and quite frankly surprised at the depth of grief that I felt. Am still feeling. I didn't even know myself how much Neil meant to me.
– Chuck P. from Vegas

I saw it on my newsfeed at work and was stunned, then I broke down and cried at my desk. It took a good two weeks to come to grips with the idea Rush will never make new music. There was always the glimmer of hope but that died the day the music died
– Todd Swift

It was very hard to deal with. I could still manage my everyday life, but it hit me harder than any other celebrity death. I, of course, never knew him personally, and I would have respected his space completely and felt uncomfortable if we

had actually met (knowing how he felt about fandom, etc.)—despite how much I might have wanted to meet him. Through his lyrics, I suppose, I felt I knew him, at least to some degree. I appreciated his way of thinking about the world, and I never had that with a lyricist in quite the same way before. At times his phrasings could be somewhat awkward, and I even appreciated that, actually. It's human and he didn't mind. It was never about being cool or anything. He just put it out there. I'm saddened by his death and feel his last several years must have been incredibly challenging for him. I don't know how he could have managed.
– Bill Garland

I was in shock, but then I felt something I call "second-hand frustration" or you can call it empathy. He never got to fulfill his role as a father. I try to think how he felt when he knew that he was going to be a dad again, after what happened with Selena. I bet he really wanted to be there for Olivia and I feel a bit of anger and I feel frustrated because I think Neil wanted to show his excellence in every aspect of his life, but time was just not enough and he had to sacrifice his family time to be the best drummer in the world, which also makes me feel guilty as a fan, I stole him from his family.
– Laura O.

Drank wine as soon as I got home from work and then went to spend an hour playing drums along to many Rush classics.
– Marc Brennan

Like a gut punch from Mike Tyson. I felt like I lost a family member. It's hard for me to reconcile that a) he's gone and, b) there will never be another Rush studio album or tour. I always held out for a couple singles or a show here or there. The finality of it, the reality of it—a part of my growing up is gone. It's tough. Sure the music is still here and always will be, but my God, a man with such talent, a genius by all accounts. Intellectual in writing, reading, playing—a brainiac, would die from a brain disease. It's terribly hard. I of course feel for his family and for Alex and Geddy too.
– Tito M. Cantafio

It was stunning, having not been aware that he was ill. Friends messaged me for days saying, "when I heard the news, you were the first person I thought of." I didn't know Neil personally, but it felt—and still feels—like a personal loss.
– Jeff Cornelius

I broke down and cried. My birthday is on January 11, so it was really hard to celebrate my birthday because I love Rush so much. Reached out and chatted with my fellow Rush friends, called my brother and we both agreed that for us, that was the day the music died. Crushed, heart broken.
– Amber Bovetti

I was surprised how really bummed out it made me. It was such a shock. And I was a little angry, as a cancer survivor myself, that the kind he died from attacked his brain where his words and ideas lived. So unfair.
– Deborah L. from Oklahoma

Tragic. Really a damn shame. Such a gifted mind, with dervish energy, and amazing talents.
– Brennanaliac

Poorly. I wouldn't consider him a hero, but he was certainly an idol and someone whose philosophy coincided with mine. A man whose lyrics and music literally helped me get through life because it made me think and [be] introspective. His passing has had a profound effect on how the rest of my life may be . . .
– Chris Carosa

My best friend from high school, Peter, who I started my Rush obsession with 35 years ago, texted me the news and I couldn't get the words out to tell my wife, even though she is definitely not a Rush fan. I wore nothing but Rush shirts to work for the next week and my car radio and phone did not leave SiriusXM channel 27 Deep Tracks, which became the Rush Tribute Channel, for almost three weeks. Not once.
– Brian F.

Complete shock. 14 hour group chat on Facebook with my music school friends, all of whom are huge Rush fans, many of whom have not talked with the other in 15-20 years
– Dan Chernow

"I cannot pretend a stranger is a long lost friend" but it is wholly possible to heavily grieve someone you've never met. Art binds us all. Neil's thoughts and feelings, expressed so eloquently in his work, certainly connected with mine making it possibly for a stranger to FEEL like a lifelong friend.
– W. Earl Brown

Disbelief, shock, sadness. I am sure most Rush fans will be able to tell you where they were when they heard the news. Similar to when John Lennon died. Not ashamed to say I did shed a few tears. Listened to Rush all weekend long. Sent messages to our fellow concert group members mentioned above.
– Mike W.

It was a very powerful and moving moment. I was aware of his illness through my friendship with Alex Lifeson but it still caught me off guard. Even though I never met Neil, I felt that I knew him through his lyrics and through the music of Rush. I started to write out my reflections on his death and this has turned into a larger project of composing my own autobiography with a focus on the importance of music in my life, especially the music of Rush.
- Metropolitan Tikhon (Mollard)

I cried for 6 hours straight. Neil's death was soul crushing. It was like losing a friend.
– Alec T.

Honestly, it has truly caused me to reflect on my life, the things I want out of it, and how I can be my truest self. Neil really inspired me as a teenager to be myself, and to not live in fear of my anxieties and insecurities. Unfortunately, those issues have been compounded by mental health concerns that I did not believe, until recently, the power of music could address.

I have been mourning, learning, and celebrating the life of this man ever since I heard about his passing.
– David B., aka Dave2112

Said a decade of the rosary for his soul and spent a couple of hours drinking beer and listening to my favorite Rush songs at a volume only those who live in the country can get away with.
– C. Carrasco

It hit me harder than any other, even my parents and grandmother. I was sad when they died and I miss them, but with Neil it went so much deeper. His lyrics, prose, and drumming have been such an integral part of my life for nearly forty years and I wasn't at all prepared to let him go. I had accepted that Rush was done as an active touring band, but I still held out hope we might get an odd song or even an album without a tour. If not that, surely Neil would write more and we might get more insight into his mindset about retiring and how he would spend his time in this phase of his life. I still hope he might have written something for eventual release, but I totally understand if he wants that part of his life to remain private. I'm so thankful for the body of work that Neil, Alex and Geddy gave to us as well as well as the additional work Neil did with his books, blogs, interviews, instructional books & DVDs, etc.
– Darren Hightower

I was at work. I work at an elementary school with some high-needs kids, so I had to compartmentalize to get through my day. I left at

4pm and on a hunch, turned on my local modern rock station (89.3, The Current). They played side one of 2112. All of it. I managed to drive over to the middle school where I needed to pick up my daughter before I started to break down. She wasn't coming out until 4:30, so I had some time. "2112" ended, and I pulled myself together in time for us to drive home. My phone kept buzzing and buzzing, but I couldn't look because I knew what all the messages were going to be. That night, after everyone went to bed, I listened to "The Garden" and had my first, real, deep cry. The man who was second only to my own father in terms of depth of influence on how I shaped my life was gone.
– A fan from Robbinsdale, MN

I was stunned. My best friend, who is also a huge Rush fan and who took me to my first Rush show, called me and broke the news. I was really in shock. Then, I had many of my students reach out to me and check on me because they remembered I had a Rush poster in my classroom right by my desk. It was so sad, I could not cry. I still have a hard time believing it is true. About a week later, my best friend and I held our own personal memorial service where we watched R40 and clips from other concerts together.
– Dustin Gentile

From these stories, you can see the connections all Rush fans seem to have, not only with what Neil Peart and Rush meant, but how so many fans felt such a depth of sorrow for a man they never met. The similarity between how fans processed and grieved is also striking; many seem to have, on their own, mourned for Peart in a manner described by Reverend Evans and Scott Webster. Maybe human beings do have an instinctual way to grieve for people we never met after all.

The upshot of this is that I shouldn't feel weird for having the feelings I did after hearing about Neil Peart's passing. And neither should any Rush fan out there. As Rev. Evans put it, art and music can bridge the gap between knowing and not knowing. It is through his lyrics and drumming that Peart spoke to us, the fans, and through their playing that Geddy, Alex, and Neil connected with countless strangers who somehow became more than strangers, dreamers and misfits united by the music of Rush.

There is nothing weird about that at all. In fact, it's rather beautiful.

CHAPTER VIII: CHOICES GOT TO HAVE VOICES

"Even I can barely make sense of our concept albums." [1]

A FAVORITE CHILD

Ask any artist which is the favorite work that they've created, and you're bound to get a plethora of variations on the theme of "I can't answer that; I'm too close to them and in a way I love them all." Some artists, indeed, might not like *any* of their own work, as counterintuitive as that sounds.

"It's always startling when an artist declares hatred for their work,"[2] begins Brian Collins in *Forbes*:

---

1 Michael Hann, "Geddy Lee on Rush's greatest songs: 'Even I can barely make sense of our concept albums,'" *The Guardian*, December 24, 2018, available at https://www.theguardian.com/music/2018/dec/24/geddy-lee-on-rush-greatest-songs, last accessed July 11, 2020.
2 Brian Collins, "Why Artists Hate Their Own Work," *Forbes*, November 19, 2019, avail-

Russian novelist Leo Tolstoy was ashamed of his masterpieces War and Peace and Anna Karenina. Irish musician Bono said about their 1997 album Pop, "It is really the most expensive demo session in the history of music."

Filmmaker David Fincher said about Alien 3, "I had to work on it for two years, got fired off it three times, and I had to fight for every single thing. No one hated it more than me; to this day, no one hates it more than me."[3]

Some of this, Collins explains, is actually a part of the creative process. Artists are a temperamental lot, so goes the cliché, but there is a lot of truth to this. After all, "[i]f artists felt satisfied, why bother pushing themselves forward or embracing a different challenge? . . . Perhaps artists also hate their work because they must stop creating and eventually ship it and all its ugly imperfections."[4]

There is something to be said about perfectionism, the fear that seizes many of us regular folk as well as artists. How often have you dreaded hitting the "Send" button on a report or brief for work, or when finishing a woodworking or automotive project to deliver to a client? What if there is something not *right* about it? Oh, it might *work* just fine. It might *do its job*. Hell, the recipient might actually *really like it*. But there's that nagging feeling that one small, tiny imperfection—an imperfection *in your eyes only*—will be noticed by the world at large. And when *you* look at your project, that imperfection is all you will see.

"A work of art is never finished, merely abandoned," English writer Oscar Wilde famously said, paraphrasing French poet Paul Valéry.[5] An artist has to get their creation into a form

---

able at https://www.forbes.com/sites/bryancollinseurope/2019/11/19/why-artists-hate-their-own-work/#12a28ce53398, last accessed July 11, 2020.
3 *Id.*
4 *Id.*
5 *Id.*

suitable for public consumption—usually having multiple passes by an editor or other such individual in charge of quality control—but after that . . . it's gone. Whether it be a painting or a book or a movie or a song, at some point the artist must let it go and let it stand. No revisions. No do-overs. No remakes.[6] It's on to the next one, and the great artists get past their dissatisfaction with their past work to push forward to something new and better.

That attitude seems to fit Rush perfectly, doesn't it? The band always seemed to venture into uncharted territory right when they were perfecting their current style, veering off into precision prog-pop right when they had mastered sprawling song structures and instrumental wizardry, or becoming for all intents and purposes an electronic rock band after successfully blending progressive rock with new wave. And these are but two of Rush's stylistic shifts. "That was the thing about Rush," says Geddy Lee in *Beyond the Lighted Stage*, "we were always overreaching." That's one of the things that endears this band to its fans, that sense that anything is possible and it all might go off the rails . . . but somehow the band makes it work. There's the "artistic temperament" for you.

But given this commonality among many artists to disparage their own work, does Rush feel like that about their own music? Do the members of Rush have favorite songs? If you ask Donna Halper, which someone did on popular Internet question-and-answer site Quora, they don't. At least, Geddy Lee doesn't:

> In all the years I've known him (more than 4 decades), he has never expressed a love for just one song. As another Quoran correctly mentioned, Geddy seems to like certain songs for a while, and then wants to play different ones. And sometimes, he will revisit a song— the

---

6 Unless you're George Lucas, I guess. Although to be fair to Mr. Lucas, he's not the only one; Frank Zappa famously, and controversially, had his band in the 1980s re-record the bass and drum tracks to several of the early Mothers of Invention albums from the 1960s.

first song I ever played by the band in the US, back in 1974, was "Working Man," and it was strongly identified with Rush for a long time. But after a while, other songs became even more popular, and "Working Man" wasn't part of their concerts. And then, a while passed, and it was time to return to playing "Working Man," which Rush did during their R40 tour.

In the 2010 documentary "Beyond the Lighted Stage," Geddy talked about the musical changes the band had undergone. That is actually quite typical of musicians, especially those with a large body of work like Rush has. So, all I can say is that Geddy has never told me he prefers one song more than all others. He may secretly have one, but I think certain songs recall for him certain periods of time in the band's long and successful career. Thanks for asking, and for being a fan![7]

Donna would know. However, a year before Donna gave her answer, Geddy did speak to *The Guardian* about a few Rush songs that held deep meaning for him. Among those are "Finding My Way," "2112," "La Villa Strangiato," "Tom Sawyer", "Roll the Bones," and "Headlong Flight."[8] Now, these really aren't Geddy's favorites. These are cuts that represented certain milestones in the Rush story. "2112" and "Tom Sawyer" are ob-

---

7   Donna Halper, "What's Geddy Lee's favorite Rush song?" Quora.com, September 27, 2019, available at https://www.quora.com/What-s-Geddy-Lee-s-favorite-Rush-song, last accessed July 11, 2020.
8   Michael Hann, "Geddy Lee on Rush's greatest songs: 'Even I can barely make sense of our concept albums,'" *The Guardian*, December 24, 2018, available at https://www.theguardian.com/music/2018/dec/24/geddy-lee-on-rush-greatest-songs, last accessed July 11, 2020. This piece also includes a twenty song playlist picked by Lee (19 Rush songs and one song from Lee's 2000 solo album *My Favorite Headache*). It's no surprise that several of Lee's picks like "Between the Wheels, "Mission," and "The Pass" were re-inserted into places of prominence in Rush's live shows after their return to the stage in 2002.

vious choices, as they fundamentally altered the course of their career.

Alex Lifeson has likewise never revealed his favorite Rush *song*. The closes he came was in a 2009 piece for *MusicRadar* where Lifeson discusses his three favorite Rush *guitar solos*, these being "Limelight," "Kid Gloves," and "Freewill."[9] And Neil Peart has often said that "Tom Sawyer" is his favorite Rush song to perform, noting that "I will never get tired of playing 'Tom Sawyer' because it's always difficult to play right . . . and anytime I do play it right, I feel good."[10]

These are fair points, and the band always seems the most excited about the *next* song and the *next* album like the true prog-rockers that they are. But while they seem either unwilling or unable to pick that one song they feel is quintessential Rush, two-thirds of our trio isn't that shy about picking the red-headed stepchild of the Rush catalogue.

WHAT ABOUT THE CHILDREN YOU DON'T LIKE?

With nary a moment of hesitation, both Geddy Lee and Alex Lifeson pick "Tai-Shan" from 1987's *Hold Your Fire* as the worst song Rush ever recorded.[11]

9   Joe Bosso, "Rush's Alex Lifeson: 'My 3 Best Solos,'" *MusicRadar*, February 4, 2009, available at https://www.musicradar.com/news/guitars/rushs-alex-lifeson-my-3-best-solos-194741, last accessed July 13, 2020.
10   *Rush: Beyond the Lighted Stage* (Documentary, 2010). *See also*, Neil Peart in Vinay Menon, *Rush: An Oral History* (Toronto Star Newspapers Limited, 2013), at 51 ("When people ask me, 'What's your favorite RUSH album,' I would hate to have to say it was something from 30 years ago. That would be awful. I know I'm playing better. I'm writing better. Everything about *Clockwork Angels* I love. There's no doubt in my mind that it's the best album we have ever made in every way. That's a great feeling to have.").
11   *See, e.g.,* "Geddy Lee Names Rush Song He Doesn't Like, Shares Opinion on Modern Extended-Range Basses: 'Alex and I had a hard time putting ourselves in it,' the musician says," Ultimate-Guitar.com, August 22, 2019, available at https://www.ultimate-guitar.com/news/general_music_news/geddy_lee_names_rush_song_he_doesnt_like_shares_opinion_on_modern_extended-range_basses.html, last accessed July 11, 2020; Jeff Giles, "Rush's Worst Songs Revealed by Alex Lifeson," *Ultimate Classic Rock*, October 14, 2016, avaialble at https://ultimateclassicrock.com/alex-lifeson-rush-worst-songs/, last accessed

"It's just one of those songs that Alex and I like to make fun of," Geddy Lee said in a 2019 Q&A session in Manchester, England while on tour for his *Big Beautiful Book of Bass*.

> At the time I was singing it, I wasn't standing on a mountain top. Because it was such a personal song for Neil, and it was such a great moment for Neil, Alex and I had a hard time putting ourselves in it. And guys in bands really need all the ammunition we can to make fun of each other. It just sort of landed on "Tai-Shan."[12]

Lifeson is more succinct in naming "Tai-Shan" among his least-favorite Rush song, simply calling it "one of the worst, easily."[13]

Geddy has another *bete noire* among the Rush songbook, one that I find quite surprising: "Lakeside Park." As he put it to *Raw Magazine* in 1993:

> A lot of the early stuff I'm really proud of. Some of it sounds really goofy, but some of it stands up better than I gave it credit for. As weird as my voice sounds when I listen back, I certainly dig some of the arrangements. I can't go back beyond 2112 really, because that starts to get a bit hairy for me, and if I hear "Lakeside Park"

July 11, 2020.
12   "Geddy Lee – BBOB Q&A Manchester – Dancehouse Theatre – June 10 2019," available at https://www.youtube.com/watch?v=o-lbS-PGcSE&list=RDo-lbS-PGcSE&start_radio=1&t=2947, last accessed July 14, 2020.
13   Paul Elliot, "Alex Lifeson on God, police brutality and 'disco biscuits," *Classic Rock*, October 13, 2016, available at https://www.loudersound.com/features/interview-alex-lifeson-on-god-police-brutality-and-disco-biscuits, last accessed May 22, 2020.; the other least-favorite Rush song Lifeson names is "Panacea," part IV of *Caress of Steel*'s concluding epic "The Fountain of Lamneth." Lifeson calls it an "innocent" attempt at "something that didn't really work out."

on the radio I cringe. What a lousy song! Still, I don't regret anything that I've done![14]

The song, apparently, wasn't bad enough to *not* be played during Rush's career-spanning R40 tour where, in my humble opinion, it sounded great. They're both wrong, of course—"Tai-Shan" is Rush's *second* worst song. "Rivendell" from *Fly By Night* is the worst. But everybody has their own rankings, band and fan alike. Jordan Hoffman of website *Thrillist* even ranked all 180 Rush songs, and he got it wrong too; while Hoffman places "Rivendell" at 138 and "Tai-Shan" at 129, he erroneously ranks 42 other songs as being worse than "Rivendell."[15] Ryan Reed of *Ultimate Classic Rock* gets it even *more* wrong, rating "Rivendell" *32* out of the 167 Rush songs he ranked.[16] This leaves me, quite literally, speechless. I suppose everybody is entitled to their opinion, even if it's wrong.

Have you heard "Rivendell"? Goodness, it's awful. Just absolutely cheesy Tolkien-inspired lyrics sung in an uncomfortable falsetto over corny Renaissance Fair acoustic guitar plucking. Mind you, I'm a guy who loves Tolkien and has a high tolerance for cheesy music, but "Rivendell" is an elven-made bridge too far. Let me put it to you this way: when I listen to *Hold Your Fire*, I'll sometimes listen to "Tai-Shan." I always skip "Rivendell" when I listen to *Fly By Night*.

---

14 Available at http://news.cygnus-x1.net/2011/05/everyone-would-gather-on-24th-of-may.html, last accessed July 20, 2020.
15 Jordan Hoffman, "All 180 Rush Songs, Ranked," *Thrillist*, July 29, 2019, available at https://www.thrillist.com/entertainment/nation/best-rush-songs-ranked, last accessed July 14, 2020. Hoffman is entitled to his own opinion, of course, and the list is pretty funny. And although it wouldn't be my personal pick for number one, I can't argue with him ranking "Red Barchetta" as Rush's greatest song.
16 Ryan Reed, "All 167 Rush Songs Ranked Worst to Best," *Ultimate Classic Rock*, available at https://ultimateclassicrock.com/every-rush-song/, last accessed July 20, 2020.

YOUR ERA OF EXPERTISE

All this talk about *Hold Your Fire*, of course, brings up another hot-button debated by Rush fans everywhere, and that is what is Rush's best *era*. A band like Rush, which has been around for so long, needs to be discussed in these terms since their sound developed so much from their early days in the late 60s honing their craft as a bar band enthralled by British blues rock and on their raw, explosive, and relatively straight-ahead 1974 debut.

But it's the different eras of Rush that keep the band interesting. Unlike some bands who retain a core sound, songwriting style, and instrumentation—I'm looking at you, AC/DC[17]—Rush's music changed wildly from era-to-era, and sometimes from album-to-album; for example, *Roll the Bones* and *Counterparts* came out within two years of each other and sound vastly different.

So what are these eras? The band themselves used four-album stretches capped with a live album to bookend various parts of their career. This pattern was stable up through the end of the 1990s. The first spans the albums *Rush* to *2112*, ending with the live album *All the World's a Stage*—this can be broadly called the "hard rock" era (1974-1976). Next, we go from *A Farewell to Kings* to *Moving Pictures*, followed by *Exit... Stage Left*; the "prog" era (1977-1981). The next four-album era stretches from *Signals* to *Hold Your Fire*, with *A Show of Hands* being the live chronicle, the "keyboard" era (1982-1988).[18] Rounding out the four-albums-plus-one-live-album cycle, there is the stretch of albums from *Presto* to *Test for Echo*, finished with the release of *Different Stages*, the "return to guitars" era (1989-1997).

The 2000s were a different beast, with *two* live albums after each studio album, one memorializing that album's tour, and

---

17 This is in no way a knock on AC/DC—they have their sound and their style and they've managed to craft an unbelievable amount of unique music and distinct songs based upon this core. But you can listen to an AC/DC song from the 1970s and one from the 2000s and the difference is minimal. Try doing that with Rush.
18 *A Show of Hands* was released in January of 1989, but recorded in 1988 on the *Hold Your Fire* tour.

another for a tour not undertaken in support of any album in particular. *Vapor Trails* was followed by *Rush in Rio* and then *R30*; *Snakes & Arrows* was followed by *Snakes & Arrows Live* and then *Time Machine 2011: Live in Cleveland*; and *Clockwork Angels* was followed by *Clockwork Angels Tour* and then Rush's final release, *R40*.

I personally don't see these as representative eras, at least insofar as they don't reflect where Rush's sound was at during these spans of time. To my ears, there is a lot of crossover between the albums before and following each live album. Rush fans have been debating this for a *long* time, but to my ears, Rush's music falls most neatly into a series of two album periods. I'm sure many will disagree, but I do think I'm on to something with my taxonomy.

The Hard Rock Era: This era is represented by *Rush* (1974) and *Fly By Night* (1975). The seeds of Rush's extended forays into complex, conceptual prog were there in "Working Man" from the debut, but especially on *Fly By Night* on songs like "By-Tor and the Snow Dog," "Anthem," and "Beneath, Between, and Behind."

The Hard-Prog Era: This era beginning with *Caress of Steel* (1975) and ending triumphantly with *2112* (1976). *Caress of Steel* began to see Rush stretch out instrumentally and conceptually: "Bastille Day" is much more complicated and challenging than your average headbanger, and the album contains not one but *two* multi-part prog suites in "The Necromancer" and "The Fountain of Lamneth," the latter a six-part, nearly 20-minute long extravaganza. The album didn't do well, but as discussed in Chapter IV, the even more conceptually ambitious title track of *2112* pushed Rush into the next level of stardom.

The Prog Epic Era: *A Farewell to Kings* (1977) and *Hemispheres* (1978) are companion pieces for several reasons. One, it is here that Rush really expanded their sound beyond guitar, bass, drums, and vocals, to include synthesizers and other keyboard instruments beyond their use on *2112*. There are also more acoustic guitars, more auxiliary percussion, and more bass pedals. But beyond increasing the scope of the instrumentation, these albums are where Rush increased the scope of their sound, creating sprawling, programmatic pieces that tackled complex subjects with even more complex arrangements. On *A Farewell to Kings*, "Xanadu" and "Cygnus X-1, Book I: The Voyage" are the obvious prog touchstones, but "A Farewell to Kings" and "Cinderella Man" are miniature epics unto themselves. Even "Closer to the Heart" proved that, when trying to write a short pop song, Rush crammed in as much interesting stuff as possible.

These predilections reached their logical fruition—some may say conclusion—on *Hemispheres*, the album which forced Rush to admit defeat. *Hemispheres* is a masterpiece, but one which almost killed the band:

> . . . I think we greatly underestimated the level of overachievement that we were shooting for. As we started writing, it became apparent that this was going to be a concept album, and then it became even more apparent that the musical attitude was going to be quite complex. That was our mistake: It wasn't that we were bereft of ideas — it's that the ideas we did have were much more ambitious than we gave credit to.
>
> We found ourselves working diligently and quite hard, but we underestimated the amount of time it would take to put that thing together. We increased the amount of time we were in pre-production, and then we finally went into the studio after about four weeks. That was a very ambitious recording, and we wanted to do most of it live off the floor, and that meant that we had to be f'ing perfect [laughs].
>
> These were long pieces of music. "La Villa Strangiato," for example, we wanted to record that in one long, perfect take. We tried for days

to get that, and eventually we had to compromise. We did it in four segments and stitched it together. I think we spent something like 11 days on that track. I remember telling the story at one point that it took longer to record "La Villa Strangiato" than it did our entire Fly by Night album.[19]

"We knew at the time, you know, we were overreaching ourselves," Neil Peart says in *Beyond the Lighted Stage*, "and we agreed among ourselves in 1978 when we finished *Hemispheres*, 'We're not doing this again,' you know? 'We're not making this kind of record again.' We knew that was the end of that era, of the epics."

And so it was.

The Pop-Prog Era: Inspired by the experience writing "Circumstances,"[20] Rush somehow managed to (mostly) condense their proggier inclinations into succinct, catchy, yet still evocative and complex song structures on their next two albums, *Permanent Waves* (1980) and *Moving Pictures* (1981). While some fans might have been yearning for more prog epics, these two albums shot Rush into the upper echelons of the rock world, lofty heights where they would remain for the rest of their ca-

19   Ryan Reed, "Geddy Lee on Rush's Prog-Rock Opus 'Hemispheres': 'We Had to Raise Our Game': The bassist reflects on writing side-long 'mini rock operas,' singing in awkward keys and Alex Lifeson's mysterious 'bedroom accident'—and offers an update on the state of Rush," *Rolling Stone*, October 22, 2018, available at https://www.rollingstone.com/music/music-news/rush-geddy-lee-interview-prog-rock-hemispheres-738828/, last accessed June 19, 2020.
20   *Id*. ("It was the end of a thing. In a way, we felt we were starting to repeat ourselves, like when we put the overture together for 'Hemispheres.' We were falling into these patterns of writing—the repetition of these thematic things that occur over a 20-minute span. They were starting to feel too comfortably organized in a way, like we weren't thinking originally enough. That's kind of a prog pattern. People associate prog rock with a challenging style of music, and it certainly can be that. But if you're starting to fall into past habits and develop a methodology that's too comfortable, it's not progressive. I think we started to feel that way by the time we finished that record. With some of the experiments on Side Two, for example, like "Circumstances," we were able to work in a shorter time frame. That started to become more challenging and more enticing, so we sort of headed off in that direction.").

reer. *Moving Pictures* remains the band's best-selling album,[21] and as we'll see later in this chapter, their most popular.

What's most astonishing is how much these two albums, particularly *Moving Pictures*, still sound like rock music of the future. Synthesizers are more prominent and integrated so well with the Rush sound in the ultimate fusion of man-and-machine. The songwriting is top notch, managing to make these thick, knotty, complex songs so accessible, the production is crystal-clear and flawless, and the instrumental wizardry is harnessed into five-minute flamethrower bursts instead of 20-minute wildfires. Plus, the extended prog epics are still there: "Jacob's Ladder" and "Natural Science" on *Permanent Waves* and "The Camera Eye" on *Moving Pictures*; they're just structured slightly more conventionally.[22]

It was the early 1980s, computers were starting to come into their own, and while we all feared we'd die of nuclear war (the next era gets more into that), there was also a sense of optimism, of fun, of better days ahead. This sense is captured perfectly by *Permanent Waves* and *Moving Pictures*.

The Synth-Prog Era: *Signals* (1982) and *Grace Under Pressure* (1984) show the keyboard beginning to take up much of the sonic space that used to belong to Alex Lifeson; *Signals* opener "Subdivisions" is striking in just how prominent Geddy Lee's synths are. This forced Lifeson to make unique choices with how he played his instrument, treating the guitar like a part of the rhythm section, or providing unique ornamentation to what the keyboards were doing. This led to some interesting music— seriously, it's difficult for anyone who has not listened to much Rush to understand just *how good* their early 80s output is—but Alex Lifeson was not fully on-board with these experiments in electronic music. This would come to a head in the next era. "At first, we were all very excited about the extra element," Alex

21 Andrew Olson, "Rush album and video sales (U.S.)," *Neil Peart News*, July 14, 2013, available at http://www.andrewolson.com/Neil_Peart/neil_peart_rush_album_sales.htm#:~:text=Quick%20facts&text=The%20best%20selling%20album%20is,Snakes%20%26%20Arrows%20(200%2C000)., last accessed July 14, 2020.
22 *Really* slightly.

Lifeson says. "It made our sound bigger. We had more impact off the stage." However, Lifeson would be the first member of Rush to sour on the keyboards.[23]

Many fans were unhappy with this left turn as well, especially hot on the heels of *Moving Pictures*. "*Moving Pictures* got us into a much broader world of rock fans," explains Geddy Lee, "and when there was a shift, we lost those some of those people. But we realized after time that there was a core of our fan base that was as curious as to where we were going as we were, and those are the ones that have sustained us through all these years."[24] Still, these two albums were immensely popular and still retained Rush's hard rock edge while throwing in elements of reggae, new wave, and electronica.

And for many Rush fans, *Grace Under Pressure* was the end of the road.

The Synth-Pop Era: As *Hemispheres* marked both the apotheosis and end of Rush's prog-epic era, *Power Windows* (1985) and *Hold Your Fire* (1987) represent the full fruition and conclusion of Rush's experiments with keyboards. Geddy Lee understood this: "There are certain periods of Rush that are more universal than other periods. Now, you can say on the one hand that maybe there are better records [than *Power Windows* and *Hold Your Fire*]. Maybe that's the best Rush."[25]

"It wasn't until *Signals* that I started having real problems with the keyboards," says Alex Lifeson.[26] "At first, keyboards were used sparingly. On *Moving Pictures* and *Permanent Waves*, it was still controlled. We used them efficiently, economically and effectively, I would say."[27]

Geddy Lee has a slightly different remembrance: "[A]t the time, he was gung ho to do it when we started. We wouldn't

---

23 Vinay Menon, *Rush: An Oral History* (Toronto Star Newspapers Limited, 2013), at 31.
24 *Rush: Beyond the Lighted Stage* (Documentary, 2010).
25 *Id.*
26 Vinay Menon, *Rush: An Oral History* (Toronto Star Newspapers Limited, 2013), at 33.
27 *Id.* at 32. ("In my heart, I really wasn't thrilled with the way it was going. But I remained silent about a lot of my feelings at the time, to be honest. I've always been like that in the band. Geddy and Neil have stronger personalities. I felt like I'm just not going to rock the boat.").

have done it if he wasn't."[28] However, Lee admits that "it was after we did *Power Windows*, that was the first time it was obvious that Al was starting to object."[29]

Lee sees *Power Windows* as Rush's "final and essential blending of keyboards and guitars."[30] Predictably, Alex Lifeson does not agree with this assessment:

> With Power Windows, I found it really, really difficult to work around the way the keyboards were developing. Why am I looking for a different place? I shouldn't be looking for a different place. What's going on with these keyboards? They're not even real. It's not even a real instrument.[31]

That said, the guitars are still loud and prominent on *Power Windows*, and it was a wildly successful album. It is also, in my humble opinion, wildly *good*. Yes, if you leapt straight from *2112* to *Power Windows*, you'd be thinking to yourself, "What the hell is this?" but underneath those sometimes dated synths and you'll find a treasure trove of great grooves, memorable riffs, vintage Rush instrumental wizardry, inspired and uplifting lyrics, and a sense of exuberant optimism. *Power Windows* might be Rush's most *fun* album, and just when you think a song is getting too cheesy there'll be some instrumental section where Geddy and Neil go to town on some odd-time riff while Alex shreds the hell out of his pointy guitar.[32] Lee's voice had also mellowed out by this point; he doesn't shriek and his singing had never been better.

Hold Your Fire continued this exploration into keyboard-led harmonic sophistication . . . and it was where many fans tapped out. The *Beyond the Lighted Stage* documentary is interesting

28 *Id.*
29 *Id.* at 33.
30 *Rush: Beyond the Lighted Stage* (Documentary, 2010).
31 *Id.*
32 It was 1985, after all.

in that Rush fans Mike Portnoy and Tim Commerford, among others, declare this their least-favorite period of the band's existence, while noted keyboard fan Trent Reznor loved it. Even Billy Corgan expressed his fondness for Rush's synth pop era, stating that what seemed middle-of-the-road for Rush was any other band's left-field.

If *Power Windows* was Rush's most fun album, *Hold Your Fire* may very well be their most beautiful, but it's also more inconsistent than its predecessor, and *far* less on the "rock" side of the spectrum. For example, Alex Lifeson seems enamored of a very thin, wiry single-coil guitar sound which is actually really nice on more somber, poppy, or introspective tracks like "Time Stand Still," "Mission," "Prime Mover," and "Open Secrets," but doesn't have the *oomph* really needed for rockers like "Force Ten," "Lock and Key," or "Turn the Page." And *Hold Your Fire* is a mite too long—personally, I think ballad "Second Nature" and the aforementioned "Tai Shan" should have been left off, which would have made the album a tighter listening experience. It's a good album, and repeated listens reward the listener with a new appreciation for its depth. It's just not really rock.

Alex Lifeson, it seems, was right after all.

<u>The Guitar Pop Era</u>: The next era commences in 1989 with *Presto* and continues with 1991's *Roll the Bones*. The band had realized that they keyboard thing had run its course, much as the prog epic thing had a decade earlier, and so decided to return to their power trio roots and make the guitar the lead instrument.

"*Hold Your Fire* was the record that told me that there was a shift in the way we were writing was pushing us away from rock and starting to move to a jazzier, softer kind of tonal area," Geddy Lee says in *Beyond the Lighted Stage*, and in 2018 admitted that Alex Lifeson was right:

> "Alex was driving at that point and he made it very clear we were drowning under a synthy noise and he wanted the guitar to return to its rightful position," Lee says. "That's fine. It un-

burdened me in a way. I accepted that maybe I had taken it a bridge too far."[33]

And yet, *Presto* sounds pretty much like a continuation of *Hold Your Fire*, just with fewer synths. Lifeson's guitar is still thin-sounding; the songs, even up-tempo rockers like "Show Don't Tell" (a true banger), "War Paint" and "Superconductor" are more sophisticated than rocking; and the production is overall sparse and spacious. Neil's drums, in particular, lack their customary punch. It's an elegiac album, quite elegant with poignant lyrics and haunting melodies, but not the much ballyhooed "return to rock" that we'd finally see in the next era.

Roll the Bones cranks the guitars up more and starts with three stone-cold classics in "Dreamline," "Bravado," and "Roll the Bones"—complete with its endearingly goofy rap—before venturing into middle-of-the-road rock. It's not bad, and the album was hugely successful, selling over 1,000,000 copies,[34] but is pretty inconsistent and, like *Presto*, a bit underwhelming by Rush's standards. But the band had fun making it, and that exuberance shows in the swaggering, groove-oriented nature of many tracks like "Roll the Bones," "Ghost of a Chance," and instrumental "Where's My Thing?" while "You Bet Your Life" is a sunny, upbeat, and appropriately frenetic closer.

The Return to Heaviness Era: *Counterparts* (1993) and *Test for Echo* (1996) answer two important questions. "What if modern Rush went back to being a straightforward power trio?" on the former, and "What if Rush was an alternative rock band?" on the latter. The results are pretty spectacular, especially on *Counterparts*.

---

33 Michael Hann, "Geddy Lee on Rush's greatest songs: 'Even I can barely make sense of our concept albums,'" *The Guardian*, December 24, 2018, available at https://www.theguardian.com/music/2018/dec/24/geddy-lee-on-rush-greatest-songs, last accessed July 11, 2020; Geddy Lee also states in *Beyond the Lighted Stage* that he was "a little bit sad" upon leaving the keyboards behind.

34 Andrew Olson, "Rush album and video sales (U.S.)," *Neil Peart News*, July 14, 2013, available at http://www.andrewolson.com/Neil_Peart/neil_peart_rush_album_sales.htm#:~:text=Quick%20facts&text=The%20best%20selling%20album%20is,Snakes%20%26%20Arrows%20(200%2C000)., last accessed July 14, 2020.

Counterparts producer and mixer Kevin "Caveman" Shirley basically told Alex Lifeson to ditch the single-coil sound and go back to playing a cranked-up Les Paul to get some "balls" back on the guitar,[35] and the results are magnificent. This is a strong album that nearly made it to number 1 in the U.S., beaten out by Pearl Jam's *Vs*.[36] There are grunge and alternative influences on thunderous lead single "Stick It Out" and "Cut to the Chase," but rockers like "Animate," "Between Sun and Moon," "Cold Fire," and "Everyday Glory" are hard-charging, quintessential Rush. The guitars and bass are thick and loud, and the drums are in your face, particularly Neil's ride cymbal. Keyboards add spice in the background, and the swaggering funk that permeated *Roll the Bones* is present in instrumental "Leave That Thing Alone." *Counterparts* is light on the prog but really sounds like three guys having a blast cranking out some heavy rock tunes.

Test for Echo continues this sonic trend. It's spottier, particularly in the lyrics department, and features softer songs like "Half the World," "The Color of Right," and the gorgeous "Resist," but Rush still brings the thunder on tracks like "Driven," "Time and Motion," "Virtuality," and the sprawling title track. *Test for Echo* is rarely fans' favorite Rush album, even Geddy Lee calls it "a creative low time,"[37] but individual songs from it remain favorites. Most bands would consider themselves lucky to sound so vital and energetic after thirty years in the business. Luckily, Rush wasn't done.

The Comeback Era: The 2000s saw Rush reemerge and gain an entire new fan base with their final three albums, *Vapor Trails* (2002), *Snakes & Arrows* (2007) and *Clockwork Angels* (2012). The sonic template is hard to explain: It's modern rock put through the Rush filter with several nods to the band's past while at the same time looking forward. They're loud, fast, and varied, with Geddy layering multiple bass tracks, Alex playing

---

35 *Rush: Beyond the Lighted Stage* (Documentary, 2010).
36 *See* "Billboard 200, Week of November 6, 1993," available at https://www.billboard.com/charts/billboard-200/1993-11-06, last accessed July 17, 2020.
37 Vinay Menon, *Rush: An Oral History* (Toronto Star Newspapers Limited, 2013), at 36 ("*Test for Echo* was a strange record in a sense. It doesn't really have a defined direction. I kind of felt like we were a bit burnt creatively. It was a creative low time for us.").

with chordal textures, and Neil continuing to improve his drumming.[38]

Each album in this era was better than the last. *Vapor Trails* is a bit too long, but shows that rock veterans are capable of learning new tricks. *Snakes & Arrows* is a confident chronicle of a band still experimenting with musical complexity in concise song structures, and *Clockwork Angels* is, to my ears, the Rush-iest (a new word I just invented) album they've ever done, forward-looking with several callbacks to each of the previous eras. It's a truly magnificent cap to a career that us fans wish could have continued for at least a few more albums.

You might disagree with my breakdown, but that's why Rush is such a fun band to talk, or write hundreds of pages about. A few big takeaways stand out when one looks at Rush's recorded output in this manner:

1. Rush rarely did the same thing more than twice in a row;
2. Rush had one of the longest winning streaks in rock history: the nine-year, eight-album span of *2112* to *Power Windows* is untouchable; and
3. With a career this long, each era is some fan's favorite.

So enough about my opinions: what do the fans think?

THE GREAT DEBATE

Given that Rush has been around for over forty years and never stopped writing and recording new music, fans have a *lot* to choose from. Questions of ranking Rush albums have been discussed quite a bit over the years—see, for example, *Stereogum*'s

---

38 It's *insane* to think a drummer as skilled from the get-go as Neil Peart got *better* as Rush went on, but then again, Rush was a special band.

Adrien Begrand's ranking from 2014[39]—but I wanted to go to the fans themselves and figure out.

My survey asked Rush fans questions about their favorite songs, albums, and eras, as well as when they started listening to Rush, how they became fans, and the first album they bought. I crunched the numbers on the two questions I think most Rush fans debate with each other and with themselves: Favorite album and favorite song. Here's what I found.

647 fans told me what their favorite album was. Now, to be fair, if a respondent included more than one and were *definitive* about it, I counted them all. If they said something like "I don't know . . . maybe *Signals*? *Power Windows*? *Presto*?" I did not count those. There's also a catch-all category for fans who said that they couldn't pick, their favorite changes constantly, or they love them all. Here's the breakdown:

Moving Pictures was the clear and unsurprising fan favorite, with 133, or 20.5% of Rush fans calling it their top pick. *Hemispheres* took second place—a distant second—with 83 fans, or 12.8%, hailing it as Rush's masterpiece. Sixty-two fans, or 9.5%, exercised their freewill and cited *Permanent Waves* as their favorite. *2112* clocked in at number four with 58 fans, or 8.9%, ranking it first. Next was *Signals* with 47, or 7.2% of Rush fans calling it their favorite, followed closely by *Exit . . . Stage Left* with 41 votes, or 6.3%. Rush's final studio album and my personal pick for number 1 *Clockwork Angels* clocked in at seventh with 37 fans, or 5.7% of respondents, really digging the adventures of Owen Hardy. Next, 37 fans, or 5.7% chose not to decide, or couldn't decide, which album was their favorite. 1985's *Power Windows*, arguably the best-loved album of Rush's keyboard era came in next with 31 votes, or 4.7% of respondents, and *A Farewell to Kings* rounds out the top ten with 27 votes, or 4.1% of fans calling it their favorite.

I wasn't too surprised by this breakdown, although I had expected *Power Windows* and *2112* to rank higher, and *Perma-*

---

39   Adrien Begrand, "Rush Albums from Worst to Best," Stereogum.com, available at https://www.stereogum.com/1685666/rush-albums-from-worst-to-best/franchises/list/, last accessed July 17, 2020.

nent Waves to give *Moving Pictures* a serious run for its money. I suppose *HemispheresHemispheres* as fans' second-favorite album makes sense upon further consideration, since it marks the apotheosis of Rush's heavy prog phase; the album is just *wild*... plus it has "La Villa Strangiato."

The remaining ranking of fan-favorite albums is as follows: *Grace Under Pressure* (20 fans, or 3%), *Hold Your Fire* and *Counterparts* (18 fans, or 2.7%), *Counterparts* (16 fans, or 2.4%), *Vapor Trails* and *Presto* (14 fans, or 2.1% each), *Snakes & Arrows* (13 fans, or 2%), *All the World's a Stage* and *Caress of Steel* (10 fans, or 1.5%), *Roll the Bones* (8 fans, or 1.2%), *Fly By Night* (7 fans, or 1%), *Chronicles* (4 fans, or 0.6%), *Rush in Rio* and *A Show of Hands* (3 fans, or 0.4% each), and *Rush, Test for Echo, Different Stages, Clockwork Angels Tour,* and *R40* (1 fan, or 0.1% each).

When it came to fans' favorite Rush *songs*, the same rules applied, and I had 651 respondents answer this question. This list is as follows:

"La Villa Strangiato" – 69 (10.5%)
"The Spirit of Radio" – 41 (6.2%)
Can't pick – 39 (5.9%)
"Natural Science" – 38 (5.8%)
"Xanadu" – 38 (5.8%)
"2112" – 34 (5.2%)
"Red Barchetta" – 33 (5%)
"Limelight" – 31 (4.7%)
"Subdivisions" – 27 (4.1%)
"Cygnus X-1, Book II: Hemispheres" – 23 (3.5%)
"Freewill" – 23 (3.5%)
"The Garden" – 20 (3%)
"The Camera Eye" – 16 (2.4%)
"Jacob's Ladder" – 15 (2.3%)
"The Trees" – 15 (2.3%)
"Time Stand Still" – 13 (1.9%)
"Mission" – 11 (1.6%)

"Tom Sawyer" – 10 (1.5%)
"YYZ" – 10 (1.5%)
"Cygnus X-1, Book I: The Voyage" – 9 (1.3%)
"Losing It" – 9 (1.3%)
"The Analog Kid" – 8 (1.2%)
"The Pass" – 8 (1.2%)
"Bravado" – 7 (1%)
"Entre Nous" – 6 (0.9%)
"In The End" – 6 (0.9%)
"Vital Signs" – 6 (0.9%)
"Witch Hunt" – 6 (0.9%)
"Working Man" – 6 (0.9%)
"Dreamline" – 5 (0.7%)
"Headlong Flight" – 5 (0.7%)
"By-Tor and the Snow Dog" – 4 (0.6%)
"Closer to the Heart" – 4 (0.6%)
"Earthshine" – 4 (0.6%)
"Fly By Night" – 4 (0.6%)
"Manhattan Project" – 4 (0.6%)
"Mystic Rhythms" – 4 (0.6%)
"The Necromancer" – 4 (0.6%)
"A Farewell to Kings" – 3 (0.4%)
"Between the Wheels" – 3 (0.4%)
"Far Cry" – 3 (0.4%)
"The Fountain of Lamneth" – 3 (0.4%)
"Marathon" – 3 (0.4%)
"New World Man" – 3 (0.4%)
"Anthem" – 2 (0.3%)
"Cold Fire" – 2 (0.3%)
"Driven" – 2 (0.3%)
"Emotion Detector" – 2 (0.3%)
"The Enemy Within" – 2 (0.3%)
"Everyday Glory" – 2 (0.3%)
"Ghost of a Chance" – 2 (0.3%)
"Kid Gloves" – 2 (0.3%)
"Lakeside Park" – 2 (0.3%)
"*Presto*" – 2 (0.3%)

"The Anarchist" – 2 (0.3%)
"A Passage to Bangkok" – 1 (0.1%)
"Alien Shore" – 1 (0.1%)
"Animate" – 1 (0.1%)
Any Instrumental – 1 (0.1%)
"Available Light" – 1 (0.1%)
"Beneath, Between, and Behind" – 1 (0.1%)
"BU2B" – 1 (0.1%)
"Ceiling Unlimited" – 1 (0.1%)
"Cinderella Man" – 1 (0.1%)
"Circumstances" – 1 (0.1%)
"*Clockwork Angels*" – 1 (0.1%)
"Distant Early Warning" – 1 (0.1%)
"Half the World" – 1 (0.1%)
"Hand Over Fist" – 1 (0.1%)
"Leave That Thing Alone" – 1 (0.1%)
"Lessons" – 1 (0.1%)
"Making Memories" – 1 (0.1%)
"Middletown Dreams" – 1 (0.1%)
"One Little Victory" – 1 (0.1%)
"Open Secrets" – 1 (0.1%)
"Prime Mover" – 1 (0.1%)
"Red Sector A" – 1 (0.1%)
"Red Tide" – 1 (0.1%)
"Resist" – 1 (0.1%)
"Scars" – 1 (0.1%)
"Second Nature" – 1 (0.1%)
"Seven Cities of Gold" – 1 (0.1%)
"Something For Nothing" – 1 (0.1%)
"The Body Electric" – 1 (0.1%)
"Territories" – 1 (0.1%)
"The Big Money" – 1 (0.1%)
"The Color of Right" – 1 (0.1%)
"The Main Monkey Business" – 1 (0.1%)
"Vapor Trail" – 1 (0.1%)
"We Hold On" – 1 (0.1%)

The only eye-opener here was that "Tom Sawyer" and "YYZ" were not ranked higher. I expected the other top songs like "La Villa Strangiato," "The Spirit of Radio," "Natural Science," "Xanadu," and "2112," but figured there'd be more representatives from *Moving Pictures*—the consensus favorite album!—among the most popular Rush songs.[40]

Anyway, this is all in good fun, but it goes to show Rush's staying power and how subsequent generations who got into Rush during different decades really latch on to a particular album or era—if your first Rush album was *Roll the Bones* or the first song you heard was "One Little Victory" and *that* got you hooked, you're bound to have different favorites than someone who was a teenager when *2112* came out. It's only natural.

For the record, if you threatened my life or that of a loved one *unless* I could name one Rush song as my favorite—and if that's your death-trap, you're a *terrible* super-villain—I'd say "Xanadu." I can't explain it, but that song just really does it for me, particularly the live version on *Exit . . . Stage Left*.

The full raft of survey questions is reproduced in Appendix A, but here are some fan explanations of why they chose one album in particular above the rest:

> Moving Pictures because it was a revelation to me, it was all I had ever looked for in music: I love high pitched voices, and I loved the technicity with no showing off. But Grace Under Pressure is a very close second.
> - Sylvie Yeranotsian

> If I had to desert island them, I'd have to go with Permanent Waves. Love the sound of that record, especially guitar tone. Love the themes expressed by that record. It's creative, smart, fun and a great blend of concept and conciseness.
> - John Heinlein

---

[40] Also: No "Force Ten"? No "Show Don't Tell"? *Really*, people?

Impossible—probably Hemispheres. That album is just so majestic and reflects Rush at the height and end of the 70s era. Side one is classic Rush taking you on a journey out of this world. Side two contains three different, yet powerful, perfectly crafted Rush songs—and "La Villa [Strangiato]" is the best instrumental ever written. I must give a shout out to Clockwork [Angels]. Another favorite, but hard to compare to the older stuff that has been part of my life for so long. But Clockwork is the absolute best way they could have ended their career.
- Mark Baldwin

Very tough to pick, but 2112. The "Overture" is a complete journey that packs an incredible amount of emotion, and is completely unique. The second ha[lf] is completely different, but has some classics also—"Tears" is very powerful.
- Chad Rutschke

Power Windows. Perfect synthesis of rock, prog, and new wave; guitars, bass, and synths; and songwriting, meaning, and atmosphere.
- Robert Matthews

Permanent Waves. It feels so full of energy, even in the slower songs like "Different Strings." It has a good mix complex but catchy "radio" songs as well as two great prog songs, including my third favorite Rush song, "Jacob's Ladder." Top to bottom I think this is their strongest album.
- Eric W.

Presto because "The Pass" helped me through family suicide attempts. It's my emotional favorite.
- Professor Cristy Tondeur

Hold Your Fire because it's the one I choose most often when I need Rush.
- Drew G.

Vapor Trails. Such heartfelt, authentic lyrics expressed through amazing musicianship
- Michael Medwick

2112—second side not so much (aside from "Something for Nothing" which I love) but I used to listen to side 1 over and over. Memorised all the lyrics. It took me on a journey. I was having a very tough time with a narcissistic stepfather at the time, so 2112 was an escape. I could identify with the character and the scenario.
- Patrick S.

Caress of Steel; because it launched their "attitude" of our way or the highway.
- Paul David Suter

Very difficult to choose as they all fill different needs depending on the day and time. Hemispheres always fascinates me the philosophical Cygnus tale to moving short song to the "La Villa Strangiato" highlighting the magnificence of the boys' musicianship. Always time and space for Hemispheres.
- Aaron Krouse

A Farewell to Kings. Hmmm. Covers a lot of ground, very catchy and complex without sounding complex necessarily. "Cygnus X-1"! "Xanadu"!
- Bri W.

Signals. I knew every word and note after listening to it over and over again. It had become permanently lodged in the cassette player of my '85 Cavalier and was all I listened to back and forth to college. Didn't mind. In fact I loved it. Never got sick of it.
- Brian F.

[E]ither Permanent Waves or Moving Pictures. Top notch songwriting, top notch playing, pristine production, album art . . . they were at their peak melding their prog tendencies with shorter, more concise (but thankfully not always) song construction.
- Drew

Hard question. Moving Pictures because that was first exposure and just a classic album, but I'm a huge fan of Power Windows as well. That was the late high school/early college aged years album that was formative for several reasons. Plus I was the only guy listening to Rush, so unique in that regard.
- Brent Rose

Snakes &Arrows. I love the way Rush continued to explore new styles of music.
- John B.

Permanent Waves—The production is light years better than on the earlier records (the

band actually sounds like they're right in front of the mics, rather than in a bathroom way down the hall) and Geddy's voice has matured to something at least slightly resembling a normal range and frequency. The awesome musical chops and complex ideas had always been present in the collective Rush mind, but here for the first time, everything really meshed into a gel. Replacing bombast with radio-friendly catchy pop riffs, but leaving in the instrumental fortitude that separated them from the Foreigner/Bad Company animals, Rush erupted with one HELL of a hit single, "The Spirit of Radio" (THAT RIFF! MY GOD! GREATEST RIFF EVER!), along with a bunch of other calmed-down, well-composed rock songs. In short, it's chock full of clever time signature changes, strong pop/rock/prog songwriting and lots of guitar arpeggios played with a chorusy sheen.
- Mark Prindle

Hemispheres. With that tour being my first Rush concert, what absolutely blew me away was the middle of "La Villa Strangiato" where the arena seemed to be so silent that you could hear a pin drop when Neil started throwing down that awesome 7/8 time signature beat and the building of Alex's guitar solo . . . And the frenzy that followed!
- Jeff P.

This might be cheating, but A Show of Hands because it contains many of my favorite Rush songs played live
- David Sanders

Clockworks Angels. They were just at the top of their game.
- A fan

Vapor Trails became my favorite in time. It was easy to dislike at first, due to the lack of solos, complex bass lines, even the absence of keyboards. But the more I let myself listen the more it all worked for me.

It's raw and yet collected, moving and yet restless. In one sense it recaptures the sonic emotions from 2112 itself. The same could be said of a number of tracks here, and the overall spectrum of sound and emotion of Vapor Trails certainly makes it one of Rush's most colorful collections.

Perhaps that's why Vapor Trails appeals to me—it offers an experience that's so distinctive and entrancing . . . Immersing us with "One Little Victory," guiding through so many emotional soundscapes, and sort of leaving us at a pleasant, sunny lake retreat with "Out of the Cradle."

That record doesn't have one wasted second on it, and I'm glad that— while I prefer the original mix—the band opted to have it remixed in 2013.
- Joe Cranford

Presto. (Sensing a theme?) OK. So on May 22, 1990 I entered the Fair Oaks Psychiatric Hospital because of severe depression and suicide. I was 14 at the time. I was there for 10 weeks and it basically saved my life . . . though I've struggled with depression through the present that time made me see the worth in myself and I found my first sense of confidence in . . . I dunno, probably for the first time in my then 14 years of life.

During my residency in Fair Oaks, I bought Presto. So: imagine the above as the backdrop to an album full of songs that are affirmative, contemplative, even a bit (befitting the album name) magical.

I get people's critiques of the album. It's certainly not their most imaginative album, there isn't anything particularly "new" about the creative direction. It could definitely use some more bass in the mix. But I think Neil brings his A-game to almost every song's lyrics. "Chain Lightning," "Presto," "Hand Over Fist," "Available Light" are all pure poetry. Geddy's voice is in that gorgeous sweet-spot where he can still belt it out but he's learned how to be nuanced and varied in his tone. Musically, these guys are relaxed and confident and still constructing songs with complexity and layers.

It's music that resonated with my 14-year-old self and the place I was in—figuratively and literally. And, after 30 years, it's music that STILL speaks to me, not just nostalgically, but as the best kind of music: the kind that contains a Truth that when you listen to it, it just FEELS right; something you appreciate in your current life and perspective.
  - Craig K.

Hold Your Fire. I think Neil was just in such a healthy and happy place while writing those lyrics. All very hopeful and about loving life and wanting to live it to the fullest. A philosophical peak for Neil in my opinion.
- David Stewart

Hemispheres. It's honestly the best 30-40 minutes of music I've ever heard in my life. I have been amazed from the first note, I still feel those goosebumps even 20 years later.
- Dave B. aka Dave2112

Currently it's Roll the Bones. It deals with a lot of the issues that I'm currently facing my life including my circumstances and what my fate is. The song writing and especially drumming are some of Rush's most tasteful work that they have ever put out.
- Mitch K.

Moving Pictures, hands down the greatest prog rock album of all time
- Alex Lioce, drummer at Nocturnal Curse

Hold Your Fire, there's just something about the aura and lyrics of that album that's always talked directly to my soul and often helped me through adolescence.
- Eric Campbell

Grace Under Pressure. In my opinion the perfect prog-pop-synthie album ever. Great sound and songwriting for eternity. Especially "Red Sector A" brings hard emotions to me, being a German.
- Bernard van Aken

Exit . . . Stage Left. Bought it after first time seeing them live. Listened to it every day. Big part of teenage years and heavily influential on my drumming.
- Dave M. Wyo

Permanent Waves, for the presence of "Jacob's Ladder," "[The] Spirit of Radio," and "Different Strings," although there isn't a bad song on the album.
- Susan C-C

Rush In Rio—I love this live album mostly because the audience is so taken with the concert. It recreates the experience of going to a Rush concert, at least for me.
- David

R40 live, because every song that a longed to see live is there for me whenever I wish to hear it or see it.
- Scott Hoelldobler

Counterparts is my favorite Rush album, as it got me through some difficult times.
- Rob Mallory

2112, because it was my first Rush album, even before I bought it; I have memories of my dad playing parts of the title track on his guitar when I was a very young child, so it feels like it's always been with me
- Jillian R. Allen

Clockwork Angels. It's a master work of the band at the height of their creativity. Not to

mention the world built around it in the novels. When they make the movie, I want to be in it.
- The Bongsisters

Hard to decide, but probably Counterparts because that was the first time I saw them live. And, I liked the return to the harder sound.
- Steve F.

Caress of Steel because I love "Fountain of Lamneth" and "The Necromancer."
- Travis C.

Still has to be Fly By Night. I still love the energy in those songs.
- Scott Fischer, a fan

I would guess the most popular response here would be Moving Pictures and though the non-conformist in me gives pause, I would have to concur with the probable consensus because aside from "Tom Sawyer," this record to me has not a single track otherwise that I'm prone to skip and I only skip "Tom Sawyer" because I feel that through the decades classic rock radio programmers had exhausted it to a degree that it hadn't for the album's other tracks.
- Nik Pfistron

It's clear that Rush fans form an emotional connection to certain songs or certain albums that stick based upon *when* they were first heard and what was going on in the listener's life at the time.

My top Rush album cycles between *Moving Pictures* and *Clockwork Angels*. *Moving Pictures* is obvious—like many, it was the first Rush album I bought, and I quickly understood why it was hailed as their peak. But *Clockwork Angels* came out at a time when I was very dissatisfied with my life, thanks mostly to my job, and the sense of adventure and wonder captivated me. "Caravan" became a favorite for its forward-looking lyrics expressing a wonder at the world I was finding myself forgetting, and "Headlong Flight" with the line "I wish that I could live it all again" gave me the courage to plow ahead.

At the time, I certainly did *not* feel like I had a life I would ever want to live again, unless it was to have a complete do-over. But repeated listens of that song, and album as a whole, made me realize that my life was what *I* made of it, not any shadowy outside forces such as an Anarchist or Watchmaker controlled me. *I* was in charge, and it was up to me to create the kind of life I would love to replay if I had the chance.

That, and the fact that the music is so powerful and confident, containing echoes of every single Rush era and album. I hear strains *Hold Your Fire* and *Presto* in some songwriting and guitar tones and vocal melodies, the raw power of the first four albums, the complex layering of guitar and bass parts of the modern era, and the same heart, finger-busting riffs, mind-blasting drums, and philosophical lyrics of that 1976 to 1985 golden era.

But it's "Wish Them Well" that moves me nearly to tears every time. The combination of the bittersweet melody and the lyrics explaining the album's main character finally having the guts to walk away from toxic people and situations really got me. I'm not going to lie: whenever I attempt to sing along to this song in the car, I choke up every single time.

So catch me one day, and I'll put *Clockwork Angels* as the peak of Rush's career, the perfect culmination of their four decades of existence . . . but catch me after listening to *Moving Pictures* and I'll tell you that *that* is their unequivocal masterpiece.

God, I love this band.

FAN PROFILE: MICHAEL OSTRICH

Name: Michael Ostrich
Location: Just outside of Philadelphia, PA
Age: 45
Gender: Male
Occupation: Project Manager

Michael first found about Rush through his sister, who got into the band in the late 80s. "I remember her going to see them on the *Presto* tour, and was envious that she was able to go. Between 1989 and 1991, I really got into them, and when *Roll The Bones* came out, it was my mission to see them live." He did on December 3, 1991, and never missed a show in Philadelphia since then.

Even cooler, Michael got to meet Geddy Lee and Alex Lifeson on the *Snakes & Arrows* tour. "I work with the band Tiles as their webmaster (since 2000), and they work with Hugh Syme and Terry Brown. Through them, I was able to get the opportunity for a meet and greet with Geddy and Alex, and that was a pretty awesome 10 seconds of shaking their hands and simply saying 'thank you' for all that they have done to enrich my life over these past 30 years."

Rush fans know that this isn't hyperbole. Like many fans, Michael feels a connection with Rush's lyrics that transcends all barriers of time and distance. "Neil Peart's words feel at times like he saw my own existence and could see what I was going through and put them into song. Musically, I tend to lean towards progressive rock and odd-time signatures, so the fact that Geddy and Alex do it so effortlessly is astonishing. The fact that they are childhood friends, 50 years later, is even more tremendous."

Such a long career means lots of touring, and Michael has been fortunate to have seen Rush on many of their tours since he first became a fan in the late 80s and early 90s. "I have been lucky. I have seen Rush in Toronto with my friend Chris back in 1997 (having parked in the old Exhibition Stadium parking lot), with my PA 1001001 license plate and getting honks of approval everywhere. I saw them in New York City, on the 2012 Time Machine Tour at Madison Square Garden (the only time I have ever been to the arena), and easily a dozen times here in Philadelphia since 1991. I am extremely fortunate to have seen them as many times as I have, and have known a time when they were an active band, putting out new material and 'progressing' in a way that made themselves happy."

"They're my favorite band, and Neil's passing earlier this year really hammered that home more so than ever. I felt a loss the likes of which was sadder than any family member." Like nearly all Rush fans, Michael feels a connection to Rush beyond the music. "While Neil or I ever met, he was a friend—one that was instrumental as part of the soundtrack to my life. His death is one that I will never truly recover from, and I am sure there are millions who feel the same way. As a single parent, my heart cries out to Olivia—I cannot fathom what she and his now widow Carrie are about to live through. There are no words that describe the sadness that I feel."

CHAPTER IX: BECAUSE WE'RE HERE

"This is, to me, a fantastic thing we've done."[1]

WHAT WE LEAVE BEHIND

The word "legacy" gets thrown around an awful lot when discussing popular musicians. However, it is also a word that all of us think about as we grow older, whether we're mothers and fathers, business owners, mentors, or just thinking and feeling human beings. Merriam-Webster defines a legacy as "something transmitted by or received from an ancestor or predecessor or from the past."[2] In light of this, it's safe to say that Rush has left a sizeable legacy, at least in the physical sense: 19 albums, thousands of live shows, and millions of lives touched.

With a band like Rush, though, it seems like their legacy is more than just the music. This is not to downplay the wonderful sounds generated by Geddy Lee, Alex Lifeson, and Neil Peart;

surely the music is the largest and most vital piece of Rush's legacy. But there is more to Rush than just the music, as I hope I have shown in this book. Rush has created a community, created a *family*. Donna Halper, I think, said it best when she told me that Rush brings people together.[3]

This is important, especially with all the bitter division and acrimony we see around us today. Maybe the world has always been like this. But until 1974, the world has not always had Rush.

IT'S A SECRET TO EVERYBODY

The relationship between Rush and its fans has always been special, one of those phenomena nobody can quite explain either from the outside or from the inside. Why this band that all the critics found so uncool inspired such a devout, some may say rabid, following appears to be a mystery. Especially mysterious was why this following was mostly smelly middle-aged white men who were total nerds.

At least, if you believed the music press in the early days of the band.

Fans know that the only "secret" behind Rush's success is hard work and relentless improvement. They were a fantastic rock and roll band who pushed the boundaries of the genre and did so with a unique level of thoughtfulness and intelligence. They were, as was often said, a "thinking man's rock band."[4] And this does appeal to a certain type of music fan.

I wrote this book partly to explore what this type was. As far as I could tell, there had been no serious attempt to determine

---

3 Donna Halper, interview with the author, February 11, 2020 (Appendix B).
4 *See, e.g.*, Greg Haymes, "Thinking Man's Rock Still Pushing, Hard-Rocking Rush Admits To Ambition, Not Pretension," *Albany Times Union*, December 12, 1991, available at http://www.2112.net/powerwindows/transcripts/19911212albanytimesunion.htm, last accessed June 22, 2020 ("'Some people, I'm sure, think that we take ourselves too seriously, but again, I think that the exact opposite is true,' Peart says. 'We don't take ourselves seriously at all, but we take our work very seriously, and we think it's incumbent on us to do the best job that we possibly can.'").

the contours of the archetypical Rush fan; whether because it was a futile and pointless undertaking that nobody cares about, or that I'm some great innovator thinking the thoughts that no one had ever thought before remains to be seen. At the most basic level, Neil Peart's passing inspired me to explore why this band means so much to me, and to discover why I am not alone in this.

And so I blasted my little survey out to the Internet and got far more responses than I expected. The fans who graciously answered my survey gave me enough raw material to at least try and create the profile of a typical Rush fan, which was not only fun but would in turn let me explore further why Rush inspired such a fervent following.

Yes, Rush fans tend to be into nerdy hobbies like table-top role-playing games, comic books, fantasy and sci-fi, and a whole lot of other interesting pursuits, as we learned in Chapter II. Yes, the odds are that your average Rush fan is white and male, as we discovered in Chapter III. This was mocked by the too-cool-for-school music press of the 1970s and early 1980s as somehow being a problem, as we saw in Chapter I. But that didn't deter fans, or the band.

In Chapter IV, we learned that Rush fans are actually mostly on the political *left*, if they're actually political at all (which most aren't), but have only a fifty-fifty chance of being an atheist as opposed to a believer. And in Chapter V we discovered that while only a plurality of Rush fans are musicians themselves, the overwhelming majority has seen the band in concert at least once.

It's been a fun trip, but you may have noticed that starting with Chapter VI, the tone of this book became a bit more serious. We had some laughs learning about Rush fans and what makes them tick on a superficial level, but when it comes to the deeper question of what Rush means to fans and why, we find some very profound experiences and ways in which the band's music has truly reached out and touched people's souls—and most importantly, done so in a positive way.

We saw how Rush's music helped fans overcome the grief of death, whether of family or friends, or the suicide of someone dear to them. It has helped fans cope with grievous physical injury, with emotional trauma such as divorce, or with mental illness. Rush's music helped shape some fans' worldviews, inspiring them to be more curious and inquisitive about the world around them. It has helped people connect with new friends, reconnect with old ones, and pass on their enthusiasm for this band to their spouses and children.

Most of all, we see that listening to Rush makes people feel good because, at some level, Rush *understood* their listeners and the struggles they were going through, and helped show that it was okay to feel these feelings, and that they had the power and ability to take charge of their lives and make them, and the world, better.

I think that's the crux of Rush fandom right there, and why losing Neil Peart hurt so much. Being a Rush fan felt like being a part of a *family*, complete with the three older brothers, or uncles, or whatever depending on your perspective, who had *been there and done that already* and were able to report from the other side that everything would be all right in the end.

And *that* is, after all my research and thinking about this and sorting through the wonderful input from fans, a damn good conclusion for the evidence to point me towards.

It also doesn't hurt that the music kicks so much ass.

Now, in the year 2020, Rush seems to be more popular than ever. They have finally earned the respect of the music press, the broader entertainment world, and even music fans who aren't into Rush but at least appreciate them. Long gone are the days of snide dismissals whenever the band's name came up. As a fan who was there when that absurd stigma was still attached to being a fan of Rush, this is all a pretty cool development.

Yet there is a dark side to this. Rush runs the risk of becoming some sort of franchise or a commodity. While Rush has had its Rush Backstage Club 1980 and still operates its Official Store, selling merchandise, collectibles, tour books, special edition albums, and various books written by and about the band, it's avoided falling into the trap of kitsch.

I sincerely hope that with Neil's passing and the end of Rush, their legacy be respectfully maintained. By and large, all of the people involved with the Rush operation have been careful to maintain the same level of integrity and respect for fans that Geddy, Alex, and Neil put into their music, as well as the same sense of humor. But the lure of money is always strong, and while I'm optimistic that Rush will avoid the trap of other legacy bands that become legacy *brands*, I dread the day I see Rush album art on t-shirts sold in shopping malls the way we see Iron Maiden and Nirvana images worn by kids who don't really care about the music involved.

Maybe that will never happen. Maybe Rush still retains enough of the "dad rock"[5] vibe to avoid this eventuality. In a world where everything is packaged for consumption as a part of a lifestyle based on the products you buy, I hope that this is the case. To be something that people buy, not for it's intrinsic value, but to show to other people how cool they are would be anathema to Rush, and a slap in the face to all that the band has accomplished.

Deep down, though, I think I know that this will never happen.

So to all Rush fans reading this, enjoy your favorite band's newfound, hard-earned popularity and respect. Rush long ago cemented itself a permanent place in the world of popular music, mainly by sticking around and remaining true to itself until the rest of the world caught up. There's a lesson there. In fact, there are several lessons there. I think it's time to run down a few of the ways Rush has taught your humble author how to be a better person. I'm sure you have your own.

5 *See, e.g.*, Rob Mitchum, "I Introduced the Term 'Dad-Rock' to the World. I Have Regrets: A dozen years ago the author unleashed the 'dad' modifier, and the world hasn't been the same since. Neither is he," *Esquire*, October 11, 2019, available at https://www.esquire.com/entertainment/music/a29419783/what-is-dad-rock/, last accessed October 20, 2020.

LESSONS I HAVE LEARNED FROM RUSH

1. **When the world expects you to do the same thing over and over, you drop a twenty-minute sci-fi epic on them and walk away.** Okay, maybe it's not as simple as this, but there is a time to stick to your guns and do things *your* way. Sometimes it works out. Sometimes it doesn't. But you'll never know unless you try, and it's far better to have your own "2112" moment than spend the rest of your life wondering what could have been.
2. **Adventures are out there if you're willing to look for them.** You don't have to fly into a black hole, scale eastern mountains, or seek lost cities of gold. There is a great big world out there waiting for you to explore, a world of *ideas* as well as *places*. Seek them out and you will be rewarded by the experience. After all, the point of the journey is not to arrive.
3. **Your mind is not for rent.** There is no shame in being "a nerd." You're not alone in whatever pursuits you seek. And even if you are, so what? Read. Explore nature. *Listen* to what other people have to say. Make your own conclusions. "[T]hey're not telling you what to think, you know?" Donna Halper told me. "His mind is not for rent to any god or government." Now, some people have taken that particular lyric . . . and said "Oh, anti-religion!" Not at all! All they're saying is don't rent out your mind to some fearless leader. You can be religious . . . the point is, don't rent out your mind. Don't just like say, "Oh okay, the Bible says, so therefore I don't have to think about anything ever again." Uh, yeah, you kind of do."[6]

---

6 Donna Halper, interview with the author, February 11, 2020 (Appendix B).

4. **You always have a choice.** The song "Freewill" is an obvious example of one of Rush's main credos. The line "If you choose not to decide, you still have made a choice" has become a cliché for a reason. Everything you do matters. *You* matter.
5. **It's okay to feel alone.** Not everybody is made for the limelight. And there will be times where you feel like you can't go on. But these feelings will pass. There is a light at the end of the tunnel. And there is a glory and nobility in enduring under the weight of opposition.
6. **Treat others, and yourself, with respect.** There is no reason to be mean or nasty to those different than you, whether those differences are in skin color, creed, or ideology. Stand up for yourself and others in the face of oppression and aggression, but do not seek out meaningless fights. Says Donna Halper, whatever it is you're into, "as a thinking human being, you still have to decide how to apply some of this stuff in the world, and if you're just gonna use it against people, that's kind of not useful, okay?"[7] We can all learn something from each other, even if all you learn is to wish them well and walk away.
7. **Be sincere, but don't take yourself too seriously.** Ennui, irony, and a smirking sense that what you're doing is a joke permeate our culture today. In Rush, we see a band free of artifice and facile nods to the camera. They meant what they said and what they did, and this sincerity was infectious. Optimism spreads. You can be that vector for positivity, yet you can also have fun at the same time.
8. **Always strive to improve.** This is an attitude we see in Geddy, Alex, and Neil's personal lives as well as in their music. The band never rested on its laurels and let success make them fat and com-

7 *Id.*

placent, and most importantly, never made them disconnected from the people around them, be they family, friends, or fans. Even if you think your job or your life is meaningless and insignificant, *it's not*. Meaning is there for you to make.
9. **Don't be afraid to put your family first.** It's clear that Rush enjoyed creating music and playing live. But they weren't afraid to set their instruments down and focus on their wives and children. And when Neil faced his unbearable losses, Geddy and Alex realized that *the band didn't matter as much as their friend*.
10. **This too shall pass.** At the risk of sounding crass, Neil's personal tragedies and the way he handled himself actually provide hope for the rest of us. No matter how bad you think you have it, a man *lost his family* and managed to get through his suffering and loss without hurting himself or others. You have the strength of character to endure. The example Neil Peart set demonstrates that it can be done.
11. **Leave the world a better place than when you found it.** Rush spread joy with their music and their message. Listening to Rush or seeing them in concert makes people feel good about themselves and about the world. Whether it's charitable giving or emotional support, you have something to offer the world. Let that be your legacy. It can be as world-shattering as uplifting millions of people, or as down-to-earth as being a good friend or spouse or parent.

I could go on, but eleven sounds like a nice number to stop on (a strange time signature, perhaps?). Not a bad legacy for a rock n' roll band from the Toronto suburbs, is it? Whenever people like to say that all rock music is degenerate or harmful, I like to point to Rush as proof that this is most certainly not the case.

There's one other part of Rush's legacy that I think is woefully underappreciated, and my hope is that this book finally gives this oft-ignored aspect some long overdue recognition: the fans.

You are Rush's legacy.

ACKNOWLEDGMENTS

This book was a true labor of love, emphasis on the "labor" (I'm never writing two books at the same time again), my small way to give back to Geddy Lee, Alex Lifeson, and Neil Peart for all that they have given us. It is also my love letter to the Rush fan community, of which not enough has been written about. My gratitude for the wonderful people who answered my survey, agreed to be interviewed, and supported the creation of this book cannot be overstated. Simply put, the Rush fan community is one of the best I have ever been a privilege to be a part of, and that's a fact, jack.

First, thank you to Donna Halper for not only letting some strange, unknown, and obscure sci-fi author interview her, but for keeping in touch and generally being an awesome human being. I can't begin to imagine the amount of hands on Donna's time as the matriarch of Rush fans, yet she always found the time for me, and her insights proved invaluable in writing this book.

Thank you to Ed Stenger for (a) running one of the best Rush websites around, (b) writing the foreword to this book, (c) letting me interview you, (d) helping promote my survey to the broader fan community, and (e) just being a cool guy. It's always fun to actually talk with people you have been reading about for years. Someday I hope we may meet in person.

Thank you to W. Earl Brown who not only answered my survey, but answered a few of my questions on Twitter and let me use them in the book.

Thank you to His Eminence Metropolitan Tikhon Mollard for answering my questions about Rush and his own Rush fandom via email. God bless you, sir!

Thank you to my close personal friend Marc Brennan, who let me interview him as well. We were supposed to do it over the phone, but when I actually had a chance to call him we ended up shooting the breeze for a few hours and never got to the questions. So we did the interview by email. Next time, Marc, it'll be over drinks and I'm buying.

Thank you to Jesse White for agreeing to paint the cover for this book. It's a true work of art and could be a Rush album cover itself.

Thank you to Mark who runs the Victory Bar & Cigar in downtown Worcester. Before the coronavirus came along to ruin everything, your place was where I got a ton of writing done for a few hours each Thursday while waiting for my son to be finished with Greek school.

Thank you to my beautiful family: My wife Demi who doesn't like Rush but doesn't *dis*like Rush either, my son John who really likes "2112," and my daughter Lola who claps whenever "Time Stand Still" comes on. What can I say? My kids have good taste.

Thank you to everyone who backed my IndieGoGo campaign, who are in no particular order: Jeff Dormer, Christopher DiNote, Kerry Frey, Christine Chase, John Tice, ProgScape, Jeff Matzke, David Andrade, Robert McCullough, Tom Driscoll, Metropolitan Tikhon Mollard, Marc Brennan, Katherine Shirk, Robert Diton, M and D, Neil Brown, Henri Leksis, Tom Dickson Hunt, Jill Mandrioli, shub542, Schuyler Hernstrom, Brett W. Stark, and Lisa LaFlame.

And a gigantic thank you to everyone who responded to my fan survey. You all are the real reason I was able to write this book, and the stories, memories, and information you provided really made this book come alive. The Rush fan community is full of awesome people, and you all showed that with your generosity. This book is for Geddy, Alex, and Neil, yes, but it's also for *you*.

APPENDIX A: SURVEY RESULTS

In this Appendix you will find fans' answers to the following questions from Chapters II, V, VI, and VII in Table A.1: "Favorite Rush concert memory or memories?" "How did you react to Neil Peart's death?" and "What does Rush's music mean to you?" "Other hobbies/areas of interest" and "If 'yes' [to 'nerd'] hobbies, which ones?" Table A.2 contains answers to the questions "When did you first start listening to Rush?" "What was the first Rush song you heard?" "How did you become a Rush fan?" "Favorite Rush song (if you HAD to pick one)" "First Rush album you bought" "Favorite Rush album and why" and "Favorite Rush era" discussed in Chapter VIII. I used responses extensively in these chapters, but there are so many more, and they're all great, so I thought it would be fun to share *all* of them.

The survey results are available on my website at https://amatopia.wordpress.com/dreamers-and-misfits-appendix-a-selected-survey-responses/

A few notes:

- There were some survey respondents who answered the questions but did not want their answers shared, so I did not include them.
- I tried to be respectful of fans' wishes and credit them as they indicated.
- If I got your name wrong, or if there's any information you want removed, please email me at alexanderhelleneauthor@gmail.com and I will make all requested changes.

As always, my biggest thanks to everyone who took the time out to share their Rush stories. I could not have written this book without you and, furthermore, this book is for *you*. So enjoy!

APPENDIX B: INTERVIEW WITH DONNA HALPER, FEBRUARY 11, 2020

Donna Halper needs no introduction to Rush fans. She is, after all, the woman who broke Rush in the Untied States by playing "Working Man" while a DJ at WMMS in Cleveland, Ohio. The song was a hit and the rest is history. Donna's role in the Rush story can be simply put as, "No Donna Halper, no Rush."

Donna was not just a DJ in the music industry. She is also a historian, a radio consultant, a Ph.D. holder, and currently an Associate Professor at Lesley University in Cambridge, Massachusetts. Being in Massachusetts myself, I had the audacity to email Professor Halper if she would be willing to talk to me about the band and its fans for my book . . . and she graciously accepted, speaking with me for about forty minutes on a cold winter night in February after my kids went to bed. She was in the middle of grading papers but still took the time to talk Rush and provide some great insights that proved invaluable in the writing of this book.

I've cleaned up the interview for readability but otherwise changed nothing. You will see that Donna is a warm, funny, and gracious person who loves the band, loves the fans, and realizes the special bond between performer and audience. You can find more of her writing on her excellent blog at dlhalperblog.blogspot.com and on Twitter @DevorahLeah.

Yeah, that's great, no but like I said in my emails, you know, I'm an independent author and I usually write, you know, sci-fi-type stuff, but I'm a huge Rush fan and have been for a long time and, I don't know if I, you know I didn't want to sound, like I said, tacky in my email to you, but, you know, when Neil died it hit me and everybody I knew that was a fan of the band much more than I guess you could say it

should have, because I didn't know him or his family, and you know, I, it was like one of these things where I talked to my brother and it was like, why does this, you know, why is this bothering us? Like I feel genuine sorrow for the passing of a guy, like I feel like I knew him. And I just kind of wanted to think about that and, you know, what is it about this band that attracts such a loyal, dedicated following, and is there a, you know, what are the reasons for that, and is there, is there a type of person that tends to really like Rush as opposed to other groups, you know, what is it about some people that when they listen to this music and hear these words it really speaks to them. So that's the kind of thing I'm exploring, and, and I know I mentioned in one email I have a, a survey out, I had . . . there's a great website I've been reading for years called RushIsABand run by this guy named Ed Stenger, I think he's from Cleveland actually—

Now, you must be, you must be on a cell phone.

I am.

Because you're breaking up.

Oh, I'm sorry!

Let me try to answer your question.

Sure.

But it's going to be very difficult to answer, and here's why. Rush fans in many cases are such a divergent bunch of people, okay? The people that love this band are in many cases conservatives, liberals, libertarians, atheists, agnostics, Jews, Christians, Muslims, shall I go on? And, I'm, I'm very serious about that.

I believe, I believe it, yeah.

Because one of the, one of the fascinating things to me as a media historian is that there are very few bands that have brought together such a diverse coalition of fans, right across the spectrum, all united around the kinds of lyrics that Neil created. If you've ever felt like an outsider, if you've ever felt not understood, if you've ever felt different, if you've ever felt not taken seriously, there's a Rush lyric for you. And, the Rush lyrics tend not to be self-pitying, they tend not to be like, let's all blame this group or that group. They tend to be about thinking for yourself, about making your own decisions, about not being over-reliant on the will of the group, and like I said, I think that resonates with a lot of people who have felt like nobody spoke to them. Like, even in the early days of the band, and I mean Neil did not write this song, but I'm saying it just started out with "Working Man."

Yup.
And, from day one, people that listened to the lyrics of Rush songs heard something in those songs that made them go, "Yeah, that. Okay, yeah, exactly. That." Okay? And I really feel like Neil just took it to the next level, and the lyrics that he composed were really resonant with so many people who hadn't felt heard, or hadn't felt understood. And what I like about the lyrics of Rush songs is that they don't invalidate you if you think something different, okay?

Right.
I mean, if you choose not to decide, you still have made a choice, okay?

Yup.
So they're not telling you what to think, you know? "His mind is not for rent to any god or government." Now, some people have taken that particular lyric in "Freewill,"[1] and said "Oh, anti-religion!" Not at all! All they're saying is don't rent out your mind to some fearless leader. You can be religious, like I'm Jewish and I used to be a chaplain, for heaven's sake, I actually can discuss Bible with people if I have to.

---

1 It's from ""Tom Sawyer"," and I know that Donna knows this, but I wasn't about to correct the mighty Donna Halper!

Okay.
But I understand that there are people who aren't religious, okay? And the point is, don't rent out your mind. Don't just like say, "Oh okay, the Bible says, so therefore I don't have to think about anything ever again." Uh, yeah, you kind of do.

Right.
Okay, because as a thinking human being, you still have to decide how to apply some of this stuff in the world, and if you're just gonna use it against people, that's kind of not useful, okay? I mean, there are so many Rush lyrics, and I don't have time to get into them now.

That's all right.
But you know some of the one's I'm talking about.

Yup.
There are so many Rush lyrics that really do encourage you to empower yourself, to get the facts, to look at the issues, and don't be afraid to change your mind. I mean, nothing used to get Neil crazier, and I've spoken to Neil, I didn't just read this in a book, not that there's anything wrong with books, I love books. But I'm saying, I've actually had this conversation with Neil, and Neil said that nothing got him crazier than people who were upset with him when he walked away from Ayn Rand, okay? Now I mean, yeah, sure, at the time Ayn Rand was a big deal, okay? But there came to a point where it just no longer met his needs. And when he got to that place, he said, "Wow, thank you very much, time for the next thing." But there are still people that are like, "But I've read everything Ayn Rand ever wrote, and how dare you?" And he's like . . .

Yeah, like some, somehow it invalidates them.
Yeah, it's like, how dare I? I just moved on. I mean, do you eat the same foods you ate thirty years ago? Do you wear the same clothes you wore thirty years ago? I mean, life goes on. So he said, I took what I could from Ayn Rand and then it was time

for the next thing. He said, that's the thing, you know? It's time to just look at these philosophies, look at them and then decide, is this still the right philosophy for me? If it is, hang on to it. If it isn't walk away and don't be ashamed. If you choose not to decide you still have made a choice.

Yeah.
Does that make sense?

It does. It makes perfect sense. And it's, it's not, um, that's one thing I—
Andrew Yang just dropped out of the presidential race.

Oh, really?
And so did Michael Bennett. Who most people didn't even know was still running.
I can confess I didn't know—
But Yang, Yang is out of here. Yang is gone.

Wow. I thought, he had some support.
No, he never resonated. He had, like, a dedicated bunch of people who wanted the thousand bucks a month. And that was . . . but no, he was, he never really took off the way anybody thought he would. But that's another story for another time.

Yeah, I confess I haven't been paying too much attention.
But it, that also is, is actually kind of interesting too, because Neil had been a Republican. Now, actually no he wasn't, he was Canadian so he couldn't vote here anyway, but I'm saying that like his views at one time, and we used to argue about this, his views aligned very heavily with what we might call conservatives in many ways. He was always socially liberal, but I'm saying like he, his, his ideology was much more fiscally conservative, you know, the virtue of selfishness, blah, blah, blah. But as time went on, the more he got out there, the more he talked to people, the more he realized, he said this to me! He said, "You know the playing field just isn't level, so he said, now I consider myself a bleeding-heart libertarian."

Yup. I love that expression.
So, he still was a libertarian, but much more center-left. And, some of the Republicans were furious, and he didn't care. And, you know, not that he didn't care about Republicans. But he never saw himself as the voice of the Republicans, or the voice of the Democrats. That's why he wrote his lyrics. It's like, don't expect me to make up your mind for you. You know? I'm just a singer in a rock and roll band, you know?
Yeah, and, and I think that's why it appeals to so many different people.
And that's what I'm trying to say.

So that's kind of what my, I guess my operating assumption was, is that I don't think the fan base is as monolithic as one might be led to believe. I, you know, I was looking for examples, I swear you, growing up too you always hear people, oh it's a, it's a nerd band, it's only dorks, this and that, and only X type of people like them.
Not at all. Not at, not at all. Not at all. Not true.

But that's not what my experience has been like. And that's not—I've had almost a thousand people, um, respond to my, my survey there, and I'm asking these types of questions and I mean, yeah, there's—the commonalities I've been finding have been that it's people that, it's all walks of life but I'm hearing things from, just wonderful stories from people like the lyrics helped me, you know, navigate adolescence, they helped me not be influenced by negative peer pressure, they helped me get over, you know, one, individual, you know, the death of a family, close family member.
Absolutely!

They helped me when my parents got divorced, so I'm finding that—
Yeah, yeah, and—

The stereotype's not true.
In my case, what Rush did for me, what Rush did for me was, it gave me a fan community and it gave me friends that I didn't have before. I mean, keep in mind, I don't want to make this about me.

That's okay. Talk about yourself!
But, um, I mean, no, but I mean, I don't smoke. I don't drink. I don't do drugs.

You sound like me.
I do remember the sixties, okay? But my point is I was mocked, I was made fun of, I was ridiculed, I was really treated quite unkindly at some of the stations I worked at. But once I discovered Rush, suddenly everybody wanted me for their best friend, okay? It was like, can you get me backstage? Can you introduce me, blah, blah, blah. And, it was like, nah, you know, I understood what that was all about, come on, I've been in the industry for a while.

Right.
Everybody wants everybody to do them a favor, I get that. But, the other thing that I didn't expect was the devotion and the loyalty that people had for this band also got transferred on to me. And suddenly, I'm okay with a whole bunch of people that I would probably in real life never have been okay with, okay?

Yup. Yup.
And not that there's anything wrong with me or anything wrong with them. But I'm saying, I have had conversations with right-wing conservatives that, we're just not going to agree on politics, I'm center-left, okay fine. And yet we can still end with, yeah and let's talk some more about the Rush songs that we like, you know? And it's all still good. And it's all still good! I can honestly say I have never lost a friend, you know? Over, you—over Rush, because Rush brings people together, and it always has.

That—that's the coolest—
And the whole myth about oh, all the, it's all guys, you know? No it isn't. Um, in the original incarnation of the band, yes. The vast majority of Rush fans were male, agreed.

Sure. Sure.
But that was true about rock and roll in general. As time went on, and the members of the band got more into different kinds of lyrical manifestations, different kinds of songs, there are some beautiful songs that Rush have done. "Entre Nous." "The Garden." I mean, come on, it's not all, you know, heavy metal thunder. And I think gradually, people got apprenticed into Rush that hadn't been apprenticed into it before, maybe it was through a boyfriend, maybe it was through a husband, maybe it was through a father, but these days? Yeah, Rush fans are just about everything, gay, straight, black, white, green, purple, and male and female.

Yeah, and, and that's the coolest thing because, you know, you hear the myth it's like, oh, just it's nerds, whatever that means.
Not at all. Not in the least.

And it's like, well no, it's almost like, I know the expression, they talk about Rush as the "World's Biggest Cult Band," and it's like, all these people you wouldn't think would be fans—
Yeah, a cult band, a cult band that's sold 16 million, has a star on the [Hollywood] walk of fame, and is—

Yeah, I laugh, I laugh every time I hear that.
What a cult band! What a cult band.

You know, sell out every single concert they've ever done.
Yup.

You know, one thing I—
So—

Oh, sorry.
No, I just, all I wanted to say with a minimal amount of time because I've got sixty papers to grade, and I—

Oh, of course.
—we're gonna have to do this in two segments.

That's fine!
But I wanted to at least see if I had something to contribute to what you're looking for.

Absolutely. Absolutely. And we can do the rest like on email if that's easier too, I know you're—
No, it's not a problem with talking. It's just like I said it's turned out to be the, the past couple of days have been rather intense and, I've got a whole bunch of stuff going on plus I haven't been feeling well . . .

Oh, I'm sorry to hear that.
Well, this whole thing with Neil, I mean, to be honest with you, come on, it was forty-five years of my life, okay?

Yeah.
And I mean, I never, I can't claim that he was my bestie. He wasn't. But we kept in touch. And when we would spend time together, I always appreciated it. I always appreciated the conversation. It was so cool to be able to talk poetry or literature, philosophy I mean, the stuff you wouldn't expect, but that's what we used to talk about! That's what we used to talk about. And I miss it. And I feel so bad for his best friend, I feel so bad for his parents, and his little daughter who I met, and his wife, and for Geddy and Alex, because another online myth was that after he retired they stopped talking to each other. Horse-puckey!

I can't imagine anybody believing that.
They used to visit each other on a regular basis!

I'm sure, yeah.
These types of things get me crazed.

Yes. I can only imagine.
So yeah, you know, the fan community lives on. And Rush left us with forty-five years' worth of great music.

Yup.
But it's still just, you asked why are people reacting to this. Forty-five years of many people's lives. And whether you saw them in concert, or whether you watched them on video, or saw the documentary, these were such down-to-earth, decent people. They were like everyman! You, you just felt like, wow I could live next door to them! They didn't seem like they were up on a pedestal. I mean, maybe you put them on a pedestal because you admired their music.

Yeah.
But as human beings, they were just incredibly human. And that may sound like a silly old, "Human beings, of course they're human." But I mean human in the sense that… do you speak Yiddish?

I do not, no.
Okay. I didn't know if you were Jewish.

No. Greek.
No, you cannot tell by names, okay?

Yup. Yup.
Michelle Obama's cousin is an internationally famous rabbi.

Huh!
Oh yeah, if you ever saw his name, it's Rabbi Capers Funnyé. Not exactly a Jewish sounding name. And yet, he's a famous rabbi.

There you go!
So, you never assume by names, okay?

Sure, yeah.
So, I'm gonna use a word, and the word is, "mensch."

Okay, I do know that word.
Okay, now, a mensch, which is spelled M-E-N-S-C-H, a mensch in the dictionary it's a human being, but it carries the connotation of a kind, compassionate person. So if you say, "Boy, you know Neil was a real mensch," well, yeah, he was living and breathing and human, yes he was. But no, I mean it in the sense of he was a kind and compassionate person. And yes, a lot of it was on his terms, but so what?

Yeah.
He had every right to decide, you know? I can't pretend the stranger is a long-awaited friend. He was not a hypocrite. And yet, he was very good to an awful lot of people. He just had to do it his way. He didn't want a lot of publicity for it, he didn't want to be in the papers about it. But he was a very compassionate person. And all three of the guys are. And that's why I think a lot of people are reacting, it's kind of like losing a friend. It's kind of like, even if I've never met them, they were such nice people. I mean, find me the newspaper articles about them trashing hotel rooms, and you know beating up women, and and—

Yup. Drug abuse, and yup.
You won't! You won't! They're family men! I mean, they're with the same people 'til the very end, you know what I'm saying?

Yeah.
If Neil's wife hadn't died of cancer, and his daughter hadn't gotten killed in a car crash, they'd still be married!

Yup, yup, I have no doubt of that either, yeah.
He'd still be with the same, okay? I mean, Geddy is still with the same woman who was his girlfriend when I met him, okay?

[Laughter]
I mean, the same, you know? I mean, there's a great scene in *Beyond the Lighted Stage* where Gene Simmons of Kiss wants to get Geddy a groupie, and Geddy's like "I gotta go call my girlfriend. I gotta go call my girlfriend." And he was serious! I've seen him do it. I've seen him do it, okay?

Yeah.
That was not an act for the screen. I was backstage with him at times when people would be like trying to get next to him and he was like, "No, no, I've got to go call my girlfriend." And he meant it! And he meant it! So I think that most people can relate to these guys because they never sold out, they never compromised, and they never lost their ethics or their compassion. And that's all I got for tonight.

APPENDIX C: INTERVIEW WITH ED STENGER, MAY 19, 2020

There are lots of great Rush websites out there that I leaned upon in writing this book to find archived articles and transcripts of radio shows: Power Windows (2112.net) and Cygnus-x1.net comes to mind. But when I want Rush *news*, there's only one site for me, and it's a site I've been visiting for fifteen years: RushIsABand.com.

Rush Is A Band is run by one Mr. Ed Stenger of Cleveland, Ohio. I remember, as you'll see from the interview, Ed quoted an old blog of mine from way back in 2006 where I wrote about Rush, and he even linked to me. That particular post remained the most-trafficked of that blog by a wide margin. So when I was writing a book about Rush fans, I could think of few people better to reach out to than Ed.

Ed was gracious enough to both tweet out my survey, and link to it on his site, helping spread the word about this book. In addition to that, he agreed to write the book's foreword, *and* took about an hour to talk to me on May 19. As you'll see from the interview, Ed is a great, passionate man with a real affection for Rush and its fans, and I am forever grateful to him for all the part he played in making this project become a reality.

I've cleaned up the interview for readability but have changed nothing content-wise. My words are in boldface, and Ed's are in regular type. Enjoy!

You still there?
Yeah.

Awesome. I guess it worked, because it didn't hang up on you. Ohio is on the Eastern Standard Time, you'd think I'd know this. I'm out in Massachusetts, so I just assume everybody's on Eastern Time, so it's a bad habit.
I know what you mean.

No, thanks for taking the time. It's pretty cool. I mean, I've got to say I've actually, I think I've been reading your site 15 years or something, 2006, 2005 is the first time I heard of it. Just a little bit of trivia, one of the very first blogs I had back in the day, you actually linked to me, which I thought was kind of funny.
Oh, yeah.

I wrote something about *Moving Pictures* yeah, I guess over a decade ago. It's cool that your site is still around. That's awesome.
I know.

That was kind of a funny bit of trivia.
That's cool.

I think I've mentioned to you in a bunch of my emails, the book I'm doing it's about fans. It's been kind of interesting just looking into fans and I've put out my little survey and I got tons of responses.
Yeah, what did you get like 600?

663 last I checked. I was hoping to get 1,000, but that's still a lot. I had some interesting people respond. I had this actor named W. Earl Brown, he was on the show *Deadwood* among others. He had a recurring role in *Deadwood*, but he's been in kind of bit parts in a whole bunch of other movies. He made a short movie called *Dad Band*. I don't know if you had seen that. It's only about 18 minutes long. You can watch it on YouTube, it's pretty funny. One of the people on it is Jerry Cantrell from Alice in Chains, but they're—
Yeah, I did see that. I did see that.

You did see that. Okay, yes. It's pretty funny. He responded and I interact him a bit. I talked to Donna Halper back in February, which is cool. She actually, because where I am in Massachusetts, I don't know how familiar you are with what

we kind of measure everything as distance from Boston. I'm an hour drive outside of Boston and she teaches at a college in Quincy,[1] which I think Quincy is on the North Shore, North of Boston,[2] but anyway she's actually really close, but we haven't been able to get together because of the coronavirus and all that. I talked to her and all the stuff, I'm doing a bunch of research. All the stuff I'm finding out about the band is cool, but also just about fans, which is cool. I'm assuming you'd have a lot more insight onto some of these things, just having been in the fan community, an active part, not just listening to the music and going to concerts and stuff, but more of an active part.
Yeah, sure.

That's where I'm coming from. I don't know, I mean, I can just fire off some questions, hear your thoughts.
Sure.

One of the things I've noticed, I'm tabulating all of the numbers. One thing I found is that 90% of the people that responded to me were men. It was more like about 89% men, 11% women, which tracks with my experience. I thought that was kind of funny. That's one of those stereotypes that's pretty true, but the thing I've noticed is that the female fans are just as hardcore, just as hardcore, into all the same kind of things and aspects of the band, lyrical content, the musicianship, all that you would assume. I always think of that movie, I always think of, I'm blanking on it. I wrote about it. *I Love You Man*, I think about those two guys, and that's what a lot of the female fans seem like. Then on your recommendation, I finally watched the *Time Stands Still* doc. I can't believe I hadn't watched it before. They talked to Jillian, they talked to the other woman that started Rush Con and it was all women and they're all into it.
Yeah, isn't wild? I always thought that was interesting.

1   I was wrong; it's actually in Cambridge.
2   I was wrong; it's actually on the South Shore, south of Boston. Yes, I actually *do* live in the Bay State.

It is. Yeah. No, that's cool.
It's a bunch of women Rush fans that started it.

Yeah, because the joke is that there just aren't any and I don't think that's true. It's definitely skews male, but . . .
The female fans, they're more outgoing and they seem to be more involved. I think the fact that the Rush Con organizers are all women kind of speak to that, in my experience.

Have you been to Rush Con before?
Yeah, I have. A couple. It's been a while. I went in '06 and '07.

Oh wow.
A couple of events. They had a couple of miniature events here and there that I went to as well.

That's cool. That's cool. They're not doing them anymore though right?
No, not really. I think they're trying to start sponsoring some events, but not doing an annual convention.

Okay.
They just did some virtual, they interviewed this popular Rush tribute band called YYZ.

Oh, okay. I've never heard of them.
A Zoom call thing.

Sure.
They did that one last week.

Oh, wow.
Stuff like that, I think they're trying to get back into that.

Hey, I guess it's not the same obviously with the band not being a band anymore. I guess after they stopped touring it was really, I guess . . .

2015 was the last one. They had a couple miniature conventions that year. They had one in Toronto when they played Toronto, and they had another one at their last show.

In LA there.
Yeah. That was the last event.

That's too bad. Why do you think, or I guess in your experience if you thought of anything, why do you think that it, the stereotype is just stuff that guys are into and guys are nerdy, guys are geeky. Number one, I guess do you think that's true? Number two, I guess just that's the question. Do you think that's true, and if yes, why and if not, why? What do you think gave rise to that, gave birth to that stereotype and what do you think dispels it a bit?
It's there, definitely. You always have your exceptions. There are plenty of "cool people" that like Rush too. You just read their lyrics, the subject matter, especially their early records, very science-fictiony, fantasy stuff, really heavy stuff that generally appeals to males I guess. Then just their musicianship, just how good they were and how proficient they were at their instruments and how much care they took in writing their songs. Just them as individuals. Neil Peers, he's a nerdy guy, he always was. Always nose in a book, real quiet. Those guys didn't have a reputation for partying or doing drugs or trashing hotel rooms, that kind of thing.

Bled over into the type of person who might have been attracted to them then in their personal life.
They stood out in that sense from other bands at the time. I think that and just the lyrics really appeal to that misfit persona. The one thing I have experienced is that I'm from Cleveland, and I think Cleveland was the first epicenter of Rush fans in the United States.

Yeah.
Where I grew up, I grew up not in Cleveland but outside

Cleveland, closer to Toronto on the lake. There were a lot of Rush fans in my school growing up. It was never uncool to like Rush.

Really?
I never experienced that, being a Rush fan I was never ridiculed or anything. Plenty of the cool people liked Rush too. I didn't experience that as much as people in other parts of the country maybe from my experience from talking to people.

That's really interesting. I was in high school, I graduated high school in 2000. I didn't get into the band until right around when *Test for Echo* came out. Even 15, 16, 17 year olds at that time "Oh, Rush. How can you deal with the guy's voice? Totally dorky." I was like "Whatever, I like them." It wasn't really until after Neil had his tragedies and the band went on hiatus, and it wasn't until then that it seems to suddenly the turn of the millennium then all of a sudden you saw a lot of people who previously sneer at them were like "You know, that band's actually pretty cool. They actually have some really good songs." I remember when *Vapor Trails* came out, it was like all of a sudden everybody was pulling for Rush. I think it might have been just a few years after that they were in, it wasn't the cover of *Rolling Stone* [yet], but I just remember it was around that time period, *Vapor Trails*, all of the sudden it became "okay" to be into them and that stigma wasn't there.
That was their second resurgence.

Right.
I'm older than you I guess, so I was, and I had older brothers. My older brother is actually who got me into the band. My older brother got into Rush when right around *2112*, when they really got popular, in '76. He was 14. He started playing bass because of it and everything.

Oh, cool.

I was only six. I didn't really tune into it, but growing up it was the background music, permeated my brain. I discovered it when I was older. When I was about 12, I went through my brother's stuff, mixed albums and cassettes and stuff and that's how I discovered them myself.

Did you get a chance to see them live? At that time, they still had plenty of years of touring ahead of them. Have you managed to get to a lot of concerts?
Yeah. My first was *Power Windows* in I think it was '85, late '85. I forget. I think it was December or '85 or something.

Okay.
I was like 15. It was one of my first concerts. Then pretty much every tour after that I would see them once. I couldn't afford to drive around and see them in multiple cities like some people were able to do.

Right. Right.
Yeah. After *Vapor Trail*, when *Vapor Trails* came out, that's when I started to see multiple shows per tour.

Nice.
Just two or three.

Still.
Two or three. Yeah. I knew people who would literally follow them and pretty much go to every show which was nuts. I don't know how they did it.

Yeah. Like Dead-Heads.
I know. Yeah. Yeah. I've probably seen 25-30 times all together.

Nice. Slightly jealous. I only saw them three times. I didn't go to, I saw *Vapor Trails*, R30 and *Snakes & Arrows*. Like a dummy I thought I really couldn't justify the expense so I missed Time Machine and the *Clockwork Angels* and I

missed the R40. All of them came up here either in Boston or there's an outdoor amphitheater not too far from Boston. I think one of the times they came to one of the big casinos in Connecticut and I'm still kicking myself for not seeing them.

It goes into another question I had, out of order of what I was thinking but it doesn't matter. Just made me think about live concerts. They're just one of these bands where they typically don't, they're not like the Grateful Dead or Phish or a jam band. They don't jam on stage, they don't change into songs very much at all. Other than a few deviations here and there, maybe they'll play "Freewill" instead of "Limelight" or something. They don't overdo it with the set lists. They really stick to the set list for the whole tour, yet people will go to every concert. Like I said, I've only been to a few concerts of theirs, but they each felt like a party. You knew what was coming, but every time they went into "Oh, they're playing 'Bravado!'" People would lose their mind. It was infectious. You're like "Yeah. They're playing the song I've heard a million times before but it's awesome. Oh, I can't believe they're playing this one." It wouldn't be changing from tour to tour, but they were still such a strong live draw with people going to them, following the whole tour.

There was one part in the *Time Stand Still* doc where I think it was [longtime Rush manager] Ray Danniels who said they could sell 100,000 tickets in 10 shows in England, but they couldn't sell 100,000 albums. He was like, ticket prices are, it could cost five, six, seven times more than buying a record. I don't know. Do you have any thoughts why even though they tend to stick to the songs, played them like they were on the record, why were they such a massive fanatical tour following? That's one that I haven't been able to really crack other than people just really like the songs.
Yeah. Good idea. I think watching them in particular, because they are so good at their craft and to see that live is a rare treat.

Sure.
I think that is a big part of it. Just the fact that they put on a good show and especially once they hit the big time in the '80s, they really took the time to put on a spectacle for the fans too. Backdrop videos, the props and everything. They always talk about that one thing they learned from Kiss, touring with Kiss was that part of it. They brought it up multiple times in interviews, but they go back to that, to touring with Kiss and seeing how they did that, learning from that, and always thinking they always want to put on a good show. They're consistent. That's another thing, you know you're going to get a good show. They don't put on a bad show.

They don't mail it in.
No, they don't. Yeah. That, and just how good they are at their instruments. It's something that's a rare thing. It's something to see.

Yeah. Yeah. Definitely not just some guys who got lucky with one song and blew up even though they can barely pluck a guitar solo.
It goes back to they don't skimp on their live show. They play the songs like they were recording. The other way around I should say. When they record a song in the studio, if they can't play it live, they don't add in an extra instrument or whatever.

That's a good point.
They will recreate it, and you see Geddy up there singing, playing his bass and a keyboard, bass pedals.

Yeah. The job of three people. Yeah.
Yeah. That's another part of it. A lot of bands don't do that. They'll have touring musicians for certain parts.

I think of Pink Floyd: Roger Waters leaves and they have to get 14 people to replace him. Not that he was a Geddy Lee-type bass player, but when you would go to see a Pink Floyd show after Roger Waters, it was like Pink Floyd and an entire orchestra of people who aren't Pink Floyd.
Right.

Not that there's anything wrong with that, but. Hard to replace him.

Yeah. One thing I've noticed, and maybe it was just the British press in particular, but I don't think I've ever seen, maybe not until Insane Clown Posse came around, but I don't think I've ever seen a group where the critics don't like the music. I don't think I've ever seen a group where the critics have an equal amount of disdain for the fans. The critics, especially in the late '70s to the early '80s, when they would talk. I don't know if you've seen some of these articles in *New Musical Express* and some of these other British publications, but man they were brutal to fans. I just I've never seen anything like that. I don't know if you notice that yourself from that era and why on Earth would they're be so much hatred directed at the fans of such three nice guys?
No. Yeah. I know exactly what you're talking about. That part for me personally as a fan, I never really ran into that too much because I didn't pay attention to music press during that time. I was more attuned to it later, especially when I started my blog and I had to dig into this stuff.

You have some good archives too, so you obviously found all of that stuff.
Yeah. I think a lot of it has to do with the fact that Rush didn't fit the mold of a rock band. A lot of the reasons Rush fans are so passionate about the band is the same reasons these critics didn't like them. Like I said, they were not into partying and cheating on their wives or doing drugs, not that they didn't do any of that, but it was low key. They were almost too serious for rock music for a lot of the critics' standpoints, too pretentious. What do they think they're doing, 20 minute songs! I think that was the key right there. They weren't used to seeing a band like this and they were like "Who are these guys?"

It was the punk era.
Exactly. A lot of there was critics who came out of that, espe-

cially New York scene or a lot of it was built around the punk and new wave stuff. Rush is just the opposite of that.

Interesting enough though, they adopted a lot of new wave, they were big fans of new wave, and they adopted a lot of the musical tropes. Alex's guitar sound starting with *Permanent Waves* really was very much. There's no way that's not influenced by The Police or some groups like that.
They admitted it.

They were huge Police fans. Yeah. I know Neil's good friends with Stewart Copeland. It's just funny, like you said, the punk-new wave scene really sneered at them yet Rush really embraced elements of punk and new wave.
Yeah. That was one thing they were good at. They would always take stuff they liked in the current musical climate and they would integrate it into their own style. It's how they evolved over the years.

Did—sorry. Didn't mean to cut you off.
No, I'm saying they don't, from one album to the next, it was subtle. If you look at their whole discography, there's a big difference between their first album and *Hold Your Fire* or something.

Yeah. Sounds like the same band though. You can still tell.
Yeah. It's still Rush.

Very interesting.
You can definitely see a progression.

The taking of influence, at least to my ears it never sounded forced, even in the *Counterparts/Test for Echo*-era where clearly there was some grunge influence there.
Yeah.

I don't know. It never sounded embarrassing. It didn't

sound like a bunch of 45-year-olds trying to be hip and cool. It just sounded like a bunch of 45-year-olds who were like "Man, that's a nice guitar sound. I like the way that sounds. Let's do some of that. That could be cool. We'll just integrate it into our regular songwriting style." I don't know how the conversations went obviously, but it never sounded forced. Even the keyboard era stuff doesn't sound forced. It doesn't sound shoehorned in. I don't know how they did that, but it's impressive.

Yeah. It is. I don't know either. Yeah. It's definitely. Like you said, you can still hear, it's still Rush. It still sounds like Rush, but just a little tweak here and there and they just sprinkle it with some new stuff every time.

Yeah. Yeah.
It doesn't sound like they're a cover band. They're not trying to write another "Smells Like Teen Spirit" or something.

That's a good way of putting it.
It's subtle. It's subtle. It's there, but it doesn't sound like, like you said, it's not forced.

Embarrassing.
Derivative. Yeah.

Yeah. It is something. Maybe, who knows? Maybe that's something that the "cool kids of the rock press world" maybe they finally grudgingly realized that. Who knows? It is amazing how the perception is changed though.
Yeah. That's true.

My take is that it's because people like you and me who were old enough now to be the taste makers, grew up as fans, and now they don't feel the need to hide that. One of the people they talked to in *Time Stands Still*, I think his name is Brian Hiatt, he looks to be maybe in his early 40s and he's a senior writer at the *Rolling Stone*. He's clearly a huge Rush fan

because he's in the documentary talking about how much he likes the band. It's like, a *Rolling Stone* writer openly admitting, he's coming out of the closet as a Rush fan. I guess in the 2010s, 2020s, that's not a weird thing to think about anymore. It's such a 180.
Yeah. All those music critics faded away. The fans, the Rush fans of that era, grew up to be successful influential people. They became movie directors or writers in magazines, or executives at companies. They were the ones in power I guess, and they had a voice. They all liked Rush so it came out. You were just talking about *I Love You Man*. The director [John Hamburg], the guy that made that movie, huge Rush fan and he wanted Rush in that movie. He made it happen. That wouldn't have happened 20 years ago.

No, not at all unless it was supposed to be at their expense.
Yeah. He was a huge Rush fan. He grew up, he made a movie, he wanted Rush to be in it somehow.

Yeah. Do you think that, and nobody likes talking about politics because Rush really isn't that political of a band at all, but that early hate, how much of that do you think was just due to Neil naively blindly assuming that talking to the press about how much he admired Ayn Rand's philosophy? How much of that do you think came from the fact that Neil had no clue that was a hot button issue?
Yeah. No, you're absolutely right. That was a big part of it. Again, a lot of that music, especially at that time was really liberal. Anything that even touched on anything that was conservative or libertarian or whatever set them off. Yeah. I'm sure that's a bit of it, although Neil toned it down later in life.

Definitely moved away from.
Moved away from a lot of that.

**Objectivism. Yeah. It's an interesting phenomenon too because it seems like as the '70s faded away, there was that

looking through archives of interviews I found that there's just a time where then suddenly they stopped prefacing everything about Neil with "Ayn Rand fan Neil Peart." It just stops at a certain point.
Yeah.

I want to say once you get into the late '80s, it's just not the thing they throw at the beginning. They just talk to him like he's just "Neil Peart, drummer from Rush" or "Rush as a band, et cetera, et cetera," and it doesn't talk about who once dedicated an album to Ayn Rand.
Right.

It just gets forgotten at some point.
. . . in there somewhere.

I'm sorry, you were breaking up a little bit. What was that you said?
I said every now and then, there'll still be a writer that squeezes that reference in there somewhere.

Yeah. Yeah. To what end? I know there's never . . .
They're still around.

They're still around.
Don't forget, it's not nearly as prevalent.

Yeah. Alex and Geddy, they really never say anything about politics, and then I know Neil has called himself a "bleeding heart libertarian" and I think that's reflected in some song lyrics, certainly starting with maybe with "Roll the Bones" but even earlier. I think it reaches a point on, why am I blanking on the name of the song, on "The Larger Bowl" on *Snakes & Arrows*. One of his things was I think people should be free to do what they want and it's good to have economic choices. Like the song says, why is it so badly arranged? I think he came to the realization that it's not, it's

what Donna was telling me from conversations she had with Neil, he realized at some point the playing field was not level and that's not right. It's just funny because when he had that gradual shift, all of a sudden the band's politics, what they were, not that they were much of a political band, all of a sudden, you never saw that discussed anywhere. I don't know. It's interesting. It's too bad too because that could maybe have made for some more interesting interviews. I don't know.
Yeah. That's true. I've heard that as well.

Yeah. Yeah. I don't know how much time you have, if I'm taking too long, if you've got to get going, let me know, but I don't know.
I can talk some more.

Okay. Is that a cat in the background I hear?
That's a cat. Yeah.

Okay. Good. I was going to say I hope it's not a little one saying "You've got to put me to bed now, dad."
Oh, no. My kids are past that. I have a son who's 18, will be 18 next week and then my daughter is 14.

Cool.
I'm beyond that.

Way past that. Like I was saying, I've got to schedule past eight, 8:30 just because my kids. My son's almost eight, he puts himself to bed sometimes and sometimes he's like "I'm tired, I'm going to bed." Our daughter is a year-and-a-half, so she's a little bit, much more of steady schedule. Okay. I don't have to worry about you putting the kids down. That's good.

One thing that sparked me to think about writing a book about the band peripherally too of course but about the fans

specifically is that when Neil died I remember talking to my brother who's a huge . . . I have an older brother, and unlike you I was the one that got my older brother into the band. Other celebrities, other musicians, other famous people, whomever that we were big fans of died, and you're like "Oh, that's too bad. That's a bummer. I enjoyed their music or their movies or whatever." It definitely felt different with Neil. It was weird because I never met the guy, I never talked to him. I'd seen him on stage a couple times, but why did I care so much, why did it seem so tragic that he died of brain cancer? Celebrity, rich and famous, had no idea who I am yet at the same token really affect me and my brother and a lot of other people. Just look at articles, blog posts, just what people were saying, other famous musicians who may not have actually met him either, everybody had this, I've never seen anything like that where a celebrity dies and there's literally nothing anything bad to say about them. Not even a joke. It just seemed like just genuine heartfelt grief, not just to call attention to the person saying "Oh my God, I'm so sad he's dead" or whatever but it just seemed so real. I can't think of any other celebrity passing recently, not even somebody like David Bowie. I'm a huge Bowie fan, but when he died it didn't feel like this. It's very phenomenal. I don't know what your take on that is. You're in the thick of the fan community.

Yeah. I noticed the same thing. It was hard to put a finger on it. For me personally, Neil's lyrics, his specifically, seem to really speak to people. You can tell that about lyricists I guess, but his lyrics really spoke to people as if they were written for them. It's also for me, I read his books. It was weird that Neil was such an introverted guy that kept things close to his sleeve but he wrote these books where he was just the opposite, he would just open up and really talk a lot about all kinds of different subjects. He had this blog that he wrote too. All of that coupled together gave you an insight into his life and his brain and how he thought about things.

For me, reading all of that, I felt like I was really close to him. I felt like he was a friend different from Geddy or Alex. Even though Geddy and Alex were the outgoing ones, I felt like I knew Neil better.

That's funny.
Yeah. For me, Neil, I've always identified with him. It felt like a friend had died. I don't know if that's, it sounded like a lot of people had that similar experience from reading all the tributes. I don't know exactly why that is compared to other artists why it's different. It's hard to say from being such a big Rush fan and being such a fan of Neil in particular, it's easy for me to see why it affected me so much. Yeah. I'm not sure why everybody else felt the same way. I didn't expect everybody else to feel as affected as me, but they were.

Yeah. It just seemed like the genuine love for this guy that so many, he would run off the stage not because he didn't like people but because he was shy. You've got this absolute outpouring of grief everybody had. It's something. It really is.
Yeah. He was a very real. He was a real guy. He was what you saw. He didn't try to be something that he wasn't. I lost my train of thought. Yeah. He was a unique dude. He's someone you can definitely identify with and he's a nice guy too. Like I said, from reading all of the stuff he wrote and his lyrics and everything, you just get a good feeling about him and the way he thinks.

Yeah. Yeah. He never talked down to anybody either.
Yeah. He's real cerebral and always very thoughtful about everything.

One thing that I noticed, I don't know if you noticed it also, maybe you didn't. It ties into the fact that so many, that Rush, the fans tend to be male and also as the stereotypical and as I discovered definitely skews "nerdy." One song that always comes up, and it was a big song for me too when I was 17-18, "Subdivisions." I can't tell you how many peo-

ple, there's some interviews with Donna that I read or listened to, articles, places even in *Vice* magazine, the last place you'd expect to find Rush fans, people who responded to my survey, "Subdivisions" keeps coming up. That's one of the songs that everybody, so many of us seem to identify with. I don't know if you've noticed that either, but that one song really struck a nerve.
He nails the teenage psyche in that song.

Yeah.
That's a great example of what I was talking about. His lyrics speaking to you.

He was like 30 when he wrote that, and like you said he nailed the teenage psyche. Yeah.
Yeah. That was him.

Right.
I was a young teenager when I listened to that song. When that song came out, I was 12. I didn't really get into the song a couple years later, but I was a teenager and that song spoke to me. People my age especially, that song really affected them in a good way. It made you feel like you're not alone.

Yeah. It's all right.
Yeah. He understands.

Yeah. That's what a song like "The Pass" is like too. That's another one that comes up a lot.
Yeah. Especially for later, Rush fans that got into the band later. That song has a similar [effect].

It gets you in the feels as they say.
Yeah.

Which of, I actually haven't read any of his prose collections. I've read the *Clockwork Angels* novel. When that al-

bum came out, that's what my parents got me for my birthday, I'm a grown man but they still got me the album and the book for my birthday. They're like "Oh, a Rush album came out, Alex likes Rush." I know he wrote it with Kevin J. Anderson. Still, it's a fun book. I never read any of his prose collections. Which one do you think, which is a good one to start with?
I think *Roadshow* is a good one.

Okay. Was that the first one?
Oh, no. I'm sorry. No. *Traveling on the Healing Road.*

Is that *Ghost Rider*?
Before that. No, I'm sorry. After that.

Okay.
His first one was *The Masked Rider* which talked about when he went on a bike trip in Africa.

Okay. Okay.
Riding a bicycle. I know it's before he got in to motorcycles.

Okay. Okay. Natural progression of course.
Then *Ghost Rider* of course. *Ghost Rider*, if you haven't read that, that's a really great book because you really get an idea of Neil's, what he was thinking at that time and the stuff he went through.

Tough one I'm sure.
It is. It's a tough read but it's really good. Then after that, the books are, there's one, *Roadshow* and then *Traveling Music*. *Traveling Music* is the one I like.

Okay. I don't think I've heard of that one.
Roadshow was . . . *Traveling Music* was I think the one after. *Roadshow* was the one that he wrote right around R30 I think. Then came *Traveling Music*. It was almost like an autobiogra-

phy. A lot of it was. It basically, he went on a ride one morning in his BMW cars and listened to a whole bunch of music that brought back memories for him and he would talk about his early life. He talks a lot about his early life before Rush, pre-Rush autobiography stuff. It's all real interesting.

That's a really interesting way to frame it also. You're driving around listening to music of his youth. Classic Neil.
Traveling Music. Then after that I think most of his, he had a series of books that were based on his blog posts.

Okay.
Ghostwriter is definitely worth the read, but probably my favorite is actually *Traveling Music.*

Okay. I'll have to snag that one then. I don't know all that much about his early life. There's a little bit in the *Beyond the Lighted Stage* doc, but they talk to his parents a little bit and they show there's some footage of a band he was in before Rush. Other than that, yeah. A little bit of home movie footage.
That's cool. That's why I liked it so much. It really was like an autobiography.

Yeah. Yeah.
His pre-Rush life.

I have to ask you because obviously Geddy was essentially the mouthpiece for Neil's lyrics, so much of the band has Neil's identity stamped on it, and he died recently and everything is Neil, Neil, Neil, which makes sense. I saw a funny picture. I just look up Rush memes one day. One of them says "How Alex Lifeson sees the band," and has a picture of the three of them and underneath it, "How Rush fans see the band," and it was the same picture but there's a black square over Alex's face. It's totally true because everybody talks about—in any other band, Alex Lifeson as the guitarist

would be all you'd be talking about, but he's the forgotten member of Rush. Why on earth, why? How can you ignore probably the most, I can't think of any guitar, the guy can play literally anything. I can't think of a single boring or bad part he's ever played.

Yeah. A lot of it has to do with Geddy being the singer and fronting the band. He's the face of the band. The singer always is. Then Neil is such a huge presence and he writes the lyrics. The lyrics are a big part of Rush too so you get those two things, the face of Rush and the mind of Rush essentially in Geddy and Neil. Then there's Alex. Naturally, he's the odd man out.

It's so weird.

He's a great guitarist, but of the three of them he's probably the worst musician, but he's still a great guitarist. There's so many good guitarists and Alex is definitely up there.

That's a good point.

Neil is always the top three. In any list you ever see a drummer, he's always in the top three. Geddy usually is too. Alex typically isn't. He might be usually in the top 20. I think that's it. He's a glue that holds that band together. I think that's why. He's just odd man out.

That's a good point. There's almost too many good guitar players.

Yeah. He doesn't stand out as much. As rock music goes, guitar is . . .

Is it. Yeah.

The instrument. There are a lot of big guitarists. Geddy didn't necessarily, I think it's more of the fact that Geddy is singing and he's a good bassist.

Yeah. Yeah. Phenomenal. Yeah.

Neil is so good, such a good drummer and he writes the lyrics.

Unfortunately, poor Alex gets the black square. He just plays guitar. That's all.

I get impressed though because I don't know if you're a musician yourself, but I'm a bassist. Every band I've been in, you tried telling your guitar player "We only need you to play a couple notes in this part, that's it because that's what the song needs," they're going to bitch and moan and start playing way too much. The one thing that gets me about Alex Lifeson was even before the keyboard era, and especially during the keyboard era, some songs he's just playing a couple things, filling the cracks here and there. I'm sure, I know that for example the *Signals/Grace Under Pressure/Power Windows/Hold Your Fire*-era he expressed he did not like that fact that there wasn't as much guitar. The fact that he actually didn't go on an ego trip about it I think is impressive. I can't think of too many guitar players who would do that, who would "I'll just play an arpeggio here and there to this."

Think of a song like Manhattan Project. Where's the guitar in that song? Where is it?
There's a lot of Rush memes about, that's the subject of many Rush memes. The Alex Lifeson not liking keyboards.

Yeah. I can't remember any right now. If I saw . . .
I can't remember off the top of my head, but I know I've seen them. I'm not a musician, I play a little guitar but not much. It's funny, just from running this blog for so long, I picked up so many things from musicians about if you talk about Rush and what they add musically to the band like Alex. When I say he's the glue that holds the band together, he is. He has to play rhythm guitar and lead at different times. He's got to dance around this awesome rhythm section with Geddy and Alex. He's underrated, definitely.

I think that's definitely fair.
He shows up on a lot of those lists too, the underrated guitars.

Yeah. Yeah. I don't know how he couldn't, then again people like you and me are a little bit biased being huge fans. What was I going to—oh. It's funny you were saying that just by running a blog you picked up so much music theory, music knowledge because one thing, another stereotype about the band, and that's by-and-large true is the fans tend to be musicians. There's a huge amount of musicians, almost a misrepresentation of fans of Rush and people who play music. Such a huge overlap, such a huge overlap. I forgot where I saw or heard it just recently. Maybe it was on *Beyond the Lighted Stage*, but I forgot who said it, saying if you know a musician, they're your favorite musician's favorite band.
Yeah.

It's so true. I've jammed with people who aren't even fans, but they'll be like "Oh, I love Geddy Lee. He's my favorite bass player ever. Oh, yeah. I'm not the biggest fan of the band, [but] he's awesome." I've heard stuff like that. Drummers, if you talk to a drummer and they don't like Neil Peart or they don't know who he is, then you're like what?
Yeah. That just doesn't happen. If you know a drummer, they're probably a Rush fan.

Rush fan or Neil.
Rush fan.

Don't like the band, but man that drummer is one of the best ever.
Exactly.

It's funny like that. Yeah. Well, I don't want to take up any more of your time. This has been awesome. I have to ask you a very unfair question, Ed. What is your favorite song that they do? You have to pick one.
That is actually an easy question for me.

For real?
It's always "2112."

Nice. Nice.
It's always been. It's the one that could hook me into the band, and for me it still exemplifies Rush for me is that song.

That's a good answer, and you also if you have to only pick one to listen to for the rest of your life, at least it's 20 minutes long.
Yeah. Exactly. Yeah.

You get a bit of everything.
It's got a lot on it. Yeah.

It doesn't sound dated. I don't know. I know it's from 1976, but I listened to it maybe a week ago and it holds up.
Oh, yeah. Yeah.

Well, thank you, Ed. This has been awesome. A lot of good stuff. I really appreciate it. I'll type this up. This program I use, you can pay a buck a word or some ridiculous thing to transcribe it, but I'll just pour a glass of whiskey and do it myself.[3] **Before I use anything or whatever, I'll send it to you. If there's anything you're like "Ah, don't say that, maybe you got it wrong here, Alex," just let me know. Yeah. This whole thing has been a lot of fun. It's cool to actually get to talk to you. Thank you.**
Yeah. No problem. It was fun.

Nice. All right, man. Thank you and definitely keep in touch.
All right, man. I will.

Excellent. Have a good night, Ed.
You too. Bye.

---

3   The program is called Rev, and I actually did just pay to have them transcribe it. I still drank some whiskey, though.

APPENDIX D: INTERVIEW WITH METROPOLITAN TIKHON MOLLARD, AUGUST 15 – SEPTEMBER 15, 2020

Metropolitan Tikhon Mollard is an Orthodox Bishop and a Primate in the Orthodox Church of America. He is also a Rush fan, a friend of Alex Lifeson, and a very interesting man. His Eminence answered my fan survey and reached out to me via my crowdfunding campaign, and was gracious enough to agree to an interview for this book. That we are co-religionists is purely coincidental.

Over the course of several emails in the summer of 2020, His Eminence took time out of his busy schedule to answer some of my questions. I'm sure you'll find his responses quite interesting and illuminating.

My first question is somewhat of the elephant in the room: How did you come to be friends with Alex Lifeson?

I first established a connection with Alex in 2008 through his participation in the annual Canadian Kidney Foundation charity auction. You are probably familiar with that event, where Canadian celebrities are asked to create some kind of artwork which is then auctioned off on eBay with all the proceeds going towards Kidney Research. Alex is actually pretty accomplished with the brush and regularly provides a painting. As far as I can tell, it always fetches the highest bids of any of the artwork. The last one sold for over $12,000, if I remember correctly.

I thought it might be cool to at least try to win Alex's painting for that year so I placed some small initial bids. I quickly realized that I would not be able to keep up with the rapidly rising bids from others so I thought of an alternate approach: Before being elected a bishop (in 2004), I lived for 15 years as a monk (at St Tikhon's monastery in South Canaan, PA) so at that time, I did not have much in the way of disposable income. However, I had saved up a little and tried to direct as much as I could towards charitable institutions. Although I had no real expectations that it would go anywhere, I wrote a letter directly to the Kidney Foundation and told them that I was making a $400 donation to their cause but was prepared to double that amount if they could convince Alex to paint me something.

I was a little ambivalent about my offer since Christian charitable giving should always be offered freely, without expectation of anything in return. However, I sent the letter and pretty much forgot about it. In fact, over the next few weeks a representative from the Kidney Foundation twice responded to my letter, saying that they had contacted Alex, that he was interested in doing a painting for me, and requesting the best way for him to contact me. For some reason, I did not notice those emails in my inbox and was completely surprised a few days later when I got an email from a certain A.L.

So, even though I had not responded to the Kidney Foundation, Alex took the initiative to write to me directly. He thanked me for my donation and added: "So, you're interested in an Alex Lifeson original painting? I normally only do the one each year for the Kidney Foundation as I'm not a painter by any stretch of the imagination but I was intrigued by your offer."

The end result is that I did make my donation to the Kidney Foundation and he completed a painting for me (he found a picture of me on our website and painted my portrait). From that point, we established an ongoing email correspondence which has lasted until this day. Since then, I have been to about 6 Rush concerts (Time Machine -1, Clockwork Angels – 2, and R40 – 3) and at each one, Alex has hosted me and provided me with great seats (usually at the light booth with Howard Ungerleider or by the stage). I have also visited Alex in Toronto on several occasions and he most recently came to St Tikhon's Monastery last Memorial Day weekend and spent a few days there.

That's the short version of the story and I will await your next question.

That's a really cool story, and not surprising given what one always hears about Alex, Geddy, and Neil, that they were very gracious, humble, and decent men. Given that the focus of this book is about the Rush fan "type," if there is one, and what draws them into Rush's music, can you speak a little bit about what it is about Rush that really grabbed you and made you a fan?

The first Rush song I heard was "The Spirit of Radio" at the time of its original release in 1980. I was 14 years old and my family had moved back to the United States from France only a few years before. So my exposure to American popular music was pretty limited. I started more with AM pop music but pretty quickly gravitated to FM album-oriented rock (Kansas, April Wine, Foreigner) which I would hear on the radio (in St Louis, MO). I enjoyed, for example, heavier songs like "Barracuda" by Heart. At one point, I started hearing a song which I thought was a new track by Heart. But it turned out it was "The Spirit of Radio" sung, not by Ann Wilson but by Geddy Lee. I would say that I was first drawn to the music itself (including Geddy's voice), which seemed to be more complex than other songs I was hearing. The transition part between the main song and the final reggae-inspired section seemed particularly wild and unusual. But it was also a very upbeat and celebratory song which somehow impressed me.

The other thing that eventually made me even more of a fan was the lyrics. I remember asking my mother about the lyrics to "Carry on, Wayward Son" by Kansas, specifically the words: "don't you cry no more." I was in 6th grade and was learning

English grammar so I wanted to know why the singer was singing incorrectly. My mother's response was something along the lines of "Most rock singers are not well educated." I don't think she meant it as an insult but as a general statement (or maybe it was just the quickest answer to my question). In any case, from that moment, I was always on the lookout for "intelligent" music. Of course, I found that in the lyrics of Neil Peart.

I had a lot of encouragement towards fandom through one of my friends. When he learned that I had *Permanent Waves* (purchased by my brother and I as one of our 12 free albums from the Columbia Record and Tape club which we joined in 1980) he gave me a cassette with *Hemispheres* and *A Farewell to Kings*, and everything flowed from there. Next came *2112* and *Caress of Steel*, each unveiling more complex and heavy music.

The other thing I would say is that I never considered Rush as part of a particular "genre." They now seem to be mainly labelled as "progressive rock" but in those early days, I considered them as "hard rock" (and I think most others would have said the same). In the early 80's, the term used for progressive music was "art rock" and it applied more to bands like Yes, Genesis, and Emerson, Lake, and Palmer. I enjoy some of that music, but I have never really understood Rush to be part of that group. They have always followed their own path and I think that is what attracted me to them. I remember being slightly puzzled by *Signals* when it first came out because it sounded so different than *Moving Pictures*. But the puzzlement only lasted a short moment once I explored the album more deeply. I think something similar happened with each new release from then on.

This is a great description of what I think a lot of fans felt upon first encountering Rush and their music (and lyrics!) and then with every subsequent release. The fact that you never knew what you were going to get was part of their enduring appeal. It would still sound like RUSH, but it would just be different. But it's truly music that hits on an intellec-

tual level as well as a visceral one, and few bands I can think of do that.

Your story leads me to my next question: Given that the topic of this book is partly about the typical Rush fan, and why their music appeals so strongly to a certain slice of rock fandom, when somebody mentions "Rush," what sort of stereotypical image does that conjure in your mind, is this fair, and does this archetypical Rush fan track with reality as you've experienced it?

I really think that the idea of a stereotypical Rush fan is something that developed in more recent years, perhaps even created by the media, which is always looking to categorize people as neatly as possible. If were to draw that stereotypical image, it would be a 1) male, 2) nerd, 3) reader of science-fiction and fantasy books, 4) player of *Dungeons & Dragons* and/or computer geek, 5) a loner or outcast, etc. While there may be some truth to all of those (for example, in my own life as a teenager, I would have qualified on most of those points (except for computer geek), I did not then, and do not now, define myself exclusively in any of those ways.

I would also say that I have not come across many other Rush fans that fulfill every single "component" of being a stereotypical fan. In fact, although they are sometimes hard to find, I think that most fans of Rush are one of the most diverse groups of people and that there really is no such thing as a stereotypical fan. What is more accurate to say about the typical Rush fans is that they are supremely loyal to the band members and to the music and lyrics they have created.

Most people will identify a particular song, or band, or genre of music with a particular time in their life. But they would probably say that the music just happened to be there at the time, as a "soundtrack" as it were. With Rush fans, I would suspect that it's the opposite: it was the music of Rush that was the central event and everything else took place around the music. I may be overstating this, but I think that the complexity of the music, the depth of the lyrics, and the overall integrity of the band demands one's full attention. A true Rush fan is one who offered that undivided attention.

This is very useful, and it makes a lot of sense. In particular, it tracks with what I've found in my survey. While there are commonalities among the over 600 Rush fans I received feedback from, they were more of this intellectual and temperamental commonalities. The other stuff—the nerdiness, the being male, and so on—was borne out by the data, but the rest of the information made it impossible to put fans into any neat little box the way music journalists and others in media like to do. I suppose it's because it's an easy shorthand way to convey a "type," but it's not completely true.

I have a bit more of a personal question. Given Rush's atheism and your Orthodox Christian beliefs and position as a Metropolitan in the Orthodox Church of America, are there any Rush songs you don't particularly care for? How do you think the band threads the needle between expressing their beliefs via their music and not being offensive or unfair to believers?

Your question is a very good one and one that I have wrestled with throughout my years of listening to Rush. My initial response is that, in terms of lyrical content, there are no Rush songs that, as a Christian, I don't care for or feel offended by. Neil was pretty open throughout his career about where he stood in terms of religion in general and I believe that Alex and Geddy fundamentally share his outlook. Those positions were never an obstacle to my appreciation of their music.

Nevertheless, if I were to isolate one song or album, I would say that one of the more challenging albums for me to listen to is *Snakes & Arrows*. Although Neil's thoughts on religion are found in some form in many of his lyrics, that album comes across to me as the heaviest in terms of a negative view of religion ("Armor and Sword," "Faithless," "The Way the Wind Blows"). At the same time, even those lyrics do not target any particular religious group or specific beliefs. Rather, they point out the sometimes irrational behavior of extremists (religious and non-religious) and speak (rather pessimistically) about the human condition as a whole. In that light, I do not disagree with his sentiments, since I understand, from the perspective of the Orthodox Church and the Holy Scriptures, the dangers of such extremism. However, I would take a more optimistic approach to the human condition he describes.

I think that Neil is often targeting "sham religiosity" as opposed to any particular religious beliefs. You can see this even in his travel books, where he likes to take note of the church signs, some of which he approves of, others not. So he is careful in his assessment of things, even if he disagrees with them.

I also think it could be argued that Neil is never criticizing directly as much as identifying certain unhealthy human behaviors or attitudes that he has observed. He then articulates those in the form of lyrics as a way to allow the listener to make his own evaluation or decision. For example, in the song "Roll the Bones," he raises the question of the suffering of innocent children in the context of faith which is "cold as ice" but frames it as a question, "If there's some immortal power/To control the dice?" While it's pretty clear where he himself stands on that question, there is a sense that he is genuinely asking the listener to consider that question for himself.

In a more personal way, I think I have never felt offended or oppressed by Neil's lyrics because I have gone through phases of similar questioning in my own journey. I first started listening to Rush when *Permanent Waves* was released in 1980 and, of course the two songs with the most active rotation on the radio were "The Spirit of Radio" and "Freewill." Musically, I was drawn more to the melody and infectious energy of "The Spirit of Radio," but intellectually, I was very intrigued by the lyrics of "Freewill." At the time, I was wrestling with a lot of "deep" questions (such as the question of suffering an the existence of God) and considered myself something of an agnostic or an atheist. Although I was raised in the Episcopal Church and was going to church regularly, there was a lot going on in my own mind and so the lyrics of "Freewill" resonated with me.

In particular, I was struck by the line: "If you choose not to decide, you still have made a choice." I can't say that that line, or even any lyrics from Neil, ever "influenced me" in a direct way. But I do think that there were elements of those lyrics, or fragments of thoughts and ideas, that I connected with and still connect with. I could even say that there are certain ideas that are clearly "Christian" or maybe even "Orthodox", even if Neil never intended them to taken in such a way. As an example, the song "Nobody's Hero" has the line: "Hero – is the voice of reason, against the howling mob/Hero – is the pride of purpose in the unrewarding job." Although Neil may have had religious fanatics in mind as part of the "howling mob", the importance of reason is important in Christianity (Christ as the "logos", the rational worship we offer in the liturgy, etc.). Likewise, the idea of perseverance in an unrewarding job is very ascetical and recalls the desert fathers who often spent their entire lives weaving baskets as they entered deeply into prayer of the heart.

Ultimately, I think Neil was searching throughout his life for "the real relation, the underlying theme." For me, those are found in Christ and the Church but for him they are found elsewhere. But the fact that he was searching for answers to those questions reveal him to be a genuinely human person looking for honesty and integrity, which is what we should all strive for.

What a great answer. I think you said it perfectly that Neil's lyrics, even when dealing with hot-button subjects like religion, never devolved into the realm of insulting or preachy.

There are unhealthy human behaviors in every realm, religion included, but not religion only.

I greatly appreciate your time, and I don't know how many questions you have the bandwidth to answer, but I'd like to talk a little bit about some particular Rush songs or albums if I could. First, I have seen in your survey answers that you have had some pretty epic Rush concert experience. This is a three-part question. First: Which was your first Rush concert? Second: What is your best or favorite Rush concert experience or story? And third, a question I've been asking everybody: What is your opinion of Rush's much-maligned "keyboard" era? (Roughly from Signals to Hold Your Fire)?

I am happy to keep answering questions as long as you are able to come up with them. But I also know that you are trying to complete your book in a timely manner. In any case, I am finding this personally helpful as I have been in the process of writing something like an autobiography. I was actually inspired to do this when Neil passed away and wanted to write a reflection on his life and death. I gradually realized that his influence on my life (both through his lyrics and through the music of Rush) could be found, in some way, at every stage of my life. So I am trying to capture some snapshots of my own life by focusing on three themes: God, friendship, and music. As you might expect, Rush will figure prominently in the parts about music.

As for your questions:

1) My first Rush concert was in 1982 at the Philadelphia Spectrum for the "New World Tour" in support of *Signals*. I know from the recently published book, *Wandering the Face* of the Earth (the comprehensive touring history book which I am sure you're familiar with), that this took place on December 13 or 14, 1982. I don't recall which exact day it was but the opening act for both nights was Rory Gallagher. I have no recollection of Rory's set, which I regret a bit since I have recently started

to appreciate his music—in part because of a recent YouTube interview of Alex Lifeson in which he speaks very highly of Rory's guitar skills. But I supposed I can be forgiven for not paying attention to the opening act since my main purpose was to see Rush, which was also my first ever rock and roll concert. In any case, I went to the concert with my brother and we had terrible seat in section A10, the nosebleed section way in the back of the arena. I recall that specifically because it was the only section I was usually able to secure seats. This was in the days before online sales, when you had to stand in line at the local ticket distributor, which for me was the Wannamaker's store in the Berkshire Mall in Wyomissing, PA. I suspect that each ticket outlet was given a certain block of seats and you got what was available. Because we were so far back, there was a delay as the sound travelled back to our ears, so we would watch Neil hit the drums and 1 second later, we would hear it. That was slightly distracting, but otherwise it was an amazing show. They played quite a bit from *Signals* and *Moving Pictures* but also did a number of the older material. I remember that Geddy introduced "Countdown" by saying: "And now, it's time to do a little space travelling" and everyone went crazy because they thought it was going to be "2112" (which they did right afterwards anyway). I also remember the funny Count Floyd introduction of "Witch Hunt."

2) I am not one of those fans who have been to hundreds of concerts. I can only claim about 8. Three of those were in the early days (*Signals*, *Grace Under Pressure*, and *Power Windows*) and for those, mainly due to age, I have only vague memories (other than a few as above). The most memorable concerts for me have been the more recent ones, primarily because, by then, I had established a friendship with Alex and that provided a lot of "perks" such as great seats. In fact, Alex usually arranged for me to sit either stage right, next to his guitar tech, or in the lighting booth with Howard Ungerleider in the center of the arena. All of that was pretty cool, including some great conversations with Howard, getting to meet Ray Danniels, their manag-

er, and meeting famous people like filmmaker Michael Moore and standing next to Peter Dinklage at the end of the Madison Square Garden show (when his brother was playing the violin on "Losing It"). My favorite memory is probably from that show (which was on the R40 tour). Alex asked me if I wanted to do a guitar exchange between songs. Of course, I immediately agreed. He wanted me to do the switch between "Xanadu" and "2112", which was really cool. As they finished "Xanadu," Alex's guitar tech, Scott Appleton, handed me the next guitar and I walked on stage. Now, I have stood in front of people before, but never such a large crowd or in the context of a concert. When I got on stage, I took a few seconds to look around and it was pretty awe-inspiring to see the crowd and realize that I was on stage with Alex Lifeson. He gave his guitar to Scott, and I handed him the new guitar. I think I made a slight bow of my head and smiled, Alex bowed his head slightly to me and then strapped on the guitar and went to work. It was a very brief but amazing experience, which I will never forget. Unfortunately, the photographer who was supposed to get my picture at that point was on Geddy's side of the stage. So while I have no photographic proof of this, I know that Alex will confirm my story!

3) Concerning the "eras" of Rush music, I don't hold as defined an opinion as some Rush fans seem to hold. I tend to reflect on the various "eras" of Rush from the perspective of my own personal journey. As I mentioned before, my introduction to Rush was through *Permanent Waves*, so in many ways, that album, for me, stands as the archetype of a Rush album. Objectively, it stands as the pivot between the progressive era and the "successful era" but for me it's simply a great album which reflect the consistent integrity of Rush's music. I definitely noticed the change in the music during the "synthesizer" period but I never felt disappointed by it. I think there may be have been some nostalgic longing on my part for the longer songs and gatefold album covers of the "progressive" era but I listened just as intently to all the "synthesizer" era albums. *Hold Your Fire* probably felt the most different to me, but at that point, I was about to "drop

out" of the music scene (and of the world as a whole) to join the monastery. For the next 15 years, I did not pay close attention to Rush (although I did not completely forget about them and did follow them as much as I was able to). So in many ways, I was not aware that there was such a thing as a "synthesizer" period. From what I can tell, no one spoke of a "synthesizer era" until they moved to the next stage of their evolution. I don't believe that there is a specific designation for this last era except for "the return to heavier rock era." But how do you define the era which gave us *Vapor Trails* through *Clockwork Angels*? One of the most memorable lines I remember from the liner notes of *Exit . . . Stage Left* where it is written (I assume by Neil) concerning their increasing popularity: "After all, we didn't change, everyone else did." From that point forward, I always took that to heart when trying to evaluate Rush's music. So to me, the synthesizer period is simply a broad title that indicates that, during that period, they used synthesizers more heavily. But the integrity and power of the music did not change.

Why do you think Rush's music resonates so deeply with fans, and with you in particularly, and What are your thoughts about Neil Peart's death and why so many fans who never met him felt like we actually lost a dear friend?

It's hard to provide an answer for why the music of Rush resonates so deeply with fans. Without trying to generalize too much, I would argue that most other bands appeal to a particular demographic or mindset, at least in terms of musical taste. AC/DC and the Rolling Stones, for example, appeal to straight-ahead rockers, the Grateful Dead preserve the spirit of the 60s and 70s, Pearl Jam and Nirvana convey the angst of the 90s, etc. Those are just some examples, but in each of those cases, I suspect that fans of those bans tend to share the same mindset or simply like that kind of music because it connected with them at a particular point in their lives. One could argue that there is a certain sociological appeal to most other bands.

With Rush, that sociological appeal is undoubtedly still there—probably most people's taste in music gets established in the high school/college years. But with Rush, I think the appeal is much more personal and much more intimate. The experience of listening to Rush is unique for each individual listener and is not necessarily generalizable in the same way that dance music makes people dance and heavy metal makes people bang their heads. There is something in the music itself, which is so rich and complex, musically speaking, which requires the full attention of the listener.

When you add in the dimension of very carefully crafted lyrics, a very full sonic and emotional ocean is created, in which people from all sorts of backgrounds can immerse themselves. One could argue that there is a "nerd, sci-fi/fantasy" demographic of Rush fans but this does not account for the wide range of other types of people who are drawn to their music, including some recent rediscoveries on YouTube reaction channels, where you find (among others) women, rappers, and young kids who are getting turned on to Rush. None of those groups fits into the stereotype and yet they are there.

My thought is that, ultimately, listening to the music of Rush is an experience and this appeals to those who look to music to engage them in an experience (spiritual, emotional, or simply musical). There is also something more mysterious about the music of Rush. It is complex, multi-faceted, and played extremely well on the technical side; but it also has a visceral impact on the listener—not the casual listener (who will be distracted by Geddy's voice or the length of the songs) but the true listener who is looking to enter more fully into the experience of the music.

Concerning Neil's death and its impact on so many people who never met him, I think there are several reasons for this. The most powerful, and perhaps most obvious, factor is the corpus of lyrics (and books, and tour books, et.c) that he wrote. He is undoubtedly intelligent but he also has some real solid wisdom as well. In this sense, I would argue that he is unique among other songwriter in the rock world. There are many songwriters who have touched millions of people but my own impression is that each of those was imposing something to their audience: Bob Dylan give social commentary, Bruce Springsteen advocates for the working person, Neil Young makes biting political commentary, etc.). With Neil Peart, one gets the sense that he is sharing rather than preaching.

Even in a song like "Limelight", which people often interpret as an expression of Neil's personal ambivalence about fame, is really not just about him, but it's about me. The lyrics clearly come from his own personal experience but he somehow makes it universal so that I, the listener, recognize these words as applicable to me. I think this is why people who have never met him see him as a dear friend. He somehow connects with me in spite of the fact that we don't hang out together or perhaps even share the same opinions about things. He engages us in a real and meaningful conversation without offending us or demanding anything from us.

APPENDIX E: INTERVIEW WITH MARC BRENNAN, SEPTEMBER 28 – OCTOBER 9, 2020

Marc Brennan is a fantastic drummer, a Rush fan, and also a closer personal friend of mine. I first met Marc in 2001 while I was in college. We both replied to an advertisement on my college's classified web page seeking musicians to start a rock band. The actual poster didn't show up, but a guitar player I went to school with and I did. We jammed at Marc's house and while the guitar player only lasted a few practices, Marc and I hit it off—one of the first things I thought was "Wow, he plays like Neil Peart!"—and not only did we spend the next fifteen or so years in various bands together, we became lifelong friends.

I had planned to interview Marc by phone, but when I managed to squeeze in some time one night to call him, we ended up chatting for two hours until my daughter woke up and needed me to put her back to sleep. So we did the interview by email. Enjoy!

What was your first exposure to Rush and what really made you a fan of the band?

When I was really young, my dad told me that I hated Rush because of Geddy's singing. I believe it was the video for "Limelight" on MTV. When I was in junior high school, both *Different Stages* and *A Work in Progress* became my additional media for learning. The musicians were cool, the music was interesting, the intricacies of how everything was created by Rush yielded context for someone to further develop themselves as musicians and meet other likeminded people. They gave us a common language for us to champion!

This was fun to think about dude, especially this year with Neil's passing.

It is fun to think about, and that's a great answer. *Different Stages* has such a great setlist, and I'm not surprised you loved *A Work in Progress*, being a drummer and all.

So people reading this wouldn't know otherwise, but you and I go way back--almost 20 years at this point. For some context for the reader, Marc and I met while both responding to a guitar players' advertisement to start a band. Another guitarist at my college and I responded to the ad and drove out to Marc's house. The original guy who'd posted the ad was a no show, and the other guitarist didn't pan out, but Marc and I not only played in bands for the next two decades, we also became friends. So thanks, guitarist whose name I can't even remember!

This all has a point, I swear: At our first rehearsal, I literally remember thinking about you, man, "Oh my God, this guy plays like Neil Peart." And this gets to my next question, about Rush fan stereotypes. One stereotype of Rush fans in the popular imagination is that we're all musicians. There are also other common perceptions about fans of this band. In your mind, what do you think the Rush fan stereotypes are, and how accurate do you think they are?

I would think that one of the Rush fan stereotypes would be that they and their immediate friends may not all be musicians but they are likely into the sci fi or alternate reality scene to a degree, be it movies, comics, gaming, etc.

As Rush songs don't always conform to the easy selling short pop song formula, I feel the fans are those who can over analyze the lyrics, for introspective reasons, as well as the music itself, for sheer exploration of the technical prowess, odd meter arrangements, and heartfelt melodies. The stereotype is somewhat accurate in my eyes.

Very cool! I have a few more questions if that's all right.

I like how you put that: since Rush's music isn't short, surface-level pop, fans can really analyze and explore both the music and lyrics. Is this the main reason you find that Rush really resonates with its fans? Do you think there's something beyond this? I mean, Rush fans tend to care VERY deeply about this band. I don't see too many rock or pop artists that inspire this level of long-term, multi-generational devotion.

In other words, what do you think inspires this rabid level of fandom?

That rabid fandom that spans generations is probably a combination of how Rush has maintained their relevant stature through decades of fresh music, not acting the part as snotty rock stars, and diving into topics of substance.

Parents and their kids, who are fans, can share stories like the parent had seen Rush in the late 70's-80's and their kids and friends are seeing them tour in the 90's or 2000s. From my experience, I was able to learn drums for "Anthem" and "Bastille Day" by listening to my Dad's record album, then I was able to jam with him because he already learned guitar parts years earlier! It's a cool experience that fosters learning, bonding, and builds confidence. All the while, there is no negative press about the band doing dumb and exploitive actions because they are famous (a road that's opposite of say . . . Motley Crue) so it's a different set of minds who care, and see that Rush is just a regular group of folks that you can identify with.

I love that you would jam on Rush--among other bands-- with your dad. Not many bands you can say the parent learned to play the songs of as a kid as well.

Speaking to this bond between fan and band, in your opinion why do you think Neil Peart's death hit so many fans, fans who never met him, so hard? And what was your response to hearing about his passing?

I think the fans that have never met him fully understood that he was an ambassador for all things music, triumph over tragedy, perseverance and dedication. Through the music of Rush, Neil was able to showcase some very eclectic non-rock styles to a wider audience, and just by listening and dissecting this music, his fans were able to benefit from him as an indirect teacher. I think Neil always appeared so humble in the public eye, and it was widely known about the tragic death that struck his family, so the fact that he could eventually regain the mental strength to make music and tour for many years after, shows that there really is a tangible healing process when dealing with personal adversity. I would imagine many fans think that as well.

Personally, when I had heard that Neil passed away, the news had struck me as a surprise and I was definitely sad. I remember finding out while I was at work and on my way home I just had Rush playing on the stereo nonstop.

When I arrived home, I opened up a bottle of Merlot and headed up to my drum room to play along with as many Rush tunes that I could for a couple of hours as part of the cathartic therapy. My playing was sloppy but I felt the significance of the songs more than I ever have.

Thanks again Alex was for this interview, it's been really cool reflecting like this!

My pleasure man!

Next time we chat it should be over some drinks.

Printed in Great Britain
by Amazon